How the Other Half Dies

The Real Reasons for World Hunger

How the
Other Half Dies

The Real Reasons for World Hunger

by SUSAN GEORGE

ROWMAN & LITTLEFIELD PUBLISHERS, INC.

Published in the United States of America in 1977
by ALLANHELD, OSMUN & CO., Montclair, New Jersey

Allanheld, Osmun & Co. Publishers, Inc.
6 South Fullerton Avenue, Montclair, N.J. 07042

Reprinted 1983 by Rowman & Allanheld

LIBRARY OF CONGRESS CATALOGING IN PUBLICATION DATA

George, Susan.
    How the other half dies.

    Bibliography: p.
    Includes index.
    1. Food supply. 2. Starvation. 3. Agricultural industries. 4. Under-
developed areas—Food consumption.
I. Title.
HD9000.6.G46   338.1'9   76-52614
ISBN 0-916672-07-7
ISBN 0-916672-08-5 pbk.

Reprinted in 1989 by Rowman & Littlefield Publishers, Inc.

Printed in the United States of America

For Maria and for Claude

Contents

Some Shorthand Used in This Book

DC	developed country (North America, Eastern and Western Europe, Japan, Australia, New Zealand)
UDC	underdeveloped country (all the others)
FAO	Food and Agricultural Organization of the United Nations
GNP	gross national product (total value of goods and services produced annually by a nation)
HYV	high-yielding varieties of food grains
ICP	Industry Cooperative Program, operates inside FAO
MNC	multinational corporation
OECD	Organization for Economic Cooperation and Development, groups the twenty-four wealthiest nations of the world
OPEC	Organization of Petroleum Exporting Countries
USDA	United States Department of Agriculture
USAID	United States Agency for International Development

One hectare of land equals about 2½ acres.
There are about 38 bushels in a ton.

The "Sahel countries" are Chad, Mali, Mauritania, Niger, Senegal and Upper Volta.

Foreword

This book grew out of my participation in a Transnational Institute project which produced a counter-report for the World Food Conference in November 1974 titled *World Hunger: Causes and Remedies.*

My co-workers on this TNI team were Silvio Almeida, David Baytleman, Jacques Chonchol, Joe Collins, Liszt Aragon Vieira and Jean-Marc von der Weid. All of them knew more about the subject than I did at the time, and I am grateful to have had people of such intelligence and experience introduce me to the complexities of the world hunger problem. Jacques and particularly Joe have been very helpful to me since then.

My interest in the subject grew as I participated in the Conference as an observer, helped to launch the TNI report—and discovered that many of the solutions that were being proposed at this international forum for the food crisis were exactly those that had been proven failures over the past three decades. As I continued reading after Rome, our report itself no longer fully satisfied me—hardly surprising, as we had worked at breakneck speed and in three languages—and I became convinced there was a need for more research that would lead to a simple and useful book exploding a few myths and possibly providing an analysis helpful to concerned people everywhere, but particularly those in the rich and well-fed countries. Here is the result, which in no way claims to be the last word on the question. If it stimulates discussion, further research and action, I shall be more than satisfied.

Some readers may find that this study is unduly controversial, tendentious and partisan. I should certainly hope so. The food crisis has, in my opinion, too long been presented as the result of nameless forces, and, so to speak, in the passive voice. Such and such happens, this or that occurs, but there are no living, visible actors on the stage. In this book I try to identify who (or what) is acting, and I name names. But I am not anti-anyone; in particular, I am not anti-business *per se*. If any business people bother to read this book, they will in fact find one example of an agribusiness project in an underdeveloped country which I describe in detail because it seems to me a model of its kind, genuinely beneficial to the country and to the farmers involved. Still, I have been able to discover *only one* such project, although I have written over a hundred letters to various agribusiness firms asking for information on their activities in the Third World. That this should be the case seems to me to be the fault of the multinational corporations rather than my own. Finally, I see no reason to make the reader pay (as part of the purchase price of this book) for opinions and statements he can get from the public-relations departments of the major firms, the World Bank *et al.* for the price of a postage stamp.

I have done the "pulling together" and the writing, but many people besides those mentioned above have contributed in meaningful ways to my work. My first thanks go to the Transnational Institute, an affiliate of the Institute for Policy Studies in Washington, which has kept me on as a Fellow since it was founded and whose grant has allowed for travel and for that minimum freedom from material chores essential to any sustained work—as any other woman with house and children will be quick to recognize. Among those who have added to this book by offering relevant documents, helpful criticism, encouragement or all three are my friends and colleagues at TNI: Eqbal Ahmad, John Gittings, Tom Nairn, A. Sivanandan, Ernst Utrecht.

To their names should be added those of friends from many countries: my teacher, friend and thesis director at the Ecole des Hautes Etudes en Sciences Sociales, Anouar Abdel-Malek; my father, Bob Akers; Gonzalo Arroyo, Rod Aya, Lakhdar Brahimi, Dick du Boff, Johan Galtung, Juan Garces, Margaret Gardiner, Ed Herman, Pierre Jalée, Peter Krieg, Ken Laidlaw of the World Development Movement, Jean-Pierre Laviec of the International Union of Food Workers, Alain Leplaideur, Heinrich von Loesch, Christopher Robbins of War on Want, Livia Rokash and Stanley Weiss.

I did part of my reading at the Institut National de la Recherche Agronomique, where I shared the rather cramped quarters of the Groupe d'Etude de Relations Economiques Internationales (GEREI-INRA) whose members, Jean-Pierre Berlan, Jean-Pierre

Bertrand, Jean-Paul Chabert and Marcel Marloie, were all hospitable and helpful. Many of the concepts elaborated by this team in a variety of documents appear in the following pages.

During the course of my research, I also visited the Food and Agricultural Organization (FAO) in Rome where I was very kindly received, particularly by people working in the Industry Cooperative Program. I take strong exception in this book to a good part of what this program is doing, but in no way do I wish to impugn the motives of the people working for it. My special thanks go to Mr. Gardner-McTaggart and to Ms. Teramo. Several other friends in FAO gave me very useful pointers, but given the tenor of some of this work, they would probably prefer not to be mentioned by name!

My husband, Charles-Henry, and my children, Valerie, Michel and Stephanie, have shown patience and helpfulness above and beyond the call of kinship. The two people to whom this book is dedicated know the role they have played both in my work and in my life.

Finally, neither passing mention nor brief thanks would be commensurate with the contributions made to this book by Pierre Spitz, the fifth member of the GEREI-INRA research team as well as consultant to FAO and to the United Nations Research Institute for Social Development. In the following pages I have shamelessly pillaged his own research—much of it unpublished or published only in limited, mimeographed form. I have further ransacked his library, picked his brains, bothered him countless times to ask a question or verify a point and abused his hospitality like that of his colleagues at the INRA. None of this has ever ruffled his patience or his permanently amiable disposition. He has saved me an enormous amount of time by suggesting what to read or simply handing it to me, and has acted as backstop and friendly critic of my work. Pierre Spitz was, however, on an FAO mission in Asia during most of the time the final draft was being written, so while much credit should go to him, he can in no way be blamed for any errors I may have made or for the uses to which I have put his own work. The same goes for all the other people mentioned above: to them and to Pierre I renew my affectionate thanks.

Lardy, Essonne, October 1975

P.S. This US edition has been updated, wherever possible, to include facts and figures for 1975 and 1976.

Introduction

This is a book about people, that is to say about the political and economic forces that shape their lives and determine how much and when they will eat. Malnourished babies, wasted mothers, emaciated corpses in the streets of Asia have definite and definable reasons for existing. Hunger may have been the human race's constant companion, and "the poor may always be with us," but in the twentieth century, one cannot take this fatalistic view of the destiny of millions of fellow creatures. Their condition is not inevitable but is caused by identifiable forces within the province of rational, human control.

The food crisis became the focus of worldwide attention in 1974, particularly during the World Food Conference held in Rome in November. This Conference, like the two that preceded it, could hardly be called a success. Most of the solutions proposed were purely technological; they stressed production rather than equitable distribution of food. Briefly, they echoed those selfsame measures that have been offered for the past thirty years. None of these "solutions" has come close to solving the problem, as the present crisis amply proves. The only point that everyone seems to agree upon is that matters are likely to grow worse.

We are going to examine the role of the affluent nations in the crisis, for it is they that have imposed a nearly universal economic system on the rest of the planet. We will look at the role of their governments, their transnational agribusiness corporations and the international institutions they largely control; as well as at the habits of consumers—meaning all of us—in keeping other people hungry. The United States merits the special scrutiny it will receive because it is the world's major seat of agripower. Although other nations may have inflated consumption patterns, food "aid" programs and their own multinational corporations, the US still remains top dog in production and control of world food supplies. In the West, we have commonly come to speak of the "oil cartel" or of OPEC's "cornering" of the oil market. This control is very paltry indeed compared to the corner America has on the world food market. Certain of its less subtle spokesmen, like the former Secretary of Agriculture, Earl Butz, do not hesitate to speak of food as a "weapon"; as "a powerful tool in our negotiating kit." The CIA meanwhile announces (secretly, to its official audience) that increasing grain shortages could give "Washington . . . virtual life and death power over the fate of the multitudes of the needy." This is exactly what food has become: a source of profits, a tool of economic and political control; a means of insuring effective domination over the world at large and especially over the "wretched of the earth."

It is my belief that many Westerners, for whom this book is primarily intended, would try to act against the forces that insure continuing malnutrition, hunger and famine if they clearly understood how—and why—these forces work. At present, most well-meaning people, encouraged by the mass media, see the hunger crisis as a result of the vagaries of nature on "Spaceship Earth," of such magnitude as to be virtually insoluble; as a scourge directly resulting from soaring birth rates in under-developed countries; or perhaps as a question of laziness and lack of initiative on the part of the poor themselves. In the following pages, I attempt to cut through official cant and popular myth— most of which is promoted by those same forces that have every interest in maintaining as thick a smokescreen as possible around the problem of world hunger.

First, I try to explain what the problem *is* and why we should be as much or more concerned by malnutrition as by outright famine. Why don't people get enough to eat and who are they? Are pigs more important than people? Is there or isn't there enough food to go around? How much more could a sane world produce using what resources? A close look at the present situation shows that only the poor—wherever they may live—go hungry and that deeply-rooted patterns of injustice and exploitation, homegrown or imported, literally prevent them from feeding themselves.

Needless to say, such analyses are not popular with those who may profit from injustice. This may be one reason so many "experts" have tried to place the burden for hunger literally in the laps of the hungry; specifically on their reproductive organs! Thus the best-publicized "solution" to the crisis is the need for population control—but population will never decline until better distribution of resources is achieved.

"Weather" or "the climate" is another convenient scapegoat because acts of God are supposed to be off-limits to rational examination and alteration.

The West has tried to apply its own conceptions of "development" to the Third World, working through local élites and pretending that the benefits showered on these élites would trickle down to the less fortunate, especially through the whole-sale application of Western-inspired and Western-supplied technology. These methods have not produced a single independent and viable economy in the entire Third World—and in fact were not meant to. "Development" has been the password for impos-ing a new kind of dependency, for enriching the already rich world and for shaping other societies to meet its commercial and political needs. Where food production is concerned, the "Green Revolution" has been a flagrant example of a "development solution" that has brought nothing but misery to the poor. Yet we continue to try to tell the other half how to live.

Perhaps the most important question we shall try to answer is, "Who has a finger in the pie?" Who has a basic interest—political or commercial—in keeping people hungry, or in feeding some of them? Powerful groups want to keep food prices at scarcity-value levels. Multinational agribusiness wants to grow cheap and sell dear (meaning mainly to Western markets that can afford to pay) and totally ignores the needs of poor people who cannot become "consumers." A multilateral institution like the World Bank would probably prefer to feed people (if this were possible without fundamentally altering the present world economic system) because it would just as soon stay one jump ahead of revolution. Western interests may seem to conflict or even to be contradictory; they can be more or less outspoken or secretive about their basic aims; but this book will attempt to prove that without any conspiracies or dark plots needing to exist, they work in essentially the same directions and against the veritable interests of the world's hungry.

In this connection, we will analyse the roles played by the agribusiness corporations, by the powerful traders whose busi-ness is food commodity speculation and price manipulation, by the US "Food for Peace" program, by international institutions like the World Bank (in which Western governments hold most of the cards). Major business interests have even wormed their way into the very structures of the United Nations.

If technical solutions like the Green Revolution, the transfer of technology and population control cannot solve the problem of hunger; if food aid is largely geared to keeping the governments of other states in line, if the multinational agribusinesses and the multilateral institutions seek to perpetuate in more sophisticated ways patterns of colonial control in underdeveloped countries; if, in a word, none of them, separately or together, can promise an era of abundance for mankind, then what?

The only underdeveloped countries that have either solved the food problem for their own people—or are on the way to solving it—have used some kind of central planning and have devised means for involving the people—*all* the people—in turning the tide against hunger. Third World countries must produce more within their own borders. Nearly everyone agrees on this now. If increased production were the only problem, we could almost discount the world food problem, for it would be well on the way to being solved. Unfortunately, the question that is almost never asked is, "Production for whom?" So long as thoroughgoing land reform, regrouping and distribution of resources to the poorest, bottom half of the population does not take place, Third World countries can go on increasing their production until hell freezes and hunger will remain, for the production will go to those who already have plenty—to the developed world or to the wealthy in the Third World itself. Poverty and hunger walk hand in hand.

Yet every time weaker nations have attempted to reallocate their resources and undertake land reform, powerful interests emanating from the rich world and its multilateral bodies have thwarted their efforts. Chile is a recent example, but it is not the only one. The inescapable conclusion is that however hard the road, the food-deficit countries must reduce their dependency on the West. They must not only produce more food crops but also allow more people access to food-producing resources. Whether the élites of these countries, nurtured and protected by the West, can be persuaded to do so without violent change—and whether Western powers will allow anything of the kind—is anybody's guess. Mine would be that they will not, and in fact cannot. But in that case we must be honest and recognize that their goal is not, and never was, to feed today's undernourished or starving millions, but to perpetuate poverty and dependence for altogether "valid" political and economic reasons.

I try to offer some concrete suggestions on how concerned citizens in the industrialized countries can attempt to organize and to counteract the thrust of worldwide agripower. This is our own task if we want to help the poor free—and thus start feeding—themselves.

If it takes you six hours to read this book, somewhere in the world 2,500 people will have died of starvation or of hunger-related illness by the time you finish.

PART ONE

Is the Problem Enough Food?

1. Rich Man, Poor Man: Who's the Thief?

Hunger is not an unavoidable phenomenon like death and taxes. We are no longer living in the seventeenth century when Europe suffered shortages on an average of every three years and famine every ten. Today's world has all the physical resources and technical skills necessary to feed the present population of the planet or a much larger one. Unfortunately for the millions of people who go hungry, the problem is not a technical one—nor was it wholly so in the seventeenth century, for that matter. Whenever and wherever they live, rich people eat first, they eat a disproportionate amount of the food there is and poor ones rarely rise in revolt against this most basic of oppressions unless specifically told to "eat cake." Hunger is not a scourge but a scandal.

The present world political and economic order might be compared to that which reigned over social-class relations in individual countries in nineteenth-century Europe—with the Third World now playing the role of the working class. All the varied horrors we look back upon with mingled disgust and incredulity have their equivalents, and worse, in the Asian, African and Latin American countries where well over 500 million people are living in what the World Bank has called "absolute poverty." And just as the "propertied classes" of yester-year opposed every reform and predicted imminent economic disaster if eight-year-olds could no longer work in the mills, so today those groups that profit from the poverty that keeps people hungry are attempting to maintain the status quo between the rich and poor worlds.

Ninety-nine per cent of the people reading these lines have next to nothing to do with the world hunger crisis, even if they are well-fed Westerners (although this doesn't absolve any of us from acting *against* it). The other one per cent know who they are. If

3

you have read the newspapers at all since the World Food Conference, you have probably not been able to esape the charge that you eat too much meat and that you are therefore directly snatching life-giving grain from some poor baby in the Sahel. Well, yes and no, mostly no.

It is absolutely true that the developed, industrialized countries (mostly Western, whether market economy or socialist, plus Japan and a handful of others), which we'll call DCs, consume a lot more food than the three continents of so-called Third World nations, which we'll call UDCs, or *underdeveloped* countries. In general, they are neither "less developed" nor "developing"— their situation is frequently growing worse—and there is no reason to adopt polite, euphemistic initials to describe them. In recent years, the world has produced about 1,250 million tons of food and feed grains annually, and DCs eat over half although they account for only about a quarter of the world's population. Their animals eat fully a quarter of all the grain, or, as some journalist has undoubtedly already told you, because we all get our figures from the same UN documents, "the equivalent of the total *human* consumption of China and India put together"— some 1.3 billion people. If the Chinese, who raise about four times as many pigs as the Americans, collectively went mad tomorrow and began to feed their pigs on grain as Americans do, there would be very little grain left in the world for humans anywhere.* UDC people eat their grain directly as bread or other pastry. On the average (although averages aren't much use in UDCs as we shall see) they consume about 506 pounds annually (1969–71). During the same period, in the USA, people averaged 1760 pounds of grain intake, nine tenths of it in the form of meat, poultry or dairy products. Figures are just slightly lower for Europe and Japan. In the past ten years alone the average American has *added* 350 pounds of grain to his annual diet— about the equivalent of the yearly consumption of a poor Indian. Obviously, this American was not seriously malnourished in 1965 and this addition has not been imperative. If *you* are eating too much meat and animal fat, this is a matter between you and your doctor. If *millions* of consumers are eating such a proportion of the world's cereal grains in this form, it is a matter between them, their governments and those economic agents their govern-

---

*It takes about twenty pounds of grain to produce one pound of beef, seven or eight to produce one pound of pork.

ments primarily serve. It is also a matter in which the consumer generally has very little to say. Taking the *individual* meat-eater to task for starving his brethren is on about the same intellectual plane as, "Think of the hungry children in India, darling, and finish your lovely peas and carrots." So please put your guilt, if you are harboring any, aside while we try to understand the *structural* nature of DC agriculture and how it relates to hunger.

The United States is generally credited with having one of the world's most efficient food-production machines—and there is plenty of evidence that it is attempting to generalize its own system in other DCs and in the Third World as well. It may be efficient, but it is also extremely costly. If you still think of farming in terms of "We plough the fields and scatter the good seed on the land / But it is fed and watered by God's almighty hand," you are barking up an entirely wrong tree. Agriculture as practiced in the US today is hardly "agricultural" at all—it is rather a highly sophisticated, highly energy-intensive *system for transforming one series of industrial products into another series of industrial products which happen to be edible.* Farming itself, inside this system, has become almost incidental: it occupies under 4 per cent of the American population on 2,800,000 farms. Not quite 4 per cent of those farms produce *half* of all the food that feeds the other 96 per cent, the farming population itself, and provides millions of tons for export besides. Forty years ago there were 6.8 million farms in America. The 4 million that have disappeared were, of course, small family farms. Such "inefficient" producers have been increasingly replaced by superfarmers: 1 per cent of US feedlots now raise 60 per cent of the beef cattle, and three streamlined producers reportedly grow 90 per cent of all the lettuce in American salads, to give only two examples. Fewer and fewer "farmers" are out in the fields in overalls and straw hats— they are, rather, in corporate boardrooms in grey pinstripes and conservative ties. Many of them are in farming only because of the tax advantages it offers. In 1972, only 39 per cent of US farms with more than $40,000 turnover reported *any profits at all*—profits are eaten up in "costs" which are made up in other phases of the business. One of the huge "corporate farmers" is the Tenneco conglomerate whose total operating revenues went over the $5½ billion mark in 1975. Although it is a major grower of citrus fruits, grapes, almonds, etc., this is just a tiny fraction of its business; for as a modern "integrated" company, its other divisions can supply tractors, fertilizers and pesticides on the input end—and packaging, marketing and even ships to carry food exports on the output end. Big processing companies like Del Monte and Minute Maid supply most of their own factories' needs from their own farms. Such farms need very little labor but they are intensely dependent on manufactured inputs like machinery, irrigation systems, fertilizers and the like.

As to the modern way to raise animals, another giant, now under development in North Carolina, will cover a total of 375,000 acres, but will employ only 1,000 people, one for every 37 acres. "Grains will be sown, nurtured and harvested by machines, including airplanes. They will be fed to the (50,000) cattle and hogs . . . those animals will never touch the ground. They will be bred, suckled and fed to maturity in specially designed pens . . . " The agricultural economist in charge of the farm (which belongs to a New York investor) says, "Meeting a need and making a profit from it is the American way . . . The era of the family farm is gone and people might as well forget it. It takes risk-capital to farm nowadays and capital investment requires a profit. The housewife will be paying more for food, but Americans spend less on food now than any other nation. The American consumer is spoiled rotten, but it's going to change."*

It is not the "spoiled-rotten" American consumers' choice that the only chicken, pork or beef they can now buy is raised on industrially processed feed on industrial feedlots. Twenty years ago, one third to one half of the *entire continental United States* was classed by the Department of Agriculture as pastureland— and thus only marginally fertile for raising anything but animals. But because it takes "too long" to fatten an animal on grassland, much of this marginal land now goes to waste and nearly all US animals—which may be regarded as animated machines for consuming inputs—are concentrated on feedlots where up to 100,000 ill-fated beasts can be conveniently stuffed with high-protein feeds and chemical additives. The animal feedstuff industry is the "ninth largest in the United States." This system wastes pastureland and it wastes grain that would be suitable for humans, but is this the individual consumer's fault? The profli-

---

*The argument that Americans spend only 15% of their incomes on food is frequently trotted out. It is accurate—if one is willing to lump Rockefellers and poor families together. Many *ordinary* American families now spend 30% or more of their income on food.

gate nature of this kind of livestock raising is further demonstrated by the fact that feedlot animal wastes do not even go back
into the soil as fertilizer but into the waters as pollution.

This energy- and capital-intensive food system model, expressly geared to consuming enormous amounts of grain and
industrial products, is the one the US is trying to inflict upon the
rest of the world. In Europe, the family farm still holds an
honorable place and most European cattle are still pasture-fed,
but this is no longer the case for Europe's pigs and chickens that
have become dependent on industrially processed feeds like US-
produced soya meal. Feedlots for beef have already been successfully implanted in Iran and in the Italian Piedmont; the Soviet
Union has also adopted this model: its massive grain purchases in
1972 and 1975 were aimed at feeding livestock, not people.
Chickens in Argentina are now being fed just like those in
Alabama. Other countries—unless their governments recognize
the dangers of dependency on feedgrains they do not themselves
produce, and unless their consumers can learn to organize *now*—
may well follow suit. Why? Because the commercial survival, and
thus status as a world power, of the United States depends
enormously and increasingly on its ability to sell its farm and
agro-industrial products abroad. Feedgrains are among its major
crops.

Some experts claim that US farming uses more than a calorie of
energy for every calorie of food it produces. The Club of Rome
says the ratio can go as high as twelve to one. If you count
everything that goes into producing tractors, fertilizers, agri-
chemicals and even the scientific research that contributes so
much to increased yields, you can make a very convincing case for
this statement. Yet these inputs, "upstream" from actual food
growing, are only half the picture: the whole industrial processing, packaging, marketing and distribution system for food
"downstream" from the farm is the other. The biggest integrated
corporate farmers can handle their produce from seeds to supermarket.

Most of the 2,800,000 farms left in the US are still, however,
family operated and according to *Fortune* many large-scale
growers have concluded "there is more money to be made as a
packer and marketer than as a farmer." These marketers (again
including Tenneco) provide brand-name, pre-packed fresh fruits
and vegetables grown by themselves or by smaller farmers **under**

contract. This produce, like Tenneco's "Sun Giant" fruits and vegetables, will cost more at the supermarket "as consumers are persuaded to upgrade their purchases. And the costs of carrying out such marketing programs could also accelerate the trend to concentration in produce wholesaling that has already taken place at the retail level." For the smaller-scale farmer, this concentration can only mean "the prospect of an even greater imbalance in the relative bargaining power of many sellers and few buyers" *(Fortune).* Food- and feedgrain-producing family farms are already largely in thrall to this system characterized by a limited number of possible customers. Unfortunately, it is logical that the system be extended to dairy products, poultry, fresh fruits and vegetables, etc. Agribusiness expert Ray A. Goldberg of Harvard urges the individual farmer to "choose vertical coordination," i.e. long-term contractual selling arrangements with a food processor, based on futures-markets prices. Such an agreement "may concern only one commodity or it may be more complicated. It may involve relating the price of feed, for example [based on the futures markets quotations for corn and soybean meal], to the price of turkeys." If the US farmer does not voluntarily choose to become "integrated" into agribusiness as a whole, Goldberg fears that "government control [of agriculture] will probably develop and a public utility approach to agribusiness set in." As we shall see in the chapter called "Planned Scarcity" the farmer can also be a victim of futures-markets prices.

Upstream, grain and energy are squandered; downstream, farmers and consumers are squeezed. Here is how the Secretary of the US National Farmers Union described at Congressional hearings what he calls the "social inefficiency" of the food industry:

I went shopping at the Giant Supermarket on the weekend. I found General Mills asking $75.04 per bushel for corn! ("Cocoa Puffs"— cornmeal, sugar, corn syrup, cocoa, salt, etc.) Farmers averaged $2.95 a bushel for corn last month. The farm price had been multiplied by more than 25 times by the time the corn was offered to the consumer.

I don't care whether General Mills makes 90% profit or 50% profit or 1% or goes broke on its Cocoa Puffs. I think that charging consumers $75.04 a bushel for corn represents a monumentally inefficient performance ... General Mills isn't the only nutritional and economic incompetent in the breakfast food business. Quaker Oats was charging ... a whopping $110.40 per bushel for what? Plain puffed wheat! Nabisco, Kelloggs,

Posts were all in the same league . . . The performance of the breakfast food industry only illustrates the kind of social inefficiency that characterizes much of our present-day food product design and merchandising practices.

The American food-system model has nearly reached the outer limits of what it can induce people to consume in *physical* terms, but since its only alternatives are expansion or stagnation and eventual collapse, it must increase the *value* of what is eaten. Although very few Americans are still involved in *farming* (the figures are also steadily decreasing in the other DCs), fully three out of ten are employed in *food* input production-processing-distribution—which makes "agriculture" in this sense easily the largest industry in America. It is this whole system, wherever it may be used, that is implied by the term "agribusiness."

Another characteristic of such highly sophisticated agricultural systems is their *flexibility*. They can adapt to market demand, or the lack of it, in an amazingly short period, considering that food still must, after all, be *grown*. Canadian officials have said they could increase food production by 50 per cent in five years if necessary. During the 1960s, the huge US food-production machine ran out of control and began to amass surpluses that could not be got rid of on the world market. The government responded by taking 50 million acres out of production and as late as the spring of 1973 was still paying farmers not to produce: subsidies stood at $3 billion that year and the country was operating at only a fraction of its real agricultural capacity. But when world grain prices shot up and world food stocks dwindled to alarming levels, those acres were put back into production. Between 1972 and 1973 (according to USDA estimates) the wheat crop increased by 12 per cent and soybeans by fully 25 per cent. Nineteen seventy-five and 1976 were also bumper years. Industrialized agriculture can, in other words, respond with exceptional sensitivity to increased demand for farm products when this demand is expressed in money.

* * * *

People most recently became aware that a food crisis was looming in 1972 when wheat stocks hit record lows and rice stocks literally disappeared. Compounding the problem were the heavy Soviet purchases and a partial failure of the Peruvian anchovy catch which increased demand for alternate sources of protein like US soybeans. Then there was a lot of talk about "catastrophic" harvests in 1972. In reality these harvests were only about 1 per cent below those of 1971, a record year. What almost no one mentioned on the other hand was that the four major cereal-producing nations had taken fully a third of their grain-growing area out of cultivation during 1968–70 in response to the "over-production" crisis of the 1960s. If these countries had merely continued to grow grain at a constant rate, they would have produced *90 million* more tons of wheat during 1969–72. At the World Food Conference, the Director General of the FAO pleaded for just *8–12 million* tons of wheat so that India, Bangladesh, Pakistan, Tanzania and the Sahel countries could "avoid the worst." This disparity may seem appalling in moral terms. In economic terms it merely shows again that DC food production is related to monetary market demand—not to the needs of human beings. If 12 million tons at most would have been enough to cover the major needs of the most stricken countries in an especially famine-prone year, this means that not even 1 per cent of the world's harvests could make the difference between life and death for the worst-off of hunger's victims. In the absolute, this should not be a problem of unmanageable dimensions. In the present world economic system, it appears to be.

If such a relatively small amount of grain could make such a difference, why don't the "hungry countries" feed themselves? That is exactly what many people recommend as a part of the only possible solution to the food crisis. But before looking at how this might be done, we should first make an important distinction: even in the Third World, there are no "hungry countries." There are only poor people living in them who cannot grow enough, or buy enough, food to meet their needs. And in this respect, there is no fundamental difference between a DC and a UDC. The US Bureau of Census itself stated in 1972 that "at least 10 to 12 million Americans are starving or sick because they have too little to spend on food." If there were no unemployment benefits in Britain or France, there could perfectly well be honest-to-God famines in both countries affecting over a million people—while both would still be thought of as "developed" and France would doubtless continue to export wheat.

The difference is that poverty so extreme as to create "starving"

Americans touches only a small fraction of the US population, whereas in a UDC half or more of the people may be in grave jeopardy at any given moment. Although our own media give most of their attention to the occasional and truly spectacular famine, poor people in the Third World who actually drop dead of starvation are relatively rare. This is why I would like to describe some of the less well-known effects of chronic hunger. It would be comparatively easy (given a different system) to wipe out famine, but the more pernicious consequences of under- and malnutrition will be harder to tackle. They will only disappear, in fact, when *real* development takes place in the Third World (or in the First, for that matter); as opposed to the shams touted by the rich nations that are passed off under that name today. When we have seen something of what hunger can *do* to people, then we shall try to examine why this should be the lot of so many millions of them.

Estimates of their exact numbers vary; certainly everyone would agree there are too many. In some areas, fully half the children can be expected to die of hunger-related illness before the age of five, but in the world as a whole, easily a fifth of *all* children (thus including some of our own) are judged to be malnourished. The UN claims that one of every eight people in the world is literally starving, and that almost half suffer from malnutrition of one kind or another. Death is only one of the possible consequences. Here are a few of the others.

In a general way, chronically hungry people are physically less developed and mentally less alert than people who eat enough; they have far less resistance to disease and are far more susceptible to invasion by the parasites that proliferate in the poor countries. Their children are fifteen times more likely to die before they reach their first birthday than ours; infant mortality rates are comparable to those that existed in Europe in 1750. Owing to the eradication of some diseases, life expectancy for adults is slightly higher than that of eighteenth-century Europeans, but these adults will not die for the same reasons we will: in France, for instance, 70 per cent of deaths are due to cardio-vascular ailments, cancer and accidents in that order; in the Third World 70 per cent of the people die of parasitic or infectious disease for which hunger provides the favorable terrain.

All of us have seen pictures of incongruously bloated or prematurely wizened little children. The first are suffering from a protein-deficiency disease called *kwashiorkor*, a West-African word meaning "one-two" because this disease may often strike an older child when he is suddenly weaned to make way for a younger sibling. The second is marasmus and occurs when the child lacks both calories and proteins. Most children will not have time to die of either—they will be carried off by some form of gastro-enteritis or a sickness like measles, whose mortality rate is, for example, a thousand times higher in Niger than in Western nations.

If a person's diet is monotonous, made up of very few foods, and not even enough of those, he will almost invariably suffer from a specific protein, vitamin or mineral deficiency with serious consequences for his health. There are 300 million people in the world with goitre, endemic in many parts of Africa, and goitre can reach the point of clinical cretinism. Some 3 million Third World people are estimated to be wholly unproductive for this reason. Pellagra, which strikes people for whom corn is the only staple food, can also go as far as madness if untreated. The World Health Organization counts one person in five as a victim of iron-deficiency anaemia. Beri-beri, which had nearly been eliminated, is reappearing especially where the staple diet food is industrially polished rice. Vitamin-A-deficiency blindess affects further millions, particularly in the Sahel, Indonesia and India. Endemic disease also prevents people from even producing their food: a huge area in Africa nearly the size of the entire continental United States cannot be used for food-growing or pasture because it is infested with tripanosomiasis-bearing flies that attack livestock. Malaria, bilharzia, yellow fever and a variety of other maladies that are nothing but names to well-cared-for Westerners also first strike the poor and the hungry.

Perhaps the most morally revolting aspect of the injustices caused by malnutrition is that it can prevent hosts of people from realizing even their *genetic* potential. Nutritionists have proved to nearly everyone's satisfaction that the baby who wants for sufficient calories and proteins during his final intra-uterine weeks and his first months on earth will be *permanently* damaged mentally, because the brain cells that were "programed" to multiply during this period were not able to do so for lack of food. Even if by some miracle the child is entirely well-fed later on, this condition is irreversible. This has been confirmed in various studies carried out from Guatemala to India, from Mexico to

Palestinian refugee camps. One study showed that for a sample of 500 middle-class children, only 1 per cent had an IQ lower than 80, but for 500 poor children who had suffered serious protein/ calorie malnutrition in their first months, *62 per cent* had IQs lower than 80. These people will not be able to hold productive jobs and their personal underdevelopment will be passed on to their children. Such underdevelopment will also be *socially* self-perpetuating. Another study, undertaken in a Chilean shanty town, showed that mothers who had themselves been malnourished as babies and thus had IQs under 80 or even under 60, were generally unable to cope with their environment effectively enough to feed their own children; whereas higher-IQ mothers living under exactly the same socioeconomic conditions with the same meagre resources still managed to feed their children adequately enough to avoid the more serious effects of malnutrition.

Such people will live out their lives as apathetic adults, prevented by disease or damaged genes from making the contributions to their own families and nations they might have made. Since only the poor suffer, and since the worst-fed among them also run the greatest risk of being ill-housed, ill-cared-for and illiterate, it will be very difficult to prod them into doing much to improve their own state if they have no help from better-off, better organized people. One wonders, in fact, if those who contribute to keeping these masses hungry do not know exactly what they are doing, since famished, lethargic, diseased people are notoriously bad at overthrowing anybody.

Why should these conditions exist? Just as we tried to look at the structural nature of DC agriculture that guarantees high consumption of industrial inputs and energy, maximum (monetary) "value" of what is consumed and consequent waste of grain; so we will now look briefly at how farming works in the UDCs. To state matters simple-mindedly, if you want to eat, you must be able either to grow your food, or to buy it, or a combination of both. Using this truism as a starting point, who can produce and who can consume food in the UDCs?

The first condition for producing food is to have land. I make no excuses for dealing in apparent clichés. It is partly because such clichés have not been taken seriously enough that there is so much confusion about the world food problem. Most Third World people live in the countryside—an average of 80 per cent in

Asia, up to 95 per cent in some parts of Africa—and most of them are dependent on land for their living. Every poor country, without exception, has a far greater proportion of its population whose only means of livelihood is agriculture than in any other sector.

Urban poverty in the Third World is appalling, as anyone who has ever seen the teeming shanty towns mushrooming around the larger cities can readily attest. But most of the people the World Bank calls the "absolute poor" (with per capita incomes under $70 a year) are to be found in the rural areas. Paradoxically, *it is the very people who are living on the land who are not eating enough*. They are the millions of small-scale farmers, tenants, sharecroppers, serfs (in Latin America), squatters, frequently unemployed landless workers and their families. Three quarters of these "absolute poor" live in Asia, but *proportionally* they are to be found all over the underdeveloped world. The Bank says they

. . . are found in roughly equal proportions in densely populated zones and sparsely populated zones . . . there are over 80 million small holdings of less than 2 hectares which generate incomes below the absolute poverty line . . . While the largest proportion of workers in agriculture is self-employed, the number of landless or near-landless workers is growing, especially in Asian countries.

Why can't these people make a living? Because the social inequities that obtain in their own countries make this physically impossible; they are held back because land—the equivalent of wealth in a UDC—is concentrated in so few hands. In South America overall, 17 per cent of the landowners control 90 per cent of the land. The situation is not quite so dramatically skewed in Asia where there are a lot more farms in the five- to fifty-hectare category. But even here, the top fifth of landowners control three fifths of the arable land (and are gaining control over more every day as is illustrated in the chapter on the Green Revolution). To describe the same situation from the opposite angle, in Latin America, over a third of the rural population must make do with just *1 per cent* of the cropland; in Africa, three quarters of the people have access to not quite 4 per cent of the land.* World

---

*The overall situation in Africa is more favorable to small farmers than these figures suggest if one excludes white-dominated Southern Africa from the averages.

Bank figures for 22 UDCs show that, on the average, fully a third of the "active agricultural population" has *no land at all.*

It is, furthermore, the case for the three poor continents (especially in Africa and South America) that *the largest holdings produce the least food.* A large landholder generally invests as little as possible in his farm and is content with a very low yield per hectare—why not if he owns thousands? The small farmer expends tend loving care on the little he possesses, giving mostly of his own labor, and the land returns the compliment. For example, in Argentina and Brazil where vast latifundia reign supreme, the smallest family farms produce, per hectare, more than eight times as much as the largest estates. In Colombia, Latin American champion in this category, the small producers are *fourteen times* as effective as the large ones in terms of output per hectare. In India, production per hectare is 40 per cent higher on farms of less than five hectares than on those of more than fifty. In other words, existing social structures in the UDCs prohibit people from producing even a fraction of the food they could grow if only a small measure of justice were applied. The poor are neither "shiftless" nor "backward"—but they have almost nothing to work with. It is the land-tenure systems that are backward—and that are a major constraint upon the productivity of the Third World. Most proclaimed "land reforms" in UDCs exist chiefly on paper.

This, you may feel, is their problem, and so it is (although Western nations' roles in nurturing local élites that exploit their own people will be discussed shortly). There is, however, another vitally important factor in keeping poor people hungry for which the DCs cannot shirk responsibility. Here again, 99 per cent of us have nothing to do with how the world economic system is set up, but all of us in the DCs profit from it to the degree that Third World people are subsidizing our breakfasts, lunches, dinners, underwear, shirts, sheets, automobile tires, etc., etc., through their cheap labor. This factor is the so-called "cash crop" that demands so much time, space and effort in the poor countries.

A cash crop can be non-edible (cotton, flowers, rubber); edible but without food value (coffee, tea); or edible and with food value—anything from sugar to bananas to peanuts, even to wheat. What distinguishes the "cash" crop (food or non-food) from the "food" crop is who eats or uses it. Bluntly stated, they are almost never the same people who produce it.

The present world agricultural division of labor which assigns the poor to producing food and raw materials for export to the rich is a hangover from the colonial period, but the system itself has flourished at least since the Roman Empire used North Africa as its granary and the same situation will doubtless continue as long as gross economic inequalities continue between nations. A cash crop is sometimes grown because one nation is in a position literally to dictate to some dependent what he will cultivate. Why did the three poor continents that must all now import such large amounts of cereals actually *export* grain until the beginning of the Second World War? Simply because that was what the "mother countries" then wanted them to grow. This does not mean that the local poor people were themselves decently fed because they were then growing wheat rather than, say, cotton. Now the United States has become the purveyor of food and feedgrains to the world at large (with some assistance from Canada, Australia, Argentina and France). Consequently, the former colonial countries have been assigned to producing other commodities. Even when legally "free" they have had relatively little say in the matter. Lord Salisbury's remark of a century ago is not so dated as it may seem at first glance: "As India must be bled, the lancet should be directed to those parts where the blood is congested or at least sufficient . . . " Entire economies have been adapted to what Salisbury tempts one to call the vampirical needs of the DCs. If you examine the transportation network, for instance, in nearly any poor country, you will see that roads and railways have not been geared to facilitating commerce between neighboring countries, or even between regions of the same country; but to getting food and other raw materials moved from the hinterlands to the capital and the ports and from thence northwards.

It is obviously not necessary that *formal* relations of dependency (imperial power/colony and the like) exist for one group to be able to control what another group will produce and to decide how much they will be paid for it. It is true that many former colonies have "chosen" to continue cash-crop agriculture and have been afraid to take the plunge into diversification because they fear their cash revenues in hard currency will drop so far that they will no longer be able to import any necessities from the industrialized world or pay their increasing debts.

Without exception, nations that have opted for continuing and intensifying colonial-type one- or two-crop economies inherited from a world they never made, have lived to rue the day the choice was taken. The "foreign-exchange-for-your-essential-imports" gambit has proved a lie. OPEC has brought higher revenues to raw-material producers because of their remarkable unity and the exceptional Western dependency on the commodity they have to sell . . . but bananas? but cocoa? even coffee? A banana OPEC was tried and has been squashed; few others have even been attempted and would have trouble. The producing countries simply do not control the international price for their products—they take what they can get. It is not that UDCs have not increased their cash-crop production *and* their exports—in most cases they have. One could say from this narrow point of view that their agricultural policies have therefore been "successful." The problem is that the "actual volume of exports by the developing world has increased by over 30 per cent in the last 20 years, whilst their value, in real terms, has increased by only 4 per cent." Bangladesh, for instance, counts on jute for half its foreign currency. Jute's price falls because synthetics are often cheaper substitutes. Bangladesh has to sell jute for less just to maintain a market and as long as this downward trend continues (and if no structural change and agricultural diversification is attempted inside the country) this country will surely continue to merit its place as the world's number-one basket case. "In 1963," says the government of Tanzania, "we needed to produce five tons of sisal to buy a tractor. In 1970, we had to produce ten tons to buy the same tractor." Similarly, a rubber-exporting nation could by six tractors for twenty-five tons of rubber in 1960 but today only two for the same effort. A cotton-growing Sahelian country has to produce two and a half times as much today as in 1960 to import the same low-priced French automobile. Cash crops have left the UDCs holding the bag—or the begging bowl.

People like Henry Kissinger make speeches at the World Food Conference stressing that "we are faced not just with the problem of food but with the accelerating momentum of our interdependence . . . we are stranded between old conceptions of political conduct and a wholly new environment, between the inadequacy of the nation-state and the emerging imperative of the global community." On other occasions, Kissinger threatened to cut off funds to the United Nations if the poorer countries tried to upset what he called "interdependence," but which seen from the opposite side of the fence looks more like dependence. Nation-states are perhaps "inadequate," but for the moment they are the only entities capable of making plans for feeding people and putting them into practice. The West recommends "give and take"; for UDCs there is very little give and a good deal of take. UDC exports are often not even allowed into the DCs—except for raw materials and cash crops which are nothing but edible raw materials. The poor rarely control the processing technology or the distribution circuits which alone could add value to the food they produce. Brazil's coffee and soybeans are largely processed by US multinationals and the same story holds true around the globe for oil and tea, timber and rubber, fish and fruit. A detailed study shows for example that only 11 per cent of the value of the world banana crop stays inside the Central and South American nations that produce it. Another recent study on Africa shows that "in this continent of greatest food deprivation, overall agriculture" (meaning cash crops) "has done better than food production since the early 1950s in *every* country listed." As late as 1967, the Sahelian country Mali was producing 60,000 tons of food crops. Today, locally produced food amounts to only 15,000 tons, while land devoted to cotton and peanuts has increased dramatically. Even so, in Mali, *cash-crop export revenues do not even cover the price of food imports alone,* much less industrial goods. At the same time UDCs devote their land to cash crops, by simple arithmetic they take it away from possible food crops, thus making sure they will get the worst of both worlds while catering to the rich nations' needs. If they tried it the other way around—more land for food, less for cash—there would be smaller quantities of cash crops on the market and the price ought to go up—or so my elementary economics textbook suggests.

The cash-crop picture is now indeed so bad that some countries may feel themselves forced to break away from the present world division of labor chosen for them essentially by the industrialized nations, whatever the price. When things reach the point that not even *food* imports are paid for by the cash-crop revenues, agonizing re-appraisals may become imperative. On the other hand, things (which is to say poverty and hunger) may remain pretty much as they are: the UN has estimated that imports of food grains by UDCs, which were sixteen million tons in 1969–71, could reach a staggering eighty-five million tons by 1985 and could cost the UDCs $18,000,000,000 (yes, nine zeroes) in hard cash. In the case of exceptionally poor harvests in the world at large, the figure might, still according to the UN, reach 180 million tons of grain imports at a cost no one has had the courage to calculate. It is patently impossible for the poor countries to contemplate anything of the kind.

Cash crops occupy enormous areas of many countries' best land (55 per cent of the cropland in the Philippines; over 80 per cent in Mauritius; groundnuts alone occupy 50 per cent of all cultivated land in Senegal, to give only three examples) and they ofen hog most of the scarce inputs that go into successful farming. Export commodities take priority for irrigation, fertilizers, pesticides or machinery—they also orient the intangible inputs of scientific research and financial credit. As usual, the small farmer gets short shrift and often has to manage with antiquated methods and the most elementary, traditional inputs. What he manages to produce, considering all this, is phenomenal. He is the answer to the food bind the UDCs are in. The manifold obstacles to giving him a chance are partly what this book is about.

Who eats the food produced in the Third World? We will be seeing how Western agribusiness is diverting more and more UDC production towards the consumers of the DCs, in an action replay of the good old colonial days. But leaving aside cash crops (which in our time include of course fruits, vegetables and meat as well as more traditional sugar, tea, etc.), how is the food that stays *inside* a UDC disposed of? There is really only one bright spot when UDC consumption patterns are compared to those of DCs and that is that animals don't—as yet—eat very much grain that would be suitable for humans. Western agribusinesses are, however, attempting to change this. According to OPIC, the government agency that insures US investments against political risks in UDCs, Arbor Acres Farms has set up poultry-raising operations in Thailand, Taiwan and Pakistan; Cargill in Indonesia; Ralston Purina is producing animal feeds across the globe; Central Soya is in Brazil, etc. These enterprises invariably depend either upon feedgrains imported from the US or on local land, diverted from food production to growing feed for animals only a small fraction of local people can afford. UDC land is also increasingly devoted to raising cattle for DC customers: Central America has increased its beef exports to the US fivefold in ten years, but this "can only be realized by rationing the local population."

The FAO publishes columns and columns of statistics showing how many calories and proteins are consumed per capita in UDCs from Algeria to Zaire. Unfortunately, these figures are not much use, partly because statistics coming from poor and understaffed countries may bear only superficial resemblance to reality, but mostly because a "per capita" figure is of little help in determining the socio-economic nature of food consumption in poor countries. Even accurate per capita figures can tell us nothing about the condition of the lower echelons of the population in countries where the top 20 per cent typically receive well over half the national revenue while the bottom 20 per cent is expected to make do with a 5 per cent slice of the national pie. FAO figures show, for instance, Cubans receiving an average of 2,700 calories a day and Brazilians a comparable 2,620. Since we know that Cuba is a relatively egalitarian society, we may assume that the entire population is well above the level of serious malnutrition, as is in fact the case. But a more detailed study of food consumption *according to income* for Northeast Brazil shows that the poorest people were at the physiological starvation level with 1,240 calories daily, while the richest were stuffing themselves with 4,290! A similar investigation in the state of Maharashtra, India, revealed a calorie gap according to income that ranged from 940 to 3,150 (one wonders that the 940-calorie group was alive to be examined!); other research in Tunisia and Bangladesh confirms this point which does not need laboring.

Could anyone be more undernourished and forlorn than a poor man at the bottom of the pile in a UDC? Yes—his wife and usually his children. The UN is gloomy: "If there is not enough food for the whole family, the working adults tend to take for themselves the largest share. This is particularly serious because children and pregnant and lactating women have additional needs." "Working adults" is UN-ese for "men"—because men are generally the only ones in poor countries whose work has a *market* value. Women work as hard or harder but their contributions cannot be quantified in what economists call "real" terms. Women are not only responsible for the preparation of food and the nutritional status of their families, but for a large measure of the food that is actually grown. "Remaining untrained and frequently illiterate they are in fact forced to perform most of the unskilled manual labor that has to be done in labor-intensive forms of agriculture and rural industries."

Meanwhile, in many societies, women do not even eat with the men, but only after they have finished—and therefore after the tastiest and most nourishing parts of the meal have disappeared. In Latin America where *machismo* reigns in all social classes, the poorest men exert their authority over the only people even more oppresed than they—their women. Globe-circling agronomist René Dumont says that the "poorest male *caboclo* in Brazil takes for himself the rare proteins available to the family, at the expense of his pregnant wife and numerous children." There *could* be an argument for giving working men the lion's share *if* this wage earner's contribution is all that staves off starvation for the whole family. But this holds no water when both the man and woman are partners in producing food, with the woman frequently shouldering the heavier burden. This is the case for something like 500 million poor rural women.

If you are landless or an urban dweller in a UDC, your consumption will depend entirely on the size of your income. According to the World Bank, for at least 900 million people, this income will be under $70 a year (it used to say $50, but now seems to be allowing for inflation!). One wonders how far this sum can actually be stretched by people who must *buy* all their food.

Farmers, one might think, are in another category, because they can produce their own food. But the number of fully "self-provisioning" farmers, or those who actually manage to feed themselves and their families all year around on what they grow, is probably extremely small, especially in Asia where the hunger crisis strikes the greatest number of people. There has not been nearly enough research done on self-provisioning or the lack of it among small farmers throughout the world. Economists elaborating "development models" seem to prefer almost any other variable in their equations to this one. However, a German research team working in North India in 1969 discovered that only 14 per cent of the peasants in the area managed to feed themselves and their families for 10–12 months of the year; 36 per cent for 7–9 months; 29 per cent for 4–6 months; and the bottom 21 per cent could only produce enough food for 1–3 months of the year. Thus half these people were feeding themselves only half the year at the very maximum. Pierre Spitz's fieldwork (carried out earlier in the 1960s in an Indian village about 100 miles from the site later chosen by the German team) confirms these results. Where population is dense and farms are small, the poorest farmers must either find supplementary off-farm employment to pay for purchased food, go into debt—or sell their land. Fieldwork in Rajasthan, India shows, however, that a small peasant would almost rather starve than sell his land, and will go to incredible belt-tightening lengths to avoid doing so. Still, many eventually have to sell out to a farmer who is already "self-provisioning," as increasing land concentration in the Third World demonstrates.

Most of the people who need employment to supplement their incomes cannot find it near their rural homes—nor often anywhere else. It is extremely difficult to determine the existing labor force in the UDCs, but 1,000 million people is an educated guess. Probably a minimum of 10 per cent is totally and permanently unemployed; if one adds those people who can find work only part of the year, often only at sowing and harvest times, the figure is doubtless closer to 30 per cent. It is wholly unrealistic to suppose that already overcrowded cities can absorb even a fraction of these 300 million people—but that is where they try to go when they are hungry, because that is where the famine-relief centers are usually organized. Sometimes they are beaten back by the army, as has happened in Brazil and in India. Sometimes they manage to join the other army, that of urban unemployed, whereas the only place these people could be *productively* used is in the countryside. If real land reform does not take place, if the hundreds of thousands of plots that can't feed their owners are not regrouped, if hundreds of thousands of rural artisanal and light-industry jobs serving agriculture are not created, UDC governmets may soon cease to be able to govern at all. Even if these nations count on the West to feed them (and this book is very much against such a "solution") they cannot count on the West to provide jobs that must be created where the people are. The Third World continents are going to remain agrarian for the foreseeable future, the population is going to grow, and the means to sustain it will shrink as more and more small farmers are eliminated. As the UN timidly puts it, before all these people have the slimmest chance of eating enough, "it would be necessary to break the vicious circle of unemployment—low food production—low productivity—low income which strangles such a large part of mankind. This, in turn, might entail very deep transformations in present socio-economic structures." Yes, it just might!

* * *

Before we go on to examine in more detail who, or what, is responsible for the world food crisis and what a rational world could do about it, it might be a good idea to state unequivocally what is *not* responsible. World hunger is not *caused* by population pressures although these do aggravate the situation. The next chapter will be devoted to an attempt at showing why this is so. Nor is hunger a result of the "climate" or the "weather" as so many people have been led to believe, even if climate can also be an exacerbating factor.

For hundreds of years, scientists have been trying to correlate the climate with any number of other phenomena, including the number of murders committed annually in New York City. At present, there is evidence to suggest that the past fifty-odd years have been exceptionally favorable from a climatic point of view, that this propitious period is not soon likely to be repeated, and that we may in fact be on the threshold of a "mini ice-age." Before we all put on our mittens, we should know, however, that the last mini ice-age began in the fifteenth century and gave way to the present favorable period around the end of the nineteenth century—an era which therefore coincided with the Renaissance and the Industrial Revolution. There were shortages and famines in Europe, of course, during these four hundred years, but the upper classes never stopped eating, whatever the weather. Surely climate cannot be the only factor that shapes our lives and our diets— social organization must have *something* to do with them. Growing seasons may become shorter, but science has already bred cereal strains that can adapt to briefer periods of sunlight. Cyclones may continue to strike, but a hurricane in Florida and a cyclone of identical force in Pakistan do not have the same consequences, even though both are disasters. The drought which is a frequent occurrence in the Southwestern United States is not at all the same thing as drought in the Sahel. Natural calamities may point up the weaknesses of underlying social structures, but they do not *cause* them. If a given social and economic system is vulnerable it may even reach the point of famine *without* natural disaster. For example, in several especially famine-prone (i.e. structurally vulnerable) countries, even a small shortfall in grain production can lead to full-scale famine when it is accompanied by less cash to invest in the following year's crop (and therefore by less employment and less income for rural workers), by hoarding and speculation on the part of local grain merchants and traders and by the consequent rise in food prices that put the poor totally outside the market.

A particularly striking, though perhaps unwitting, refutation of the "climate" explanation for hunger comes from a report by the *National Geographic* on the world food crisis. It cites satellite photographs of the Sahel—one of the world's great food disaster areas—and a particular picture that shows

a hexagonal island of green in the great tan sea of the Sahel. Inspection revealed it to be a quarter-million-acre modern ranch, fenced off with barbed wire from the surrounding desert. Inside, other fences divide the ranch into five sectors, with cattle grazing a single sector at a time. Though the ranch has been in operation only seven years, the rotational grazing has made the difference between pasture and desert.

This magazine does not say who owns the ranch, nor does it ask why such green plenty fenced off with barbed wire should exist in the midst of tens of thousands of starving people. The ranch, whose exploitation corresponds exactly to the six-year period of severe drought (even drought does not exist equally for everyone), unquestionably belongs either to a foreign agribusiness corporation or to local wealthy landowners, and it is probably producing beef for foreign cash sales. In neither case does it give any relief to the nomads of the Sahel who depend on pasture for a livelihood.

The same *National Geographic*, hardly a radical magazine, in another article shows that even in the case of natural disaster, abundance of food can and does exist alongside generalized famine—caused by classic and uncontrolled economic forces. The following passage concerns Bangladesh after the 1974 floods:

Despite loss of foodstuffs, however, there is an estimated four million tons of rice in Bangladesh during the famine—enough to feed the entire nation for a third of the year. But the vast majority of the people, subsisting at the poverty level in the best of times and now also victimized by the flooding, are too poor to buy it.

Relief officials tell of widespread smuggling of rice into neighboring India where it sells for up to twice as much. Hoarders at home drive rice beyond 50¢ a pound in a country with a per capita income of $70 a year, among the world's lowest.

Taking command, inflation triggers price jumps of from 200 to 500% in other food. The black market thrives, but at prices hopelessly beyond the reach of the hungry.

Another eye-witness account describes how rich Bangladeshi farmers stood in line all night at fiscal registration bureaus in order to buy, literally at "famine prices," land that famished small peasants were selling as a last resort. *Each famine takes more land from the poor and thus sets the stage for the next one.*

Supporters of the "free market" or "free enterprise" system, if they are consistent, actually ought to admire such activity. The fact that its consequences are more visibly unpleasant in a country like Bangladesh should not, intellectually speaking, cause them to change their opinion; for here we have, in the raw, so to speak, a dynamic entrepreneurial class in action. As a Bangladeshi professor from the University of Dacca explains,

> Fundamentally, hoarding, blackmarketing and smuggling, although decried as "anti-social," are only rational behaviors of "profit maximizers", the heroes of private enterprise, in situations where scarcity is combined with a structure of command over the scarce goods unrelated to the structure of needs.

People who need food are not part of this "structure of command" and small, poor farmers are

> . . . victims of financial compulsions that force [them] to sell much of the paddy [rice] they produce and would need for their family consumption for the season at give-away prices soon after harvest or even long before harvest to pay off debts and meet immediate cash needs . . . the better end of this bargain belongs to the money lender, the big landholder and other such parties who take advantage of the poor bargaining conditions of these small farmers . . . while the farmers themselves, the producers, are ironically compelled later to buy rice from the retail market at much higher prices and often consequently have to go into further debt . . . "

The situation can be even worse for landless laborers whose "wages reflect the supply and demand for labor" (Bangladesh is not noted for its undersupply of people) but which

> . . . bear no relation to the movement of food prices which dance to the speculator's tune . . . In times of floods or drought when work on land diminishes, they are deprived of work altogether and hence of any command whatsoever on food, ironically again at a time when food prices shoot up abnormally.

Berthold Brecht once said, "Famines do not occur, they are organized by the grain trade." Flood or drought can help to create the conditions under which famine thrives—but they do not create the human action and inaction that insures that the wealthy alone will eat—come literally hell or high water.

The world is still full of famine flashpoints. The most stricken areas can be identified by a quick glance at the headlines and at FAO press releases for the past three years. The Sahel still needs hundreds of thousands of tons of grain, cyclone victims in Burma and Madagascar need emergency rations . . . "For thousands of children, Somali drought aid arrives too late." "Famine threatens half a million peasants in Haiti." "Major food scarcities faced by states in India." "Natural catastrophes and flare-ups in world food prices cause fear of serious famine in India and Bangladesh." "Refugees, drought victims in Sudan, Ethiopia to receive World Food Program aid." "375,000 Mozambican victims of floods and war in need of help." "Food airlift to Angola resumed." "Sri Lanka receives $4.5 million emergency food aid." "Major emergency program for stricken Lebanon." These victims reach the headlines because their fate seems to journalists in some way exceptional. The brief interest they arouse is almost invariably related to war or natural disaster. Yet the common denominator of these flashpoints is that any rockslide can start an avalanche— none of these countries have social systems immediately capable of mobilizing the energies of the government and the people as a whole against the threat of food crises or the effects of weather. It is safe to assume that other such nations may join the preceding ones in this year's headlines. Climate and the vagaries of nature will doubtless continue to be useful scapegoats for lack of planning, lack of investment and lack of justice.

The world is presently living from hand to mouth and from harvest to harvest. We, the global population, have consumed more cereals than we have produced every year except two between 1969–70 and 1974–5. Nineteen seventy-two was not a good year; 1974 was worse. Calls for a World Food Conference were prompted by the frighteningly low levels of world grain stocks in 1972–3, but in 1974–5 they reached new all-time lows for the postwar period. The 1974 harvest of wheat was down 4 per cent (down nearly 8 per cent in India) and the rice crop was down 1 per cent. Nineteen seventy-five and 1976 were good years, particularly, in the US and in India, but this merely represents a return to "normal" conditions. It would take several years of good harvests to bring food stocks up to safe levels, and in late 1976, the Director General of FAO called the outlook for poor countries still "disturbingly inadequate." If two or three bad years were to occur in a row, and if major producers like the US were also hard hit, the world's food stocks could be reduced to zero as the well-fed continued to give themselves and their animals priority. The poor countries might not then find grain to import *at any price*.

Reports of renewed massive grain purchases by the Soviet Union in the summer of 1975 sent prices spiralling again on the futures markets. Any small shock, climatic or commercial, will be enough to cause major price fluctuations—most detrimental to those who have to import food—for a long time to come. In this context, the UN prediction that food-deficit countries could be importing upwards of 85 million tons of grain in 1985 at a cost of $18 billion takes on a coloring of total unreality. Who knows what prices will be in the years to come; who would swear that the poor nations could afford them? Even the 10 million tons they needed in 1973–4 were not *given* to them as aid in spite of the plea from FAO, but were largely purchased with precious foreign exchange. How long, O Lord, will they be able to stay afloat in the world food market if they don't start producing more and distributing it better themselves?

Public interest in the food crisis tends to decline when the media decide that people have had enough of looking at emaciated bodies for a while, and when there is no really spectacular localized famine to photograph. Chronically hungry people and the structural conditions that keep them that way are thought to be very dull subjects. But we shall probably not have long to wait. The crisis has not gone away. Many countries are worse-off than they were a year or two ago. Short-term aid measures, even if they increase, can be effective only so long, and in conditions of worldwide scarcity, we can count on the rich to fill their own exaggerated needs first. Any day now, the tormented faces of the starving will again be staring at us from our television screens.

* * *

Some readers may find useful the Appendix in which I give some facts about the inputs that go into farming (like fertilizers, pesticides, credit and research) and explain how the DCs monopolize nearly all of them. For those who are interested, now would be a good time to turn to page 265 before going on. I assure the others, who may find this rather more technical information heavy going, that it is not at all necessary to understanding what follows: I hope they will turn the page and will not feel burdened by the Appendix.

PART TWO

Telling the Other Half How to Live

2. The Population Myth

Life for a small farmer or landless peasant in the poor nations can be hungry, brutish and short. He has very little control over the forces that shape his life. But what is, in a certain sense, even worse is that it is the rich who consider themselves best equipped to propose remedies for his problems. This may be done in a well-meaning, "charitable" spirit, or for reasons much less frequently admitted or admittable. One of the chief targets for Western assault on the Third World has been its people themselves. There are too many of them.

Population control measures should definitely be introduced—in the rich countries that consume so much of the world's food supply in the form of meat. If you think this statement sounds strident, you should listen to the far harsher indictment of René Dumont:

> The rich white man, whith his overconsumption of meat and his lack of generosity for poor people, behaves like a veritable cannibal—an indirect cannibal. By consuming meat, which wastes the grain that could have saved them, last year we ate the children of the Sahel, Ethiopia and Bangladesh. And we continue to eat them this year with undiminished appetite.

I have explained why I do not agree with Dumont that this is the *individual* Westerner's fault. Still population control in the West is not exactly the focus the media have brought to bear on the "population problem." Swelling numbers in the poor world are on the contrary the media's favorite—in fact, sometimes only—way of explaining to readers and viewers the reasons for world hunger.

So much garbage has been printed, so much bad theory circulated, so much brainwashing of innocent bystanders attempted that a debunking effort like this one is tempted to go all out in the other direction in order to prove that the earth can

31

sustain, as Harvard Professor Roger Revelle has persuasively argued, a population of 40–50 billion people. I shall try to resist this temptation for obvious reasons rooted in human dignity—no child should arrive unwanted—and in concern for the environment. This book is a plea for rationality and social justice, but it does not suppose that necessary structural changes and reallocations of wealth will occur overnight. Even taking for granted that current knowledge and technology are equal to the task of providing a decent diet for every human being now on earth or for a much larger number—given a radically different world order—it would still not be ecologically desirable to decimate the last natural forest in order to provide arable land and food for tens of billions of people.

The mere fact that the rich and powerful have shown such enormous interest in limiting the birth rates of the poor and downtrodden should in itself make us suspicious. Is it their milk of human kindness spilling over? Such charitable intentions have been less evident in areas where they would do more good. It seems fantastically easy to get money for birth-control studies and programs in Asia whereas research geared to more equitable distribution of food, "soft" technology and the like must go begging. Could it be that philanthropists would rather have countries like India tailor their populations to *existing* capacities of agriculture—capacities limited by reactionary land-tenure structures—than see them undertake the thoroughgoing reforms and overhaul of the social system that would be necessary to feed growing populations? Let us keep this healthy suspicion in mind as we proceed: first to make an inventory of the "garbage," then to try to discover what really influences population growth and what might be done about it.

Here is a typical example of what the mass-media feed to their readers every day. It gives the argument in admirably condensed form.

1. The world's resources, including food, are limited.
2. There are too many people in the world, and everyone knows that the poorest countries have the highest birth rates, therefore
3. It is the poor who are consuming the world's resources.

                                                                QED

This is unworthy even of a third-rate editorial page. We have already seen that it is the rich who consume over half of the world's food supply in the most wasteful possible manner. World Bank figures show that "on average the one billion people in the countries with per capita incomes below $200 consume only about 1 per cent as much energy per capita as the citizens of the United States." The Bank's Mr. McNamara also hopes that "once the people of the United States understand that they, with 6 per cent of the world's population, consume about 35 per cent of the world's total resources, and yet in terms of economic assistance as a percentage of GNP rank 14th among the 16 developed nations... [they will not] turn away in cynicism and indifference." For another audience, he could, with slight modifications in the figures, have spoken just as well of Western Europe or Japan. The least one can say is that the media are doing little to aid the citizens of the developed world attain the kind of consciousness McNamara hopes for.

What about less popular-oriented, more scientific approaches to the question? The German economist–demographer, Heinrich von Loesch, speaking of 150 years of population theory and attempts at prediction (and backing his conclusions with econometric models too complicated to reproduce here) sums it up rather admirably.

This predictability suggests a measure of understanding on the side of the projecting demographers which in reality does not exist. In fact, even the most sophisticated population projections of today are only extensions of past trends into the future. If the motivations which produced these trends remain the same the projections are likely to be accurate. If the motivations change, the demographers will have failed.

In other words, it is far more important to learn *why* people want and need to have children than to dither about mounting population figures.

Personally, I am so tired of reading about how we could reach the moon if the world's people were stacked vertically (or is it horizontally?) or how quickly the continental shelf would sink if they were all concentrated between Boston and Washington that my favorite prediction, admittedly tongue-in-cheek, is the one headlined "Doomsday: Friday 13th November A.D. 2026" in which the authors prove from present trends that the population will become infinite on that date!

For the moment, let's forget the year 2026 and try to understand the present. According to UN figures, world population in-

International Herald Tribune, April 5-6, 1975

'Chomp, Chomp, Chomp.'

creased by 2.1 per cent in 1973, or 78 million people. Fifty-five per cent live in Asia, about 10 per cent in Africa, 8 per cent in Latin America—or just about three quarters of humanity in the Third World. It is not so important to grasp the UN's contention that "if this trend continues world population will double in 32 years and will reach 7.5 billion people in 2007" as to recognize that the world *presently* contains about 3,900 million human beings, and we had better get on with feeding them *now*. This is, in fact, the only hope we have of reducing their numbers *later*.* As the *New Internationalist* quite correctly states, "The number of people in the world is going to double in the next 30 years and there is absolutely nothing that anybody can do to stop it. Even the most spectacular, sustained and successful family planning program imaginable could only serve to slow down an even more dramatic rise in numbers during the 21st century." But if *we* can devise the social means to provide our present world with food, the chances are that our children and grandchildren can take the twenty-first century in their stride.

*The only hope, that is, outside of letting them starve to death. A late 1976 report from The Worldwatch Institute states that declining birthrates in some countries and "unforseen deaths from hunger have slowed global population growth to the point where doubling of the world population by the year 2000 is no longer anticipated." [International Herald Tribune 1 November 1976]

It is quite true that population growth rates have increased faster than food production in some UDCs, but in many of them that have been prime targets for Western advice on the subject, the opposite has been the case: Angola, Bolivia, Brazil, Egypt, Ethiopia, India, Mozambique, Niger, Senegal, Sri Lanka, Sudan and Upper Volta are among them. Still one could argue that even in such countries populations are too large to allow a decent diet for all. But doesn't this argument itself indicate that the basic problem is one of *distribution* (both of food and of food-producing resources) and of the political will to increase food production since it is technically possible? Population could even decrease and food production increase, but if the broad majority of the people still lacked the purchasing power to pay for their food or the means to produce it, hunger and malnutrition would still affect the same number—or a larger one—proportionally to the total population. There are indications that just such a trend has taken hold in Brazil which has a highly respectable growth rate both for industrial and for overall food production. It is lack of equitable distribution that keeps so many Brazilians hungry, even though the population growth rate has been 2.9 per cent and GNP per capita growth rate a praiseworthy 5.6 per cent (both figures averages for 1965-72). By comparison, growth rates of GNP per capita for the US and the UK during the same period were 2 per cent.

People are going hungry partly for lack of investment: without going to ecological extremes there is still plenty of useful land that could be farmed if investment were directed that way. (See Appendix.) They are going hungry especially for lack of justice: we have seen that in UDCs those with the least land produce, proportionally, the most food and we have cited some individual country figures to back this claim. But the worst news is yet to come and it relates directly to the population problem: *a mere 2.5 per cent of landowners with holdings of more than 100 hectares control nearly three quarters of all the land in the world—with the top 0.23 per cent controlling over half.* These revealing and horrifying figures come from the world land census conducted by FAO in 1960. Figures for the 1970s are not available, but it is known that land concentration has everywhere increased, particularly in the poor and populous countries that have adopted the Green Revolution.

How do land distribution (simply a different term for social justice), ratio of population to land (density) and hunger correlate? The World Bank gave the following indications in 1974. There are four developing countries in Asia, the world's most populous continent, generally credited with feeding their entire populations tolerably well. Two of them have market economies; two are socialist. They are China, South Korea, Taiwan* and North Vietnam. When we look at the ratios of cropland to total population or to agricultural population, we discover that these four countries have the *least* land per person of all the countries in Asia. In China there are 0.13 hectares per person; in North Vietnam 0.10; in South Korea 0.07 and in Taiwan only 0.06 (Land available for every member of the agricultural population is also less in these four countries than in any of the other Asian countries. Japan is a special case: it imports some food for hard currency but also has a highly successful agricultural sector—and only 0.05 hectares per head.) Compare these figures with India, which has 0.30 arable hectares for every Indian, Pakistan with 0.40—or even with two other chronically underfed countries, Bangladesh and Indonesia, with 0.16 and 0.15 respectively—and the truth will become clear. The *structure* of landholdings has far more to do with erasing hunger than the amount of total population.

Here is further proof that density of population simply does not correlate with actual food supply: famine exists both in Bolivia with 5 inhabitants per square kilometer and in India with 172—but there is no famine in Holland where there are 326. As for availability of cropland per person (total, not farming populations) there are 0.63 hectares in Bolivia, the 0.30 we mentioned for India—but only 0.06 in Holland. Many Indians and Bolivians are starving, while Holland adequately meets its own needs and exports besides. Up to now, the press has not been clamoring for birth control for the Dutch, who nevertheless dispose of only a tenth the land of Bolivians or a fifth that of Indians. The most obvious and final example is, of course, China which experienced famine somewhere nearly every year when it was a country of 500,000,000 people. Now it furnishes over 2,300 calories a day to a population of 800,000,000. *The first thing to realize when trying to think straight about population/food is that hunger is not*

---

*Paradoxically, one of the reasons for Taiwan's success is that it used to be a Japanese colony! Japan organized it to produce a maximum; it has gone on doing so.

caused *by population pressure. Both hunger and rapid popula-tion growth reflect the same failure of a political and economic system.*

"But why," you are entitled to ask as a media-influenced Westerner, "do the poor persist in having more children than they can afford?" The answer is, "They don't." Another baby for you means visits to the pediatrician, formulas, strollers, snowsuits, orthopedic shoes and disposable diapers; followed by an expensive education and myriad other outlays. When you finally get your costly progeny on its own feet, does it contribute to your income? Perhaps—for a short time. But usually it will go off without a thought to raise its own babies with the money it can now earn itself, thanks to your years of care.

Another baby for a poor family means an extra mouth to feed— a very marginal difference. But by the time that child is four or five years old, it will make important contributions to the whole family—fetching water from the distant well, taking meals to father and brothers in the field, feeding animals. Later the child will help with more complicated tasks which would all devolve upon the mother of the household if she could not count on her children. Women may have to suffer the biological servitude of pregnancies, but at least they can be spared—in poor, "overpopulous" families—the much longer and far more burdensome servitude of carrying out all the household and many of the farming tasks without even simple conveniences like running water and without any help whatsoever. Most Third World mothers have only a 50/50 chance of seeing their children live beyond the age of five. Once we realize that children are an economic *necessity* for the poor, then we can understand that poor families will have to plan their births every bit as carefully as couples in Westchester or West Harrow—and allow for the predictable mortality rate.

Would you think quite the same way about children if you lived in a country which had never heard of old-age pensions, social security, health insurance and the like? Outside of societies like China, Vietnam and the other planned economies, the only safeguard against an indifferent world in old age is the family. The poor age quickly. One of the family's sons may turn out to be bright and will get some education followed by a paid job in the city. He will help to support his parents, but they know they will be able to count on all their children, educated or not. How else are the poor to survive when they are too old or exhausted to work?

In the West, the usual attitude toward the population explosion (reminiscent in its very terminology of atomic bombs and similar disasters) is that the poor multiply because they are ignorant of biology, illiterate, and don't know any better. So they have more children than they actually want. A forthright critic of the "lesser breeds without the law" even explained the problem by the absence of television! "When the sun goes down on an Indian village, the people are left in darkness. They have no books, no movies, no television. There is only one thing to do— go to bed. There they find their sole source of recreation and amusement . . . At the root of Asia's problem of population is copulation." And no "Kojak." More recent words of wisdom from the West are somewhat less simplistic, but they still stress a purely technical approach:

> There are appropriate technologies which make it possible to abate population growth. What appears to be lacking is a universal will to embark upon this effort aggressively and continuously. Some nations are still not convinced that the population threat is real, growing, and is contributing each day to a deteriorating world economy which, in turn, determines what standards of living shall prevail.

This comes from one of the major foundations supporting family planning in the Third World. One wonders if the standards of living invoked are theirs or ours. If we stopped looking just for a moment at what *we* consider to be the problems of the poorest people ("too many children") and tried to look at life from their point of view ("my children are my only wealth"), then we might realize that "appropriate technologies" to lessen population growth without social changes making children less *necessary* cannot possibly have any effect.

It is not even true that governments of the most populous nations have not tried to do something about the problem. According to a study by the Population Council, thirty-one UDCs representing 74 per cent of the underdeveloped world's population had public birth-control policies in 1972, and twenty-eight more representing another 13 per cent of the total Third World population supported family-planning programs in one way or another. Thus birth-control policies have been implemented more or less forcefully in the recent past by governments representing 87 per cent of the total citizens of UDCs. Why, then, do most of them seem to have failed?

If we examine an Indian's assessment of his own country's attempts at population control, we discover that the effort has been phenomenal—and the results miserable. Yet the outlay for family planning in five successive Indian Five Year Plans has zoomed from a mere million and a half rupees in the first plan to 560 million in the current (1974-9) budget—an increase of nearly 2,700 per cent. D. Bannerji explains that in order to "motivate" its citizens, the Indian government has done everything from handing out free condoms to suppressing maternity leaves for working mothers with "too many" children; it has paid bounties to doctors and health workers for every sterilization candidate they can haul in; it runs "mass vasectomy camps"; it has raised the legal marriage age for men and women and maintains a fleet of IUD-mobiles to take contraceptives to village women—not to mention saturation public-relations and "communications" campaigns. Well over 100,000 people are employed in population-reduction extension work. "However, despite the enormous investment, despite the good will of planners and political leaders, and despite the recourse to means that [are] questionable on social, moral, ethical and political grounds, the programme has abjectly failed even in terms of reduction of the birth rate." Goals have had to be "revised" constantly: although the goal was 25 births per thousand by 1980, the rural birth rate has been hovering around 38 or 39 per thousand for several years now and shows no signs of beginning a rapid decline. Bannerji wonders how "the decision makers [could] 'succeed' in making so many mistakes, and how they could get away with them."

He suggests that their worst mistake was to put the cart before the horse by not understanding that

. . . for controlling population growth, a family planning programme is a mere component of a wider spectrum which has to embrace a combination of programmes for dealing with different social and economic problems of the country. Population control [is] considered—rather simplistically—to be a precursor of development in other social and economic fields.

The methods that were tried—and failed—such as "motivation techniques" were thought of by planners as "some sort of magic

. . . . The so-called 'communications/action research' were West-ern-induced ideas that gained in importance in this country because [they] happened to be in tune with the research back-ground of some of the *key foreign consultants* [emphasis added]."

Such pitiful (though expensive) attempts at Western-style human engineering would be bad enough, but Bannerji says the overall picture is even worse. He finds fault with political leaders who want, they say, "revolution" without standing up to the forces that perpetuate the status quo, with a bureaucracy holding "steadfastly to its colonial traditions"; and he states that "heavy dependence on foreign agencies for 'technical assistance' [is] a natural corollary to the unwillingness of leaders to squarely face the basic problems of the country." A population policy guaran-teed to be ineffective fits right into this pattern:

> It is indeed the same forces which have found a common interest in raising the spectre of a runaway population growth in India . . . the bogey of a rapidly rising population came in very handy for covering up the massive failures of the leadership to comply with the Directive Principles [a Bill of Rights set forth in the Indian Constitution]. It is not surprising that, in dealing with the population problem, the decision makers simply circumvented the basic problems of poverty, social injustice, ill-health, primary education and illiteracy. Nor is it surprising that they tried to cover up the inherent weaknesses in their own approach by stooping to use "incentives" to procure "acceptors" [of contraceptive devices or sterilization], to use police methods, to "motivate" the people . . . As a result, it is also not surprising that, despite recourse to [these questionable] means, they fell far short of their objectives of rapidly bringing down the birth rate.

It seems worth quoting Bannerji at some length not only because he is Indian and most readers have no ready access to Indian sources, but also because he is writing in one of India's most respected journals—and one of the most outspoken, at least until the axe fell on free speech. His message is clear: no amount of money, inducement or externally imposed "motivation" is going to change birth rates in any significant way unless the root causes of the "explosion" are eliminated. Hunger and popula-tion growth are both *symptoms*—one is not the cause of the other—and to single out population growth for *direct* attack is both a costly and a tragic illusion. As long as profound inequali-ties subsist within the Third World countries, the poor will continue to have many children because they cannot logically or humanly do otherwise.*

The Overseas Development Council report *Population* quotes a 1971 study by William Rich showing that where decrease in birth rates is concerned, variations between UDCs with similar gross national products per capita result primarily from differences in the *distribution* of this GNP. In more equalitarian countries birth rates tend to decline more rapidly and vice versa. These conclusions are also borne out by the comparative figures for five UDCs published by the *New Internationalist*. (See pp. 42-43.)

This chart shows that if you want to get your national birth rate from 41 down to 26 (Taiwan) or from 45 to 30 per thousand (Korea), the best way to go about it is not to distribute condoms and IUDs and hope for the best, but to give people effective land reform and more income. They will reward you with fewer babies. (Note also the far higher density of population—coupled with very high yields—in Korea and Taiwan.) This should be so obvious from the experience of the developed countries themselves, where population growth rates began to decline only *after* the stage of relative affluence was reached, that one wonders why such arguments should seem so novel to so many.

It is also amazing how little attention is paid in UDCs to those who actually have the babies. I am not being facetious. Governments outwardly professing their desire to reduce birth rates simultaneously do little or nothing to educate women (especially rural women) and give first priority to boys. A woman's "education" in any number of cultures is limited to preparing her for a marriage which may take place before she is fifteen years old.

One of the heaviest pressure factors on population growth, as Heinrich von Loesch points out, is nearly universal "son preference." Girl babies are no longer being exposed on mountain tops—at least as far as I know—but the birth of a girl is still regarded in many quarters as a family disaster, while poor fathers will sacrifice an animal in thanksgiving when a son is born. So long as these ingrained attitudes are unchallenged—even encouraged—by government policy, it is hard to see how much progress

*The current compulsory sterilization campaign in India will place further burdens on the poor for this reason. It will also give local authorities means to increase coercion, extortionate measures; indeed, blackmail.

Comparison of the Economies of the Philippines, Taiwan, Mexico Brazil and Korea

		Philippines
Per capita income	1960: 1969:	$169 $208
GNP growth rates in 1960s		—
Annual increase in industrial jobs		—
Unemployment and gross underemployment		14.5% (1961) 15% (1968)
Ratio of income controlled by top 20% of income recipients to bottom 20%		12:1 (1956) 16:1 (1965)
Income improvement of poorest 20% over past 20 years		Negligible
Investment cost of increasing GNP by $1 in 1960s		$3.50
Exports ($ millions)	1960: 1970:	$560 $961
Effective land reform		No
Agricultural working population per 100 hectares		71
Percentage of farmers belonging to cooperatives (late 1960s)		17%
Yields per acre for food grains		1,145 (1968–70)
Literacy		72%
Life expectancy		55
Infant mortality per 1,000 births		72
Rural households electrified		6%
Consumption of electric power kilowatt hours per person)		39 (1951) 184 (1968)
Crude birth rates (births per thousand)		— 45 (1960) 44 (1970)

Taiwan	Mexico	Brazil	Korea
$176	$441	$268	$138
$334	$606	$348	$242
10%	7%	6%	9%
10% (1963–9)	5.4% (1969–70)	2.8% (1966–9)	—
10% (1963)	Significant	—	—
4% (1968)	and rising	10–12% (1970)	7.5% (1970)
15:1 (1953)	10:1 (1950)	22:1 (1960)	—
5:1 (1969)	16:1 (1969)	25:1 (1970)	5:1
200%	Negligible	Negligible	**Over 100%**
$2.10	$3.10	$2.80	$1.70
$164	$831	$1,269	$5.2
$1,428	$1,402	$2,310	$835.2
Yes	No	No	Yes
195	35	43	197
Virtually			**Virtually**
100%	5%	28%	**100%**
3,570	1,225	1,280	**2,850**
85%	76%	67%	71%
68	61	64	64
19	66	94	41
75%	—	—	27%
116 (1949)	162 (1948)	200 (1952)	55 (1953)
745 (1968)	481 (1968)	390 (1966)	200 (1968)
41 (1947)	44 (1950)	41 (1950)	**45 (1950)**
36 (1963)	44 (1960)	41 (1960)	42 (1960)
26 (1970)	41 (1970)	38 (1970)	**30 (1970)**

Emphasis added by S. G.

can be made or how the vast numbers of illiterate, sometimes cloistered women can even be reached with the news that they can exert control over their own bodies.

Because control over one's body is important. None of the foregoing discussion is intended to discount the necessity for effective methods of contraception and safe, legal abortion when contraception fails—simply to state that *by themselves* they cannot be expected to make a dent in world population.

The above chart helps to make useful comparisons for certain market economy countries. The system used in China is at base the same—greater social equality—but there are interesting variations. In addition to social services and freely available contraceptives, solidarity among the women plays an important role. Novelist and surgeon Han Suyin reported after a recent trip to China that although family planning began in China in 1956, it has only reached the rural communes where 85 per cent of the women live in the last three or four years. She explains that the program is carried out

> . . .street by street and village by village. Women talk with other women. They get together and decide how many children should be born that year in that particular street. Supposing they feel the street should have only five children that year and there are seven prospective mothers, there will always be two volunteers to say, "I'll wait until next year." If a woman disagrees, nothing is done to coerce her. But someone else will have to sacrifice for her and she will feel bad about it. There are still women in China who have six, seven, or eight children. The difference is that before many of these children died. Now they all live.

"Say the husband wants another child and the wife doesn't. It is the wife's decision that prevails. That doesn't mean the husband is not consulted." Abortion is also freely available; the decision rests solely with the woman, but most Chinese women rely on the "paper pill"—a block of postage-stamp size chemically impregnated squares for each day of the month. "In the fields and the communes, they have a system whereby one woman is responsible every day for calling out to the others, 'Have you taken your pill?'" Han Suyin suggests that you can't get this sort of result by giving orders "but only when the population is pulling together. This is solidarity."

Another recent visitor to China explains that the type of social organization chosen for the rural areas provides a built-in material incentive for limiting the number of people. He points out that in the communes the production team is the basic social unit.

Each production team is governed by a revolutionary committee including representatives of households, cadres, and others, who collectively decide how assigned quotas shall be met, what crops will be planted, what management system will be used and so forth. Income is dependent upon productivity achieved *above the assigned quota* and all produce other than market barter is sold to a State Cooperative Agency. This system of operation encourages limitations on population growth *since the area farmed is static. Unless productivity increases proportionally with an increase in manpower, per capita income must fall.*

Instead of "telling the other half how to live" and how many babies to have, we in the West would be better advised to examine our own motives. Certainly we are afraid—afraid that increasing numbers in the Third World will one day demand from us their due and lower our own standard of living; fearful that the pressures of population may finally demonstrate that the "only solution is revolution." Even the most well-meaning of the pills-for-the-poor contingent cannot escape the charge of arrogance. Father does not necessarily know best; neither do ex-colonial powers. Rockefeller Plaza is not necessarily the best vantage point for understanding life in Andhra Pradesh. The objects of so much Western solicitude will take to IUDs, pills and condoms with startling alacrity and in their own sweet time—that is, just as soon as real development and a fairer deal in their own countries allow them to do so.

3. Local Elites —
And How to Join Them

Even if we in the West admit that we try to tell the other half how to live, the question remains, "Why do they listen to us?" Why do UDC governments so often seem to act as if the adoption of Western values and methods were the only road to salvation? This frequent acquiescence of the Third World is in part the result of a long-term Western strategy. I am hopeful that by making this strategy explicit, it will be possible to meet head on the kind of counter-attacks analyses like this one so often encounter in the rich countries themselves. Some of these, more or less elegantly expressed, are:

"Our Western life-style is the best there is, and the proof is that the rest of the world imitates us, or would like to." "The first thing those black presidents (oil sheikhs, banana republic generals, *et al.*) do is buy a big fleet of American cars." "Aid money just goes into the pockets of corrupt officials anyway." "If the multinational corporations are so bad, why don't they kick them out?" And of course, such remarks are all at least partially justified. It is not, naturally, poor and hungry people who benefit from imported whisky and limousines, nor is it they who make the budgetary decisions in the UDCs any more than they do in Washington, London or Paris.

On the other hand, it is decidedly unfashionable in many liberal circles to chide the locals: *everything* is the fault of the nasty imperialists, and to suggest otherwise is to be a racist. But isn't it less racist to affirm that given a certain social structure and sufficient opportunity, *people*—not black ones or yellow ones or brown or white—will demonstrate greed and selfishness and will resort to oppressing those beneath them if it proves necessary in order to hold on to what they have acquired? Will they not also cooperate with whomsoever holds out a promise of help in maintaining them in positions of power and privileged status?

Clearly, all is not well with the local élites and there would seem to be certain natural affinities between them and powerful groups in the developed world. But are these affinities natural—or nurtured? Is is entirely fortuitous that in Third World countries the classes in a position to do so have so often aped Western affluent society life-styles or that they welcome Western aid, foreign advisers and the "contributions" of multinational corporations to their economies? I am not going to subject the reader to a five-century history of colonialism but simply ask him or her to bear in mind that for at least that long there have always been local élites eager to collaborate with colonial powers in exchange for a slice of the cake. It is more enlightening to look at what passes for the post-colonial period of history—beginning at the end of the Second World War, also frequently labelled the Cold War period—from which we have not yet entirely emerged. How and why is it that so many post-colonial local élites have become so tractable, so amenable to the dictates of the rich world's interests?

A remarkable official US government document, ingenuously titled "Winning the Cold War: The U.S. Ideological Offensive" will give us a clue. It is a stenographic record of testimony by US Agency for International Development and Department of Defense (USAID and DoD) officials given in January 1964 at the height of the Cold War when the US was less self-conscious about flaunting its interventions in other peoples' affairs. Little commentary on the following passages would seem necessary to prove that the US has made a conscious, costly and long-term effort to bring key foreign citizens around to "thinking American." (European countries have attempted to do exactly the same thing, but have had to work with lower budgets and less personnel.)

Here is some testimony from Mr. Coffin, Deputy Administrator of USAID:

> Our basic, broadest goal is a long range political one. It is not development for the sake of sheer development. . . . An important objective is to open up the maximum opportunity for domestic private initiative and to insure that foreign private investment, particularly from the United States, is welcomed and well treated. . . . The problem is . . . to evaluate the manner in which the program can make the greatest contribution to the totality of U.S. interests. . . .

Mr. Coffin then explains that, "the AID program planning process recognizes that the program is an instrument of U.S.

foreign policy. AID country programs . . . are developed in the field on the basis of . . . instructions from Washington." After recalling AID's role in military assistance, "counterinsurgency" and the orientation of local police forces, Coffin explains that in the area of general policy "we give serious consideration to how we can most effectively influence [countries] in the direction of policies and programs which accord with U.S. objectives." There are various ways of doing this, but one of the most important is the Participant Training Program which

. . . is at once the phase of the program which is probably most critical from the standpoint of the opportunity for the effective communication of ideas, and the most sensitive if the opportunity is not handled with restraint and sensitivity. . . . The Agency annually brings to the United States 6,000 foreign nationals [the participants] for study and training in technical and professional fields . . . their training is directly related to development objectives in their home countries. They live and work with us, they travel throughout our country and share our recreational and social life. They return to their homes to add not only increased skill and competence, but *whatever they have absorbed of the values of our society.* . . . The opportunity for *broad social and political orientation* exists at every point in the total experience the participant has while in the United States [emphasis added].

Participants, who usually remain in the US from five months to a year, get pre-departure orientation, and once in the US they are exposed not only to intensive English language and professional training but also to a series of university seminars on subjects like "U.S. institutions, traditions and values," guided tours, leisure-time activities and social contacts. The latter are organized through the generosity of the Ford Foundation, which maintains a volunteer network called COSERV grouping 26,000 people in 150 American cities—all of them prepared to entertain USAID's guests. The Director of International Training at AID describes the results:

CHAIRMAN [DANTE FASCELL]: When you get through with this participant he is upgraded to do a better job in the skill in which he started?
MR. KITCHEN: Yes.
CHAIRMAN: To go back to his country.
KITCHEN: Yes, sir.
CHAIRMAN: I assume also he is then a strong supporter of the US Aid Program?
KITCHEN: I would hope that the capacity to participate in the AID program is what I would call the visible part of the iceberg. It seems to me

there are far larger areas of understanding the total interest of this country, its ideals, its aims. . . . There is a tendency to ask that they be particularly loyal to AID. We are not hurting at all if it facilitates the conduct of our program, but I would say, having spent 10 years abroad and now being back here, this is certainly a by-product.

In case the participant might not feel such loyalties strongly enough, Coffin specifies that "we make special arrangements . . . that they will want to be a continuing channel and point of contact when they return home." He provides the Subcommittee with an annex to his testimony giving a list of the present positions of some of the 80,000 participants from 80 countries (as of 1963!) who doubtless serve as "continuing channels and points of contact." They include ministers, undersecretaries, directors of major government departments, judges, parliamentarians, governors of national banks and the like. Coffin proudly points out that "there are very few countries in the free world where former participants have not had a real impact in government, private industry and the professions."

AID nevertheless sometimes has a hard political row to hoe when pushing the American way of life. This is because "In many of the less developed countries, particularly those with a colonial past, 'capitalism' is synonymous with foreign exploitation" so many of these countries tend to adopt a "vague and idealistic 'socialism' [as] a cardinal tenet of the dominant political philosophy." Therefore, among other goals, Coffin explains,

The fostering of a vigorous and expanding private sector in the less developed countries is one of our most important responsibilities. . . . We can and do endeavor to influence relevant attitudes directly. . . . Already we can see evidence of such ideological evolution in some key countries. For instance, Colombia, Venezuela, Ethiopia, the Philippines, India and Pakistan have taken practical measures to improve the climate for private foreign enterprise.

Coffin also details the way in which contacts are kept up with participants once they have returned home to responsible positions—these range from "old-boy" networks and alumni associations ("an important source of support for the USAID country program and U.S. policy") to social events, workshops, conferences and seminars, continued English language training, newsletters, membership in American professional societies and the like.

AID is also heavily engaged in "winning the cold war" inside the foreign countries themselves. It works in every social area from "labor" to "public administration" and stresses the study of English, for "new leaders who read and write English are far more likely to grasp the essence of the American way than those who do not." AID-supported educational institutions "have been highly successful in communicating American educational theory and practice to key groups. They serve, in fact, as living models of the American approach, not simply to education, but to life in general" which "students learn both consciously and unconsciously."

AID is also, not surprisingly, strongly interested in agriculture, because

> ... virtually all countries we assist are primarily rural with 70 or more per cent of the people earning their living in agriculture. *U.S. assistance to the agricultural sector of the developing countries is therefore, to an exceptional degree, significant in the influence it has in the ideological contest.* . . . As in our own countries, the fundamental political character of the country which emerges from the development process will be determined largely by the rural institutions designed to achieve agricultural development [emphasis added].

In 1963, 18 per cent of all AID participant training was for key people in agriculture. Only education ranked higher with 24 per cent. In-country AID activities include "development of agricultural extension services, development of agricultural universities (with participant training of faculty in the US) and the sponsorship of rural youth clubs." Particular attention is devoted to students of agriculture because "universities in many underdeveloped countries are centers of unrest and focal points of expression of discontent" where students "direct their energies into protest, often of a violent and usually of a political nature." AID's program is aimed at redirecting these energies by integrating the universities into the practical life of the country, reorganizing the curriculum, etc. "This is the process by which universities are developed into highly responsive, creative centers supporting their national development rather than isolated centers of protest. As progress is made toward this end, students tend to organize into professional rather than political societies." One might translate this by saying that as the students themselves are drawn into the élite and see careers opportunities in collaborating with US-defined development goals already pursued by their elders, they can be successfully coopted and will leave immature "political" goals behind them. The witness claims that for both students and faculty "the overwhelming majority of such trainees become thoroughly convinced that economic development of his own country can be most easily achieved under a comparable [to the US] system . . . ."

In the case that these countries, in spite of so much US effort on their behalf, might still express discontent of a "violent" or even of a "political" nature, the Department of Defense maintains a much larger Participant Training Program (28,000—30,000 people invited yearly, compared to AID's 6,000) for UDC military and police forces. All the features of the program are similar to AID's.

The Chairman wants to know how effective the program is compared to similar efforts on the part of the Russians.

FASCELL: [I take no responsibility for the Chairman's grammar.] Whether we like the title, I am assuming and hoping that the reason we are training these people is so we will have friends in camp. I also hope we can assist the technical caliber of every military establishment which understands and supports us. Furthermore, I hope our program is flexible enough so that we can focus in on a particular country which might be a problem area.

MR. SLOAN [of DoD International Security Affairs]: We hope the impact of our program will be more successful in the political and ideological areas than theirs [the USSR's].

FASCELL: Have we any way of measuring that?

SLOAN: It is difficult to measure, except when the chips get down and you see who is supporting a US position, whether it be in the UN or in some dispute that is going on in the country, or whether it be a problem of a new government and its attitude toward the United States; we can see—I think I can report confidently—that *those who have been trained here have a great friendliness for us* [security deletion]. . . . While it is definitely true, of course, that we have the key countries [security deletion] in which we do concentrate larger parts or segments of our program, because of all our operations to influence people world-wide, the training program is the one least expensive to us, relatively, and we certainly get more for our training dollar than we do for a dollar invested in a truck, for example. [Emphasis added.]

Part of the military/police training is carried out in the US, and includes the Civic Action Program which encourages armies to participate in rural development activities in order to prove to the people that the Army is their friend.

SLOAN: A very dramatic example of the success of the [civic action] program from its ideological viewpoint as distinguished from the physical building of a road was in Bolivia recently, with the recent uprisings down there. The truth was that until this [program] came up, President Paz did not know whether he could risk using his army or not in coping with the miners. The army was a pretty unpopular outfit. So he mostly kept them in defensive positions, perhaps even to defend the government. [But now that the Bolivian army has got out into the countryside] President Paz decided the Army was in pretty good favor with the people and he could use them to put down the rebellion if necessary and he sent them. I think this is a pretty dramatic illustration of how it can work in a non-hot-war situation. I have always felt that the limits of a civil action program are almost the limits of your imagination of what you can do with organized people.

It is also a pretty dramatic illustration of how US military training assists repressive régimes in crushing their own people with legitimate grievances, but we have had many and far more horrendous examples of this sort of intervention in the years that have elapsed since these hearings.

Surely ordinary pride and national self-respect in the UDCs should counteract such pressures, however great? It is true that a Western education has been the first step in forming many a militant Third World revolutionary.

But put yourself in the shoes of the average bright young man in an underdeveloped country. You are suddenly transplanted to the most developed, not to say overblown, industrial society on earth, exposed to its manifold pleasures and to intensive—but not heavy-handed, AID is careful about that—ideological indoctrination, to the overwhelming (and quite genuine) hospitality of some of the 26,000 citizen volunteers of COSERV; in the bargain you get a chance to upgrade your professional standing. All of this is not only absolutely free but is accompanied by a generous allowance. What will be your normal reaction—fear, hatred and suspicion of your benefactors? Your stay in the US has also given you added prestige at home and a boost up the career ladder (as the list of positions of former AID participants shows). You may even have the unconscious feeling that your own country may some-how become "like" the society you have experienced, if only you follow the same policies and keep listening to those who formulate them. This is not at all incompatible with a real desire to see your own people better off.

If you are less generous and idealistic, if you are merely interested in capitalizing on your training and extra prestige for your own power and position, you may become more selective about the "values" of a "free society" you are supposed to have absorbed. In an article entitled "The Geography of Disgrace," Robert Shelton details the number of political prisoners held in many of the countries from which a disproportionate number of AID/DoD participants come. The most AIDed nations—in Asia or Latin America—are also those that Amnesty International places at the top of its lists: South Vietnam (until recently), Indonesia, Brazil, etc. One could use many other indicators besides political prisoners to show that most of the nations with which USAID and the DoD have been especially preoccupied have indeed adopted US-inspired economic systems while simultaneously rejecting such values as freedom of thought and political action. If the introduction of "democratic ideals" into the UDCs via their élites is to be the criterion, AID's efforts have failed dismally. If, on the other hand, we assume that the nurturing of private enterprise, country participation in the free market and freedom for the penetration of American capital were the real goals—as most of the cited testimony suggests—then we may safely say that the US government's money has been well spent on procuring docile partners in the UDCs.

One should be neither shocked nor suprised by such testimony. Expansionist powers have been cultivating local collaborators since long before Rome found indigenous help in getting rid of a popular rabble-rouser called Jesus Christ. Great Britain created a landed élite in India along British lines which had not previously existed. As Noam Chomsky says about Lord Cornwallis,

> There is no reason to doubt the sincerity of his belief that this civilized arrangement could only benefit the Indians in the long run. Of course, the new squirearchy also happened to serve British interests; as the British Governor General Lord William Bentinck put it: "If security was wanting against popular tumult or revolution, I should say that the "permanent settlement" . . . has this great advantage . . . of having created a vast body of rich landed proprietors deeply interested in the continuance of British Dominion and having complete command over the mass of the people." [1829]

What is interesting is not that "popular tumult and revolution" is now, in the US view, "communist" directed and inspired— it is the worldwide scale of élite-building that has been undertaken and the near-total collusion of the American political-intellectual Establishment in the enterprise. This Establishment, on the whole, has a nice disregard for anybody else's values or achievements. Here is another pearl unearthed by Chomsky, dropped by a well-known Columbia University professor:* "America has become *the* creative society; the others, consciously and unconsciously, are emulative." Cold-war politics is one motive for intervention; common or garden arrogance is another. If there is only one source of creativity, then it follows that the creators have a moral responsibility to intervene when and where they please; to apply development models of their own devising to other societies; and, of course, to train leaders in various spheres who will be capable of "emulation." Harry Truman was as usual more honest than most when he explained what is really behind the logic of constructing local élite power-bases: "All freedom is dependent on freedom of enterprise. . . . The whole world should adopt the American system. . . . The American system can survive in America only if it becomes a world system."

One of Orwell's principles in *1984* was that real control is thought control and that the pinnacle is reached when the controlled person (or society) *no longer realizes* that the concepts and the terms of reference he uses have been superimposed upon his mind by an outside agent. We have taken a short look at one great power's state policy for the training and education of Third World development cadres, but we would also do well to examine the collusion of the intellectual Establishment in winning hearts and minds in these same countries. On the whole, governments, foundations and universities are all pulling in the same direction. Certain uses of the social sciences, certain methods for devising "development models" may come to seem—at least for a time— the *only* uses, the *only* methods in developed and underdeveloped countries alike *if* the scientific and intellectual élites of both can be made to share the same non-explicit postulates, the same unspoken attitudes. If this can be managed, one may fairly consider that the models and methods of the more advanced countries will prevail; that specific local conditions and needs will affect decision-making in poor nations only marginally, and that on the whole, poor people in UDCs will be regarded by their own high-status compatriots as "inferior and in need of civilizing by anglicization" as S. Goonitalake puts it for the case of

*Who has lately attained particular eminence: Zbigniew Brzezinski.

officials' views of peasants in Sri Lanka. This author also says that

. . . the bureaucracy, where the decisions pertaining to the country's development were to take place, accepted Western socio-economic models unreservedly as representing modernity and the scientific ethos. The question of whether these models and the assumptions on which they rested were at all relevant to Sri Lanka was not raised.

D. Bannerji, speaking for India, says,

Because of the colonial heritage and the continuing affinity and strong links of the ruling élites of India with their counterparts abroad— particularly in the Western industrialized countries—almost every facet of the social, economic and cultural activities in India has been considerably influenced, if not often actually controlled, by the bigger global system.

Part of this "bigger global system" is embodied in the private foundations which have been involved in the hearts-and-minds business since the Harkness family (Standard Oil) founded Yale in China in 1902. Its then Chancellor believed that "once we have won over the students and the educated people, we shall have won China itself." The Rockefeller Foundation followed suit with the China Medical Board and the Peking Union Medical College (in 1914 and 1921). These may have been dress-rehearsals for the Rockefeller-financed All-India Institute of Medical Sciences founded in 1956. The Rockefellers also support several "independent" research organizations in the US like the Agricultural Development Council and the Population Council—obviously not concerned with examining problems of agriculture or population in the United States itself. A recent Rockefeller effort, concerned with food, the environment and other pressing issues, bears the somewhat sinister title of Worldwatch Institute. The estimated (1971) capital of the Rockefeller Foundation is $800 million.

The Ford Foundation also keeps its eye on the world. It has an estimated capital of $3 billion with which to do so. Under the guidance of Paul Hoffman, former Marshall Plan Administrator, it set up a permanent bureau in India in 1951, established itself in the Middle East the following year and from 1959 onwards operated in Africa and Latin America. The teaming up of the Rockefeller and Ford Foundations to promote the Green Revolution in the Third World is important enough to merit a separate chapter, and the enormous sums of money they have poured into population control (along with Mellons, Carnegies and sundry others) has been well documented elsewhere.*

The US intellectual Establishment's greatest international political *coup*—in the literal sense of the word—was perhaps its decisive contribution to bringing Indonesia back into the Western fold. This long-term effort was spearheaded by the Ford Foundation, working through several universities. Here was the most populous nation in Southeast Asia (120 million people) drowning in oil, with deposits of tin, nickel, copper and bauxite on an Eldorado scale, vast tropical forests and natural rubber plantations—and all of it under the control of Nationalist President Sukarno whose followers included members of his own Nationalist Party and the Indonesian Communist Party (PKI). This was seen as an affront to Western interests.†

In the late 1950s, the Foundation confronted the following situation: national elections in 1955 and local ones in 1957 had given a clear mandate to Sukarno's Nationalist Party and to the PKI; the government began nationalizing foreign holdings. Aristocrats and landowners grouped in two tiny, Western-oriented minority parties attempted a rebellion "briefly supported by the CIA" which was a total failure. The leaders were exiled, their parties were banned.

The Ford Foundation determined to right this apparently hopeless situation through the creation of what it called "a modernizing élite." "You can't have a modernizing country without a modernizing élite," explained a Foundation official. "That's one of the reasons we've given a lot of attention to university education." One finds this élite, in his words, among "those who stand somewhere in the social structures where prestige, leadership and vested interests matter, as they always do." Ford worked through top American universities, especially MIT, Cornell, Berkeley and Harvard, to study various aspects of Indonesian society including "political obstacles" to development. The other side of the medal was the training of aristocratic Indonesians in the US in lavishly funded programs. Many stayed for four years, particularly those who came to be known as "The Berkeley Boys."

*See, for example, Steve Weissman's article "Why the Population Bomb is a Rockefeller Baby," *Ramparts*, May 1970.

†The following account is summarized from David Ransom, "Ford Country: Building an Elite for Indonesia" in *The Trojan Horse*, Ramparts Press, San Francisco, 1974.

Exchanges became common: "While the Indonesians junior faculty studied American economics in Berkeley classrooms, the Berkeley professors turned the Faculty in Djakarta into an American-style school of economics, statistics and business administration." Sukarno protested, but when Ford threatened cut-offs of all aid, backed down. "Ford felt it was training the guys who would be leading the country when Sukarno got out," recalls another Foundation official: to do so it was spending $2.5 million a year. Back from Berkeley with their degrees, the Indonesian economists began a studied *rapprochement* with the Army, and became its civilian corps of advisers. Together they prepared "contingency plans" nominally directed at "preventing chaos should Sukarno die suddenly." In reality, they were more concerned with the PKI and the immense popular support for the President. Army officers were simultaneously being trained at US military bases and universities thanks to the DoD participant program: by 1965 over 4,000 of them had been through the mill. They increased their political and economic influence to the point that journalists spoke of a "creeping *coup d'état*." An American professor explained that this was a "new form of government—military/private enterprise." The PKI reacted by trying to "keep the parliamentary road open," participated in coalition cabinets with the Army, and hoped its hour would come. By the time repeated peasant clashes with the Army over back-pedalling on land reform had proved to the PKI the necessity for a peoples' militia, it was too late. "The Army had become a state within a state. It was they—and not Sukarno or the PKI—who held the guns."

Now it was time for the students to appear on the stage—students trained by the Berkeley Boys, by the University of Kentucky's 'institution building" program and by the CIA-sponsored Foreign Student Leadership Project among many others. In addition, "students in all Indonesia's élite universities had been given para-military training by the Army . . . advised by a [US] colonel on leave from Berkeley." They formed alliances with "extremist Moslem youth groups in the villages." When word came down from the Army high command that the purge was on, students joined the Army in carrying out orders, to wit: "the extermination, by whatever means might be necessary, of the core of the Communist party."

Time described the pogrom: "The killings have been on such a scale that the disposal of the corpses has created a serious sanitation problem . . . travellers from these areas tell of small rivers and streams that have been literally clogged with bodies; river transportation has at places been seriously impeded." Graduate students, assigned to assessing the number of victims, came up with the figure of one million; other observers say from three to five hundred thousand. Students not out massacring peasants were holding anti-Sukarno demonstrations in Djakarta. The bloodbath began in September-October 1965; by March 1966 Sukarno was deposed and the formal government was composed of pro-Western elements. The United States was back in the saddle. A Harvard professor wrote the new government's "economic stabilization plan"; the US Embassy helped to draft the new Investment Law. "We were all working together at the time," recalls an AID official, "the [Indonesian] economists, the American economists, AID." By September 1966 the plans for a new Indonesian economy were ready and the Stanford University Research Institute was able to bring 170 American business executives to Djakarta to discuss future plans. At another meeting with foreign businessmen, the Ford-funded Berkeley Boys now in power explained the advantages of their country: "political stability, abundance of cheap labor, vast potential market, treasurehouse of resources" among them.

Modern Indonesia now indeed has political stability: its chief ministers, allied with the Army, all have PhDs from the US. It has cheap labor, or even no-cost labor provided by the Army and by tens of thousands of political prisoners. Its treasurehouse of resources has been allocated:

> Freeport Sulphur will mine copper on West Irian; International Nickel has got the Celebes nickel . . . [US], Japanese, Korean and Filipino lumber companies will cut down the huge tropical forests . . . A US-European consortium of mining giants headed by US Steel will mine West Irian's nickel. Two others, US-British and US-Australian will mine tin. . . . The Japanese will take home the shrimp and tuna.

The vast potential local market is something else again. Indonesians are among the poorest people in the world (the World Bank ranks the country fourteenth from the bottom) with a per capita GNP of $90 annually. But the Western developers and the élite they created are still in there fighting: Ford-financed Harvard, Berkeley and MIT economists are sharing offices with their old Indonesian friends, and the Foundation, faithful to the last, in 1969 was sponsoring a project in "developing human resources for the handling of negotiations with foreign investors in Indonesia."

At this point, let me say that in describing the various ways in which Western interests collaborate to build up local power bases, I am not indulging in an irrelevant, though perhaps interesting, digression. The economic choices made by these alliances bear directly on how the great majority of poor people in UDCs will live. They even decide, to put it crudely, whether or not they will eat. Unless we understand how and why the poor have been sold out through the joint efforts of their own privileged countrymen and their foreign cronies, we will continue to ascribe food shortages and even famines to "natural forces," "population pressures" and so forth.

For the case of Indonesia which we have just examined, the US-inspired economic choices have had clear results. Land reform, which Sukarno called "an indispensable part of the Indonesian revolution," has been halted. The 1960 legislation was imperfect, the result of many compromises, but at least it limited landholdings and granted real property in most cases only to those who tilled the soil themselves, for, as Sukarno observed, "the peasant who owns his own land cultivates it more intensively" and "properly implemented land reform [will] result in a more just distribution of income among citizens and create a social structure that [will] open the way towards higher national production." After the 1965 pogroms,

Land reform, from the start stigmatized by its opponents as a product of the Communists, was stopped. A considerable number of former landowners tried to get their property back. The next-of-kin of murdered or arrested new landowners were prevented . . . from tilling the soil. . . . New landowners who were accused of having sympathized with Communists simply dared not appear on their piece of land, and many of them fled to the city. All this provided opportunities to bring redistributed land back into the hands of the former owners and so to nullify the hard-won results of land reform. . . . Since [the *coup*] approximately 300,000 hectares land has fallen into the hands of third persons, in many cases military people . . .

Rice shortages have increased. In 1974 the shortage was over a million tons—in spite of large-scale implantation of the Green

Revolution. During the especially bad year of 1972, "in many rural areas only the rich could afford to eat rice every day" as inflation sent food prices up drastically. (This account is from a study by Ernst Utrecht, exiled Indonesian agronomist.)

Western "development" cadres in Indonesia and elsewhere would surely claim innocence. After all they did not themselves wield the knives that murdered so many peasants, nor subsequently take rice and land away from them. The same claim would be made by the other battalion of the Western "development" shock-troops in the Third World—the universities that practice "neutral" social science. We have already seen them at work, hand in hand with the government and the private foundations, training students, elaborating "modernizing" development models and carrying out their projects directly in the complying countries. It is in the groves of academe that the ideological justifications for intervention are concocted and the bases for subsequent government programs hammered out. Recall the repression of the Bolivian tin miners and the military civic action program Mr. Sloan was so proud of. This program did not just happen: it was the brainchild of scholars belonging to the Massachusetts Institute of Technology Center for International Studies in 1957. Their specific proposal was for deeper military involvement in rural development so that peasants would be less inclined to support "internal insurrections." The American intellectual élite has consistently shared its government's assumption that it has a right, in fact a duty, to practise universal intervention—peacefully if possible; if not, through violence. Thus it was entirely "normal" for a respected Professor of Government from Harvard to press for "urbanization" of the Vietnamese, which in plain language meant saturation bombing of the countryside so that peasants would have to take refuge in cities where they could be more easily controlled. It was also normal for New Frontier intellectuals to advocate the most brutal forms of warfare when they attained positions of power in the political hierarchy. Mr. Kissinger, who did so much for countries like Cambodia and Chile, is also a former Harvard professor.

Most of these men go about their business quietly and their names are not known to the general public. The business they go about includes, of course, the training of key foreigners in Western ways. On the whole, the professors are quite content with their accomplishments. As former Harvard professor Hollis

Chenery (now Vice-President for Development at the World Bank) commented,

> To a great extent, and increasingly, the ideas upon which economic policy in the developing countries is based are derived from research done in the advanced countries, particularly the United States. . . . Scientific research on economic development has been extremely dependent on American resources and initiative . . . Latin American economists frequently remark that the only way they can acquire a regional perspective on their own countries is by coming to study in the United States. . . . In most underdeveloped countries (with the exception of Africa) the United States is the priority choice for economic training of students. . . . The effects of this research effort are more and more visible in the policies implemented by developing countries. Since the majority of economic policymakers in underdeveloped countries have been trained in Western institutions, *transmission and acceptance of new planning ideas and methods have been altogether rapid* [emphasis added].

US academics also stand ready to help their government get the most out of its food-aid legislation and US Food Aid Acts have directly provided for the training of local élites. Thus the Indian Emergency Food Aid Act of 1952 called for an allocation of $5 million (from interest on the loan) for reform of higher education in India, to be accomplished partly through exchange of students and faculty. Subsequent bilateral agreements allowed six American state universities with particularly strong departments of agriculture "to send teams to India and to divide up its entire area among themselves. It was onto this network that the Ford and Rockefeller Foundations grafted their Green Revolution policy in the 1960s."

Another task of the university Establishment is to elaborate development models through field studies—and whenever possible to translate them into action. Harvard's élite Development Advisory Service has been especially active in Pakistan, Greece, Argentina, Liberia, Colombia, Malaysia, Ghana and, of course, Indonesia. It may have up to eighty social science experts in the field at any given time, often working as local government advisers.

The models put forward at home in the US and into practice abroad tend to examine social problems like unemployment, income distribution, land tenure and even hunger only in so far as these may tend to contribute to social discontent and possible revolt. Their universal characteristic is the "trickle-down" theory of development strategy emphasizing growth to be accomplished by "modernizing élites." In urban areas, these will be local entrepreneurs in cooperation with government bureaucrats and foreign investors; in rural areas, the wealthier, more "progressive" farmers should be given priority, since they will presumably do most to boost national production. Progress is to be measured in all cases by increase in the growth rate of the GNP and of per capita income, not by the *distribution* of this income. Cooperation on the part of the élites is the obvious prerequisite as they are designated as the motors of growth. The broad majority of the population—that is to say the poor—are regarded at best as passive objects; at worst as obstacles to development because their attitude is "traditionalist" and supposedly resistant to "modernization." "Of course, there are also those two-legged beasts of burden that one stumbles on in the countryside, but as any graduate student of political science can explain, they are not part of a responsible modernizing élite, and therefore have only a superficial biological resemblance to the human race." So Noam Chomsky characterizes the kind of development thinking which, carried to its logical conclusion, decrees that in extreme cases, such as Vietnam, obstacles (the people) must necessarily be eliminated so as to allow the nation builders to get on with their work without interference.

Such, then, are the techniques of the benevolent government agencies, the humanitarian foundations and the disinterested scholars of one of the world's great powers as they pave the way for the corporations that have their own contributions to make to the Third World. The United States has concentrated its élite-building efforts on Latin America, Asia and the Middle East—although its wealth has allowed it to devote at least a smattering of attention to the rest of the world as well. The role of Great Britain in training Indian, Sri Lankan and African leaders is prominent; France has concentrated on its former colonies, and Germany now has development missions and institutes operating in many Third World nations. To a considerable extent, educational systems of the recently liberated poor nations are themselves based on Western models their élites have absorbed abroad, rather than on relevance to the pressing needs of their own poor citizens. The rare child who succeeds in jumping the academic hurdles will himself join the élite—the others will be taught early on to consider themselves as failures.

René Dumont suggests that one of the reasons for the low priority given to agriculture and especially to small farmers in so many UDCs is to be found in the prevailing educational system:

> Education servilely copied on our own in wholly different conditions has slowed down agricultural development by pushing the best farmers' sons out of farming. The gap between the exploiting town and the exploited countryside increases the rural exodus and the size of the shanty towns. Agriculture cannot find the trained personnel necessary for its modernization. Many of the extension workers in agriculture have lived in the cities, are sometimes European educated and they cannot reintegrate into the rural atmosphere.

Does all this mean that had they been left in some idyllic state of nature Third World upper classes would be paragons of virtue and selflessness? No more so than anybody else. After the decolonization process, the so-called "national bourgeoisies" were supposed, especially by Western liberals, to plunge with no further ado into the exalting task of creating modern, egalitarian societies in their countries the moment the colonialist masters departed. Frantz Fanon, the black psychiatrist from Martinique who put himself at the service of the Algerian liberation struggle and then travelled widely in Africa, took care of *that* myth. Whereas, he said, in an underdeveloped country the "national middle class ought to consider as its bounden duty . . . to put at the people's disposal the intellectual and technical capital it has snatched when going through the colonial universities," in reality these élites have betrayed every hope placed in them. "Intellectual laziness," "spiritual penury," "cowardice at the decisive moment" are some of the milder charges Fanon levels at UDC upper classes. He also finds them narcissistic, "completely ignorant of the economy of their own country," "stupidly, contemptibly, cynically bourgeois." Fanon finds in them most of the nastier traits of the colonialists, plus some of their own—they lack, in fact, only those attributes which have made the Western nations what they are; i.e. capital and a spirit of initiative. They follow "the Western bourgeoisie along its path of negation and decadence without ever having emulated its first stages of exploration and invention." They are not forging ahead, but "beginning at the end," "already senile." They do not invest or share their profits with their poorer countrymen, so the economies of their fledgling nations tend to become more, not less, dependent on the former colonialists.

The national economy, formerly protected, is today literally controlled. The budget is balanced through loans and gifts, while every three or four months the chief ministers themselves . . . come to the erstwhile mother countries or elsewhere, fishing for capital. The former colonial power increases its demands, accumulates concessions and guarantees and takes fewer pains to mask the hold it has over the national government. The people stagnate deplorably in unbearable poverty.

We may or may not share Fanon's conclusion, which is no less categorical: "The national bourgeoisie of underdeveloped countries must not be opposed because it threatens to slow down the total, harmonious development of the nation. It must simply be stoutly opposed because, literally, it is good for nothing.

But we must admit that it has had a little help from its friends.

4. Technology: Now Who Pays to Do What and to Whom?*

A rose is a rose is a rose, but Gertrude Stein notwithstanding, a tractor is not a tractor is not a tractor. No instrument, no skill, no crop introduced into a society from the outside is "neutral." No so-called technical solution for any problem remains technical longer than about five minutes. Any innovation is going to have far-reaching consequences on people's lives and will affect their jobs or lack of them, the direction their children will take, and how much they will or won't have to eat. Large-scale development schemes, budget decisions and Five Year Plans work the same way, only more so. If the social consequences of innovations are disastrous, the people whose lives have deteriorated or been ruined find little consolation in the fact that the innovators meant well or that solutions imposed upon them looked terrific on paper.

The last chapter was devoted to an attempt at understanding why many poor nations should be so receptive to the all-purpose answers held out to them on the silver platters of the rich. The next one will discuss a world-wide phenomenon *cum* horrible example of backfiring technology known as the Green Revolution. This one will talk about technology and its consequences. Most people think of some sort of machinery or apparatus when they hear the word "technology." The definition here will be much broader. First, it will mean the choice of the *crop itself* that is to be grown. These crops will tend to orient the kind of *research* that is carried out and the *inputs* that will be required. They will also alter consumption and income patterns where they are produced. The crops grown will also take their place in a worldwide system of *trade* which will in turn deeply influence the avenues of choice left open to countries as to the *orientation of*

*Tag line of an otherwise unprintable limerick.

their economies. Technology—understood as any physical means to an end—is also implicit in the overall *development models* adapted by—or forced down the throats of—UDCs and will determine their degree of dependency or self-reliance. The style of development chosen will profoundly influence relationships between social classes—particularly in the area that most concerns us, the importance attributed to farmers and their place in the whole society. Tools and machinery are only a part of the picture. The word "ecology" has been used to cover the concept of the overall effect of the social system on nature. "Technology" is my choice for the concept of the *effect of the physical environment on the social system* until someone coins a better word.

It is a sad fact that many nations have by now been almost wholly dispossessed of their own freedom of choice as to the kind of society they will have—and thus of the means to attain their goals. The decision-making initiative has all too often fallen into the hands of the more powerful nations. We have seen how the latter have laid the foundations for dictating their own development strategies through the ruling classes they have nurtured. Any change in this pattern will imply a 180-degree turn by these élites, or their replacement by independent, nationalistic elements dedicated to wholesale social change—both of which the rich countries would naturally oppose. Still it is worth making a plea for self-reliance and truly autonomous development as the only way of averting misery and hunger for the masses of the rural and urban poor in the UDCs. So here goes.

For all the recent talk about "transfer of technology," "technical assistance" and the like, these are in no way modern inventions. Transfers of technology have been occurring as long as people have been able to travel; and especially as long as superior force has allowed one group to use another's land and labor for its own purposes. Take the simplest level of technology in agriculture—the crop itself that is to be grown and the seeds to plant it. Take, again, the example of sugar cane. Indigenous to Asia, it was introduced all around the Mediterranean by the ninth century through the offices of Arab merchants. Christopher Columbus took specimens with him on his second voyage to the Antilles in 1493; the following year sugar cane had reached Hispaniola (now the Dominican Republic and Haiti) and Cuba. By the early sixteenth century, the Dutch had a monopoly on sugar shipping and sales, with refineries in Antwerp and Amsterdam. During succeeding centuries other nations moved into this lucrative trade, but in order to keep their plantations producing, were "obliged" to indulge in another kind of trade—slaves from Africa. The ships that carried the slaves out brought new plants in: among them groundnuts, corn, sweet potatoes, tapioca and tobacco.

So much for the "neutrality" of even the least sophisticated techniques. The introduction of just one plant species profoundly altered the lives of generations of people in Europe, the Mediterranean area, Latin America, and especially Africa—although the cane was not yet even grown there. One could make a similar case for the introduction of cotton and wheat into India by the British or of cotton and tobacco into the southern United States.

Agricultural research did not exist as such before the nineteenth century. It only got under way then because settlers introducing cash crops into newly colonized areas found their plants being attacked by myriad diseases and pests in unfamiliar environments and the planters themselves were being wiped out financially. Research stations sprang up throughout the colonial world, but predictably paid no attention whatever to local food crops. This research lag between cash and food crops is, alas, still with us.

To sum up with a quote from Pierre Spitz, whose research provides the foregoing examples,

> Human history has been profoundly affected by transfers of seeds, plants and animals from one region to another, from one society to another. In areas adopting new varieties, agricultural techniques necessary for cultivating the seeds in a new environment markedly influenced the social and economic organization of the local farmers, and henceforward that of the whole society; they introduced far reaching changes in the organization of local and international trade and altered patterns of consumption both in the producing area and abroad. Previous producers of the same crops—or rivals to them—in other areas of the world were often seriously affected; social and economic conditions in rival producing areas were often radically transformed.

The following modern example of far-reaching effects of crop transference is drawn from a report commissioned by the French Government Center for External Trade. It concerns the recent introduction of soybeans to Brazil. The FAO has predicted that demand for soybeans in UDCs will go up 53 per cent during 1965–85 and countries like Japan are actively seeking to diversify their sources of supply. Brazil can produce and sell its crop between the two US soybean harvests, so the government's official agricultural policy encourages soybean production for export.

The price is attractive, so farmers have, the report says, "abandoned corn, a traditional crop," as well as wheat to a lesser extent because soybeans demand less fertilizer. The crop is "easily mechanized" and the study notes that in the areas of intensive mechanized soybean cultivation the labor costs account for only 11 per cent of total production costs; that the "labour factor is thus gradually diminishing in importance." In plain language this means that fewer people need be employed—besides, Brazil had 250 per cent more tractors in 1970 than it had in 1960.

Soybeans are not like most other grains—they need complex processing (into oil and feedcakes for animals) before they can be of much value. In Brazil, it is the world's most competent processors—the top American firms—that are taking over this function.

We have witnessed in the past two years [in 1971-3] a double movement: small processing factories are closing down and enormous units are taking their place. The Cargill Co. in 1973 will inaugurate its new plant with an annual capacity of 360,000 tons . . .

Management imported by the American companies has markedly improved the productivity of this sector: for example, Anderson-Clayton, whose capital investment is only 61% that of SANBRA [a "very traditional" firm belonging to the Bunge group], made a net profit of 11 million cruzeiros in 1972 compared to only 0.6 million for SANBRA. These companies are highly integrated: they have their own purchasing offices in the producing areas and their private export corridors to the seaports.

These "corridors" were necessary because the infrastructure for loading and transportation in Brazil was definitely not up to the mark—trucks were constantly getting mired down or breaking parts—so private roads became a must. The authors of the report note further along that the World Bank has been kind enough to contribute half the price of the "corridor policy" the Brazilian government has been kind enough to declare for the multinational grain firms. The authors also feel sure that the soybean sector in Brazil has a great future since

. . . this very strong penetration of foreign capital has the advantage of opening the sector towards the outside and guarantees that it will find it easy to adapt [to the international market] . . . In addition, the sheer size of these firms allows for large-scale investment . . . From our discussions with executives of these companies we may affirm that they are entirely capable of increasing their production by 15 to 20 per cent a year for at least the next 5 to 10 years.

The increase in plant capacity during 1973–4 was 30 per cent.

There is no doubt that the introduction of soybeans into Brazil has had exciting and profitable consequences for the multinational agribusinesses. Have the consequences been as beneficial for the Brazilians themselves? Leaving aside those hapless small businessmen whose undersized plants have gone bankrupt and those workers who are no longer needed, we learn from this study that since soybeans caused a drop in the corn crop, corn for animal and poultry feed was scarce and prices for meat went up 60 per cent while those of chicken rose by a third in 1970–72. Brazil, like Argentina, was one of the few developing countries where meat was cheap enough to be a staple food for much of the population. The authors are cautious, but suggest this can no longer possibly be the case. They are, however, entirely certain that soybeans have drastically reduced the amount of land previously devoted to another staple food crop—the *feijao* or black bean—whose price went up, owing to its scarcity, 275 per cent in the few months between the end of 1972 and August 1973.* "Rice production has also suffered from the competition of soybeans." The "consequences were that not only did a great price increase for the principal food products take place, but it also became necessary to import large quantities of foodstuffs."

"In addition, real estate prices in areas suitable for soybean cultivation have undergone a spectacular rise: one hectare in the Rio Grande do Sul was worth about 1500 cruzeiros in 1972 . . . a hectare of good soybean land there now [i.e. not even a year later] goes for up to 10,000 cruzeiros." The end result will, of course, be that the smaller, unmechanized farmers will gradually be eliminated by those who can afford to buy more and more land.

The Brazilian government encourages soybeans because they are a profitable export crop, but the authors of the study find this policy has certain contradictions: "Soybeans, directly or indirectly, have been the cause of a great many price increases. Commodities essential for the average Brazilian have been the most seriously affected. Soybean production thus directly counteracts the efforts of the Government which is determined to limit inflation by any means available."

*"Rio de Janeiro, October 12, 1976 (UPI): Scuffles broke out in several parts of the city yesterday as people lined up to get rationed supplies of black beans, the Brazilian staple source of protein.

Police used clubs to disperse unruly lines in front of a supermarket in Campo Grande, south of Rio, and similar measures were taken in Rio's northern sector."

No comment.

If it can be so easily demonstrated that the most elementary technology—i.e., the crop grown—is in no way neutral, what can be said of the far more sophistica'ed development models foisted upon the UDCs by the foundations, the social-science experts and the governments of the developed world? These models stress "growthmanship" and speed-ups of the kinds of processes that are supposed to have produced development in the now advanced nations. If enough momentum is built up, the UDCs will then qualify for what W. W. Rostow called the "take-off" phase and "modernization." The implicit myth of such models is a kind of linear progress; their implicit assumption is that *all* societies are on the same ladder, but on different rungs, and that all should want to reach the top of this same ladder. The corollary is that this can only be done through the use of Western-manufactured inputs and the adoption of processes and technology that have brought growth to the countries that invented them. Nobody, figuratively, is allowed to stand on a stool, build a flight of steps, use a rope, climb a tree or invent any other way of reaching the top—nor can he decide to stop along the way. The developers assume that "West is Best"; they also imply that in the UDCs the problem is that certain rungs of the ladder are missing: if only these are supplied by outside aid and techniques the UDCs will be able to scurry up much faster and we in the rich nations will be able to clock their progress by measuring their GNP. So one builds a road here and a dam there, and the piecemeal supply of such items in proper combinations will—presto!—create development. This approach also facilitates subsequent private foreign investment which does not want to carry the cost of building infrastructure itself—the soybean corridors are a good example. If the UDCs are to become "like" the DCs, they will have to concentrate on urbanizing and on shifting labor from the traditionalist rural backwaters into the dynamic, modern sector. Prosperity will seep down from the upper strata to the lower. Finally, one day they too may have 1.3 automobiles per head, just like Los Angeles.

Although it can't be proved statistically, I'd stake my typewriter on a bet that such conceptions have been specifically responsible for the shameful neglect of the poorer agricultural sector and the needs of the peasantry in any number of UDCs' development plans. In return for such neglect, they have got urban shanty towns, massive unemployment and rarely is anyone, rural or urban, eating any better, to put it gently. In one country after another, "rural development" has been *intended* to reach only the most "modern"—i.e. richest—farmers who frequently have ties with the rest of the political-economic élite. The small peasants who actually produce most of the food supply have been rendered functionally invisible.

These development conceptions have another advantage for the West. They are conveniently tailored to obscuring certain historical facts. If everyone is on the same ladder, but some have simply climbed faster than others, then it follows that there can be no possible *organic* or causal link between the development of some and the underdevelopment of others. As André Gunder Frank says in a now classic essay,

Even a modest acquaintance with history shows that underdevelopment is not original or traditional and that neither the past nor the present of the underdeveloped countries resemble in any important respect the past of the now-developed countries. The now-developed countries were never *under*developed, though they may have been *un*developed. It is also widely believed that the contemporary underdevelopment of a country can be understood as the product or reflection solely of its own economic, political, social, and cultural characteristics or structure. Yet historical research demonstrates that contemporary *underdevelopment is in large part the historical product of past and continuing economic and other relations* between the satellite underdeveloped and the now-developed metropolitan countries.

If it is true that today's underdevelopment results in large part from a history of colonialism and satellization, then it would seem to follow that the faster the poor countries extricate themselves from the grasp of Western development models, techniques and institutions, the better off they will be. Such models will *necessarily* be conceived along lines most applicable and beneficial to Western interests, even if one allows the benefit of the doubt that this will be done unconsciously.

It is, for instance, very important for the developed world that poor countries continue to supply enough raw materials and that they be in this measure reliable trading partners. They must not, on the other hand, become rivals. In the world food arena, their role is to continue to supply the cash crops the rich countries have come to rely on. If the Third World accepts this Western assessment and the resulting development model that concentrates on the "modernizing élite" and on plantations, they *will* produce food for export and for cash, not for local people, so as to have necessary foreign exchange for their imports of industrial and luxury goods.

Senegalese economist P. Kane describes how this process worked in his country. Following independence, the government decided to reinforce the cultivation of groundnuts which represented about four-fifths of Senegal's total exports and 40 per cent of all the funds in the national budget. In the framework of "Senegalese Socialism," cooperatives were set up, rural extension work and technical assistance schemes for peasants were launched with the aim of "teaching the peasants cultivation techniques which, because they are scientific, are effective factors of productivity and consequently of social liberation," in the words of President Senghor. "Unfortunately," Kane points out, "these new structures merely contributed to spreading results of agronomic research that had been developed in Africa with a colonialist perspective and which was entirely geared to producing crops for export." While Senegal was devoting a disproportionate amount of its physical and human resources to groundnuts, the price for the crop was constantly falling on the world market. The results, even in terms of productivity, were disappointing, so in 1964, Senegal called in a private French technical assistance company, which itself was able to get considerable funding for the development project from the EEC. The company promised a productivity increase of 25 per cent in three years which would offset the drop in world groundnut prices. It could not be bothered with cajoling and cosseting peasants—more advanced technology including a lot more fertilizer was the answer. Three years after the experts' arrival, groundnut production in Senegal had *dropped* by 10 per cent and in 1972 was approximately at the level of 1962. And yet many African countries, including Senegal, still rely on outside assistance which must be paid for in precious foreign exchange. Kane observes that the patent failure of such methods is "not due to the frequently advanced 'resistance of peasants to innovations' but to the non-concordance of such innovations with the felt needs of the peasants themselves. A true development strategy with some chance of success would be one based on the satisfaction of the needs of the vast majority of the population." Kane adds that the orientation of African governments in seeking outside aid is reinforced by the policies of multilateral aid agencies which prefer to finance large-scale or "macro" projects.

Leaving the question of what crop will be grown and for whom and looking now at the more conventional sense of "technology" —the tools of production—there is another quite obvious notion that does not yet seem to have been fully recognized: any choice of technology automatically means also the choice of its *supplier*— the seller—and thus of a long-term partner. Without discussing the industrial sector, for here there is nearly general agreement that Western technology will have primacy for some time to come, what does this imply for poor rural economies? To produce food, you can choose techniques and inputs supplied by multi-nationals and consultant companies—or you can develop a strong local artisan sector to provide your farmers with adequate and improved tools. You can try to produce your own fertilizer from many sources, or import all of it. If you choose the multinationals over the artisans and imports over local produc-tion you have also chosen dependency over self-reliance. You have further chosen, in a sense, to invest less of your total resources in agriculture (or whatever other sector in your country needs investment) because you will have to pay out that much more to the man who supplies your technology. Investing less, you will produce less. Producing less, you may be tempted to call on other outside help to solve your dilemma. And so forth and so on, down the spiral. In this sense we are not talking about technology but about *capital*. What may appear to be the most advanced techniques—and those that may thus most appeal to development planners who want "only the best" for their coun-tries—may actually *increase and perpetuate underdevelopment;* because of their initial and maintenance costs, the relationships of dependency they establish, their effects on local society and their long-term setting of wrong national priorities.

Another truism is that expensive technology will produce expensive goods—including higher-priced food. This is particu-larly true when Western-style, highly energy-intensive growing methods are used. *Someone* is going to pay the cost of such items as spare parts, imported fertilizer, sophisticated distribution systems and just plain energy. If you then want to keep food prices down for urban consumers, you will have to reduce the prices and wages you pay rural producers and laborers. You can also simply let prices follow "market" forces and fix themselves at the level commensurate with the technology that went into producing the food. If this places the food beyond the reach of the poorest consumers, too bad. You will sell to the upper classes, or to foreigners.

Here is an example of how advanced technology can *contribute* to hunger. It is deliberately chosen from the technical assistance program of a country which hardly qualifies as a nasty imperialist with a dark colonial past: Norway. Johan Galtung recounts how his country conceived and implemented a fisheries project in the Indian state of Kerala. The idea was to improve the standard of living—especially protein and calorie consumption—for the poor population of fishermen living along the coast and plying their trade with age-old techniques. The plan was also to reach poor consumers beyond the immediate area. Before this program came to Kerala, the fishermen's catch was slim, their productivity low; but they and their families ate some of the fish they caught themselves. Enter the Norwegians, who generously felt that what was best for Norway was also best for Kerala. They brought with them "impressive modern steel and fiber-glass vessels" with "electronic fish-finding devices" and deep-freeze facilities on board. Galtung tells what happened then.

Because of this [new technology], the producers are no longer the traditional fishermen trained through imitation of the older generation, benefiting from the experience handed down by their ancestors. For the pattern of modern fishing that is introduced is industrial fishing, whereby the fisherman is an industrial worker. As to the consumers, they are not the same as before either, and here comes what is perhaps the crux of the story. Briefly told, it may be said to have three phases, all of them part of this developmental project.

In the first phase . . . fishing is less labor intensive and more capital and research intensive . . . The Norwegian government makes the effort to introduce new methods of marketing, partly to make it more effective . . . reaching consumers farther out, and partly to eliminate the middlemen, the fishmongers. One key element in connection with the expansion is the method of preservation. Beyond simple ice-cooling, there are many alternative methods; the alternative chosen is deep-freezing of the catch . . . Instead of old bicycles transporting baskets of fish, insulated vans with considerable carrying capacity are introduced . . . The difficulty now was that the finished products became too expensive. Consumers were not obtainable at realistic market prices. There was certainly need [for protein] but not demand, articulated in the language a market economy will understand: the language of money. Before there was consumption at a very low level of technology; now there is a high level of technology, but a very low level of consumption.

In the second phase attempts were introduced to improve the situation. The choice was between using cheaper technology so as to produce cheaper consumer goods or finding consumers who could pay the price. The second method was the one chosen . . .

Unfortunately, the Indian upper classes persisted in their unwillingness to consume fish and there was not enough demand to pay for the cost of the technology and supply a profit margin as well.

The solution came during the third phase: to concentrate on the part of the catch consisting of shrimp and lobsters . . . elegant seafood indeed . . . Needless to say, the price of these products was extremely far beyond what the very poor local population could pay, but years had passed and the goal was no longer local consumption.

Expensive technology had now produced expensive goods; where were the consumers willing to pay the price? The answer was very simple. In the rich countries . . .

And thus the cycle has been modernized not only in the sense that it has been expanded and integrated into the world economy in general, but also that all elements in the cycle are modern. What is caught is caught with modern technology, by modern fishermen, marketed with modern techniques to modern consumers.

Did anything else change locally? Indeed it did. The leading local entrepreneur caught on, "built his own ice factory" and bought fifteen insulated vans. By late 1969

His own profit was estimated at 4 million rupees; some of it was given back to the village in the form of a blue and white five-storey temple, much of it was invested in his own house, a palace protected by a high fence and guards with machine guns.

Meanwhile

. . . most of the local population continued as before, and those who were employed in the lobster and shrimp factories were very poorly paid, usually not even with a guaranteed daily income—they worked on an hour-to-hour basis depending on the incoming catch.

All Western technology has been aimed at getting greater productivity for fewer man hours—that is why less than 4 per cent of the active population in the US still farms. *All* UDCs have vast rural populations and only one really abundant capital resource: people. There is no need to insult the reader by pointing out the contradiction these opposites entail.

Even some of the multinational input-producers in the West have begin to worry about such contradictions between capital-intensive and labor-intensive technologies in UDCs. One of them, Massey-Ferguson, commissioned a very thorough scholarly study entitled *The Pace and Form of Farm Mechanization in Developing Countries*. The study aims at understanding to what degree mechanization of agriculture actually displaces labor. We can accept its conclusions that mechanization (except in the case of combine-harvesters) does not *always* reduce the need for human labor; we can even assume the disinterested nature of the study even though it is published by a major farm-machinery corporation. Unfortunately, disinterested or not, the whole text rests on the kinds of premises we have been attempting to discredit:

> On balance, it is difficult to see any lasting solution to social and employment problems in developing countries without rapid growth of GNP and foreign exchange earnings and the availability of consumer goods to a balanced and planned population. There seems little doubt that these over-all aims can be most rapidly achieved by adopting the latest technologies and by inputs of foreign knowledge and experience.

Given this approach, it is not surprising that in commenting on a study of Pakistan showing that one tractor displaced an average of five workers and depended for its economical use on the eviction of tenants, the author says, "While the arguments sound convincing, the data used are suspect. The information relating to the period before the introduction of tractors was obtained from the farmers' own recollections with few written records." Yet who should know better, if not the farmers—especially if they were themselves displaced? It is also not surprising that among the sixteen advantages of mechanization listed, we learn that "the ownership of a farm tractor confers many important social and non-economic benefits on developing country farmers. These must not be overlooked when considering workable public policy." Among the six possible disadvantages listed, we find nothing at all about the social implications of mechanization (it is assumed these all fall on the "plus" side) and the questions— Who owns the tractor? Did the owner displace several tenants to make mechanical farming possible on a larger area? How is tractorization changing food consumption patterns and prices locally?—in other words the social questions—are not raised. A tractor lumbering over land formerly farmed by forty evicted tenants is not at all the same machine as the one used on a cooperative in, say, Bulgaria, even if both have the same horse-power and both are contributing to increasing overall yields and GNP.

In any case, wherever mechanization is not integrated into a social system favoring small farmers and farm workers, it *does* tend to create unemployment. The *Massey-Ferguson* report cites, for example, a study on mechanization in Latin America—but discreetly avoids quoting its conclusions—which are that wealthy landholders have increased their profits while two and a half million jobs have been lost due to use of agricultural machinery (as of 1972). The author adds that this is a "very cautious estimate."

One is almost ashamed to write such an apparent cliché as The Definition of Social Goals Must Precede the Choice of Technol-ogy, but it must be worth saying since so few countries seem to have observed it. If a nation has no explicit ideas about the degree of self-reliance it wishes to attain versus dependency on outside suppliers—both of food and technology—if it is not clear on who it wants to do the producing and consuming of how much and of what kinds of food; then it cannot possibly make any intelligent technical choices. In this case the ends not only *justify* the means—they must *determine* them.

A Pakistani economist who works for the World Bank describes the kind of sloppy thinking about social goals that has obtained in far too many UDCs:

> In most developing countries there has been a confusion in policies combining very weak economic incentives with bureaucratic interven-tions in systems vaguely described as socialistic. If these countries were frankly capitalistic, if they had used all their institutions and policies to accelerate their growth rates, if they had done it rapidly over the course of a decade or so, they could hold out the hope that through increased employment and the "trickle-down" process, conditions would change.
> . . the developing countries shied away from a clear choice between capitalism and socialism because . . . they did not wish to make a commitment as to what kind of political framework they were going to adopt. They felt they could combine the good features from all the systems and be very pragmatic about it . . .

(We have seen how they were also pressured into accepting foreign private enterprise when their inclinations were towards nationalism and/or socialism.) They also, poor things, thought they were going to get massive aid from the West: according to this same economist, "The feeling was that this would be in the magnitude not only of the 'Marshall Plan, but much larger." They forgot that, as far as the West conceived it, their role was to be that of raw-material purveyors and markets for industrial goods—not competitors.

Well, massive aid has never materialized and even non-massive aid is drying up; trade terms are steadily worsening for the poor nations' exports, the prices of imported food and fertilizer are not about to decline, so perhaps the time has come to eliminate woolly thinking about development goals and to make some difficult social and resulting technical choices in the UDCs. These choices will be made even more difficult by the very degree of dependency on the West most of them have now reached. If this book is an indictment of the West's role in the hunger crisis, it is also a plea for self-reliance in the poor nations as the only strategy of escape. Self-reliance does *not* mean closing one's frontiers to *all* outside influences (although this may have worked in extreme cases like North Korea about which we know very little). It does not mean producing *all* one's necessities of life and abstaining from commerce with others. What it does mean is making maximum use of one's own resources—including people—before calling on external aid, and regaining the capacity to choose and to take initiatives with the ultimate goal of standing on one's own feet. The choices will necessarily include where one wants to go, how fast, and at what economic and social cost. As the British economist Phyllis Deane has said, "After more than two decades of development planning and internationally financed programmes for progress, not a single one of these plans has produced an independent, viable economy." Surely, then, it is worth giving self-reliance a try.

How does one go about this? One very good way is to begin by using one's own most abundant basic resource—the population. It is possible to listen to one's own peasants instead of always attempting to impose technology on them from on high, "for their own good." Peasants have been doing research and development for generations—otherwise they would not have survived. If the farming base—the poor peasants—is not taken into consideration and heard, technological innovations will universally tend to benefit only the richest, best educated farmers who can afford them and specific measures must be taken to counteract this tendency. Naturally, there may be strong initial resistance—not from peasants, but from the scientists, technicians and economists who have been trained to go out and shower their knowledge upon the underprivileged, undereducated peasants—not vice versa. The problem will not be so much to "train" the peasants as to retrain higher echelon personnel.

The gap between two possible attitudes toward farmers themselves can be illustrated with examples from Pierre Spitz's report on field work in India in late 1974.

The first concerns the new Rahuri campus of the Maharashtra State University of Agriculture, the most recently established (1973) center in India for post-graduate agricultural research and for the training of rural extension workers. The campus is situated in an area where agricultural progress has been slow, farmers are poor and there is little irrigation. Spitz reports that

Students are not responsible, together or separately, for farming plots or for animals. They do no manual work except that which may be necessary to understand the workings of machinery. Nothing is done to counteract the separation of the intellectual work of the student and the manual work of the peasant . . . no time is set aside for work in the villages, no discussions are organized between students and peasants. The only activities in which the peasants of the area participate are the demonstrations organized by extension-work specialists. These [demonstrations] are given in English [the peasants speak only Marathi so everything has to be translated]. One should recall that the researchers and extension workers do not lose their monthly salaries if the innovations they propose are harmful or irrelevant. The peasant and his family, on the other hand, have their lives at stake, for there is nothing to protect them against the consequences of error . . . The kind of agronomic research [taught at Rahuri] is closely linked to that carried out in the United States. In 1973–74, ten students from the University were doing post-graduate work in the US; one of them studying for an advanced degree in rural extension work.

The total area of the campus is 8,191 acres, of which 6,781 is made up of lands from which *peasants were expelled.* Legal proceedings concerning payment of indemnities to these peasants are still pending. Whatever the nature, more or less fair, of compensation offered, the fact remains that because of the scarcity of land in the area, these farmers will not be able to buy new land to replace that which this counter-land-reform has caused them to lose. The most fortunate among them have found employment as day laborers on the campus.

The Vice-Chancellor indicated to me, with reason, that this state of affairs did not enhance rural extension work coming from the campus, nor participation of the peasants, who, he said, formed a "hostile environment."

Small wonder!

The other example, also from India, also from Maharashtra, concerns a private, non-profit foundation created in 1952 and directed by a disciple of Gandhi, Mr. Manibhai Desai. It was originally financed by Mr. Desai himself; now it is funded by public and private contributions (including official development-aid money from Denmark), government subsidies for certain parts of the program, income from operations, and loans. It is called the Bharatiya Agro-Industries Foundation (BAIF).

The BAIF is concerned mainly with rural improvement and livestock-raising techniques. Its programs include a technical school teaching 1,500 students subjects as diverse as agricultural techniques, carpentry, electricity, mechanics, etc., in a three-year curriculum. There is also a rural-development center including a pilot-project farm where new methods of cultivation are tried out before being suggested to peasants in the area. Livestock-raising techniques include improvement of breeding stock, disease prevention (BAIF hopes soon to produce its own vaccines with the help of a French institute) and the medium-term goal is the artificial insemination of a million local cows. The foundation employs about one hundred veterinarians and sixty agronomists. "From discussions I had with [technicians] and with Mr. Desai, and from what I was able to observe," Spitz states,

. . . this is a very different kind of research-extension effort from what government agricultural extension services offer . . . The liaison between local farmers and the research workers/technicians appears to be on the whole very good . . . One of the principles stressed by Mr. Desai is that during the development process, no one should be left out. This principle seems to be applied in rural improvements and irrigation works which by mid-1973 had reached 46,000 families occupying 32,000 hectares. If an irrigation network is built, it must serve all the farms. This is possible only through close contact with the peasants, encouraged by constant discussions during which the people are listened to when they speak . . . Such discussions also orient the research undertaken at BAIF to develop techniques best adapted to the needs and possibilities of various categories of farmers. All the workers here . . . stress the necessity for well-adapted, intermediate technology as opposed to that [proposed] by State services . . . which are so-called modern techniques, adapted only to the needs of the richest farmers.

And yet BAIF is hardly a revolutionary outfit. It is merely working intelligently inside the system.

Obviously, any such successful projects will be confined to limited areas so long as they depend upon courageous (and selfless!) private initiatives and do not receive both sanction and guidance from the state. It should be made quite clear at this point that I am not trying to make a case for "counting on the spontaneity of the masses" or any other such romantic notions. The "masses" indeed have a great deal to contribute, but they are not going to do so all by themselves. It is again China that seems to have struck the best balance between listening to the people, making use of their knowledge, and centrally planning agricultural development. It has also been very careful to maintain a system through which innovations are adopted because rural workers perceive them to be in their own best interests.

Taking the peasants' views into consideration does not mean merely sticking to traditional methods either. More modern inputs can and should be introduced at various points in the food production and distribution chain to overcome bottlenecks, improve quality, etc. Probably the worst course a UDC can pursue is to buy foreign technology "packages" which leave absolutely no freedom to combine various modern and traditional elements. Farmers cannot be left with the whole job of figuring out how best to mix modern and traditional inputs. They need help from scientists and technicians. For example, in North Vietnam, twice a year after harvests, students and professors of chemistry go out into the communes to do soil tests in order to recommend the best fertilizer mixes. This is done with very simple equipment and methods—simple enough that they can be explained to local twelve to fourteen year old high-school students so that they can do the tests next time. Students and peasants talk together about problems encountered—these discussions then orient the research done in the university.

Another good example of fruitful interaction between intellectual and manual workers comes from Sri Lanka where metal working and tool making are ancient arts. University students of metallurgy were sent out to share their knowledge with village blacksmiths. To their total surprise, the students discovered that the Bethlehem Steel color-for-temperature charts they brought along corresponded exactly to techniques local smithies had always used. Now that the initial shock has passed, the students are learning at least as much as they teach. But on the whole, Establishment science anywhere does not want to have to answer too many hard questions. What do you tell a peasant who can't afford the fertilizer that is your only "scientific" solution to his problem? It is much more difficult to discover plant strains that fix nitrogen naturally, or to devise complex systems of crop rotation to do some of the same jobs as chemicals—and such challenges are not always cheerfully accepted.

The disasters that can ensue when local people are neither consulted nor involved in the processes of technological changes can be illustrated with another disheartening example from India, where more than 150,000 new wells have been sunk in the last ten years. A UNICEF employee who has spent the last two years in India and has drawn upon surveys of the whole country reported in the *New Internationalist* that "at any one time 60 per cent of the new water wells are not working." Why should people be reverting to using ponds and ditches for water with all the attendant risks of disease? "The main cause of the breakdown," says the author, "is the superficial imposition of the new technology on a deep-rooted and traditional society." There are also many material problems and financial ones:

> It should be a relatively simple and minor job to redesign a more appropriate and sturdier pump, but it has not been done. Even when the village people have tried to maintain the new wells, they have often found that meagre funds, the unavailability of spare parts, the handful of service engineers to cover an area of thousands of square miles, have made it an impossible task.

But mostly the problem is one of non-involvement.

> A truck appears, a 150-foot well is sunk, a hand pump is installed, cameras click, speeches are made, and the truck is cheered on its way to the next village. The villager often does not know how the rig and pump work, where they have come from, why they have come to this particular village, what advantages they offer. He has not contributed anything to the planning, money, labor or time. He is uninvolved. And then it is taken for granted that he will feel responsible for it. Rarely is a film shown, or the danger of impure water explained, or the local doctor or midwife consulted, or the related problems of drainage, sanitation and waste disposal spelt out. . . .

The larger social context has also been ignored. In such societies,

. . . who takes water from where, with whom and for whom, is a key element in the social structure. . . . The introduction of a new source of water is therefore not just a matter for the geologist or the engineer. It is also of concern to the local community, the doctor, the sociologist, the politician and the priest. This is yet another reason why the deep wells in the earth have such shallow roots in the community.

What are the "right" tools and techniques for a self-reliant agriculture? Their whole range will be different for each country depending on the resources it has and the problems it needs to solve. But usually they can be grouped under the general heading of "intermediate technology" which means just that—"intermediate" between primitive, unproductive stick-farming methods and *dernier cri* technical packages like the one Norway brought to Kerala. The inventor of the term, and largely of the thing itself, is British economist Ernest F. Shumacher, author of *Small is Beautiful: Economics as if People Mattered.* He has devoted years to finding simple, low-cost solutions to some of the problems of UDCs and one is tempted to quote his life's work as a shining example of beneficent "intervention" in other peoples' affairs.

Shumacher founded the Intermediate Technology Development Group several years ago with seed money of just one hundred pounds, and although the group still has a very small staff it has been a wizard at getting existing technological workshops to work for and with it and now has several panels of advisers. The building panel, for example, works with the engineering department of Cambridge University and devotes its attention to local building materials and to upgrading their use. The water panel

. . . developed various small-scale technologies to hold the water where it is wanted and where it has to be protected. This meant underground water catchment tanks. We adjusted the technology to the level of the poor; in economic terms that means that outgoing expenditures to build the tanks must be minimal, ideally zero. The labour content can be what it has to be, because there are a lot of workers who for a long stretch of time during the year have nothing to do. Funded by . . . Oxfam, we demonstrated these tanks in Botswana. The Botswana government told us that having water where it is wanted had changed their entire prospect . . . I was recently in quite a different part of Africa [Shumacher continues] and I found these catchment tanks being built there. They are also being built on a large scale in Jamaica and other non-African states.

The group made another marriage with the College of Agricultural Engineering in Bedfordshire which had been looking for projects for its students to work on. They came up with seventy ideas for low-cost agricultural implements that could all be village-manufactured and designed the blueprints for them. The Group has helped countries design and produce everything from mini-turbines (Pakistan) to egg trays (Zambia). But its members emphasize that requests for help must come from the people involved—otherwise the Group will not intervene. If they go into a UDC, they start from the principle that the local people know something about their own situation. For example, in Malawi, a previous aid mission had introduced techniques allowing the local farmers to double their yields, but went back a year later and found the people had reverted to their old methods. The aid people returned home, grumbling about "backward farmers" and the "cultural gap." Shumacher says:

> We happened to be in Malawi and were asked to have a look. We did not assume these people were stupid. We found the answer, namely, that they had been subsistence farmers and consumed everything they produced. Now that they had produced twice as much this extra crop had to be taken to market. But there was no means of transport, except for the beast of burden in Africa, the woman. The women carried the extra food to market in baskets on their heads, walking for miles and miles. They did it for one season, but they said, "Never again."

At this point the Group put its transport panel onto the problem which found a very simple oxcart design whose few metal parts could be procured "from an inexhaustible source of material in Africa, namely, wrecked motor cars. . . . Once they had the oxcart, their problems disappeared."

There are other intermediate technology groups working on such problems of UDCs in Europe and in the United States. But here again, however profitable their help may be to the rural poor, their effect will necessarily be piecemeal, a drop in the ocean, so long as UDC governments themselves do not make it *public policy* to seek out and produce intermediate, low-cost solutions to their problems involving maximum participation on the part of rural people themselves.

Before we leave the question of the social consequences of innovations, does anyone care *at all* about the effects of technology on the planet's most underprivileged group of all—Third

World women? I must confess I would not have been sensitive to this aspect myself if Shumacher's Malawi example had not made me think, and if I had not come across an FAO brochure prepared for the International Women's Year. This document, pointedly titled *The Missing Half,* is full of illustrations showing that technology usually benefits men first and can often actually make women's lives *harder.*

In Africa, women have the honorable, but little-honored, job of taking care of the subsistence food plots, while men tend the cash crops. Therefore, when any inputs are available they go to the men's sector first, and women are expected to make do. Not only must women throughout the Third World fetch and carry water and firewood—they also provide, in spite of one refusal in Malawi, convenient transportation for farm products. A woman gets no training from rural extension services, so she would not know how to use modern inputs if she could get them. Often she cannot hold title to land even if she is a widow. If she does work as hired labor, she receives lower wages for it than men. "Modernization" can set her back. "In one African country, poultry schemes were introduced, but no arrangements were made to provide extra water. The result was that the task of fetching extra water (about 25 quarts a day for every 100 chickens) fell—literally—on the women's shoulders." "In [another] African country, it was found that women performed 55 per cent of the agricultural labour in a traditional village and 68 per cent in a modernized one." As modernization increases, the more desirable jobs, like running the tractor, go to men. This is "normal" because only men can read printed instructions. The result of all this is that "the gap between levels of male and female technology increases and women are relegated to the marginal role of unskilled labourers."

The FAO brochure also indicts development projects that pay no attention to the fact that women are half the society, and frequently part of the labor force, yet "most projects have been planned, formulated or implemented with scant regard for the employment of women or their production of income." If programs for women do exist, they are usually limited to the home economics field and they are the first to be cut off in times of budgetary problems. "In short," says FAO, "the first people needing to be developed are the developers themselves."

＊ ＊ ＊

If it is true that no meaningful progress towards the elimination of hunger can be made without a reasonable degree of self-reliance, and therefore of public policy aimed at attaining it, what must be the steps in elaborating such a policy?

First—again, again and again—one must set the social objectives. These may range from free whisky and cigars for every male urban citizen above a certain income level to reducing the infant mortality rate and assuring every family of three square meals a day. When the goals are set, one must assess the available *resources* for attaining them—both material and human. Someone has said that natural resources can be defined as the "estimation a civilization makes of its environment at a given time in its history." In other words, beauty (and wealth) are in the eye of the beholder. You can look at a dung-heap as valuable or smelly. You can look at a river that floods every year as a scourge or as something to be controlled and used for irrigation. You can look at the land and the minerals under it as belonging to all the people or to some of them—or to foreigners. And you can see your own compatriots as a precious advantage, or ignore them. But a clear idea of what you have to work with is vital. Next, you must determine the *restrictions* you will encounter. These may be geographic (tropical climate problems are different from temperate ones) or economic (other people's trade policies) or ecological (what happens if you cut down the forests?) etc. Finally, you determine the economic *instruments* that are in line with your objectives, resources and restrictions: your policy of income distribution, prices and wages, tariffs and so forth. If the job of definition has been done thoroughly, appropriate technology should appear almost by magic as an integral part of the goals, stemming from the resources, limited by the restrictions and paid for by the economic instruments.

When the careful planning is done, there remain the imponderables. We know the techniques of the present and some of the techniques of the past, but we are ignorant of those that human ingenuity will provide for the future. And only yesterday, a small nation defeated the world's most formidable technological power using one twentieth the arms and equal doses of determination, courage and bamboo.

5. The Green Revolution

And he gave it for his opinion, that whoever could make two ears of corn or two blades of grass, to grow upon a spot of ground where only one grew before, would deserve better of mankind, and do more essential service to his country, than the whole race of politicians put together.

—Jonathan Swift, *Voyage to Brobdingnag,* Part II, Chapter 7

Most readers will be familiar with the term "Green Revolution" if not with the thing itself, for the public-relations job that has been done around this technology-package approach to UDC farming has been admirable. We will try to define it through a series of questions: what it is, what it does, who profits from it. The least one can say is that it is a very mixed bag and an even more mixed blessing.

What does the term mean, technically speaking? It means breeding plants that will bear more edible grain—the "two ears where only one grew before"—and thus increase yields without increasing cultivated crop areas. Traditional grains, especially those grown on the three poor continents, tend to be tall on the stalk for reasons of natural selection. That way they can get more sunlight, grow higher than the surrounding weeds, and resist flooding when heavy rains come. If one tried to produce double kernels on these long stalks, the plants would be top-heavy, keel over and lodge in the soil. So the problem was to produce plants with short, tough stalks that could bear new fertilizer-sensitive hybrids. These dwarf varieties, capable of producing spectacular yields under ideal conditions, were eventually bred: they go under the name of high-yielding varieties, or HYVs for short.* These plants can be adapted to any number of environments, but they are not as adapted as thousands of years of natural selection could

*The term "high-*potential* variety" is really more accurate for reasons shortly to be explained.

make them—so they present problems of disease resistance. And they will not bear full fruit unless heavy doses of fertilizer are applied, and unless optimum irrigation is supplied. In other words, to get full benefit from the new "miracle" seeds, they must have plenty of water, plenty of nourishment and plenty of chemical protection—pesticides and fungicides against disease; herbicides against the weeds that also thrive on fertilizer. The rub is that if a *single one* of these elements is lacking, HYVs can sometimes produce *less* grain than what could have been obtained with traditional varieties.

How did the Green Revolution get started? The official birthplace and birthdate are Mexico, 1943. Four American plant geneticists/pathologists financed by the Rockefeller Foundation were sent to Mexico, which at that time imported much of its food from the United States. There they founded the ancestor of CIMMYT, the Spanish acronym for what is now the International Wheat and Maize Improvement Center. The fact that Rockefeller holdings in Mexico had recently been nationalized and that the climate for US private investment was in definite need of improvement may or may not have had something to do with the Foundation's choice of location and purpose. In any event, early results of the team's scientific efforts seemed unhoped for. As soon as the new seeds were introduced (mostly on large farms in the Sonora district) yields began to increase. Between 1944 and 1967, wheat output tripled and corn doubled. Mexico began to export commercial grain surpluses. With this success under its belt, the Rockefeller Foundation teamed up with Ford to repeat the performance in Asia—this time with rice—and founded the International Rice Research Institute (IRRI) in the Philippines in 1962. Here again, research was so effective in producing revolutionary HYVs that Dr. Chandler, Director of the IRRI, was moved in 1969 to interject a word of caution about "miracle" rice, reminding people that it was only miraculous insofar as it was protected against disease and received appropriate fertilizer, irrigation and drainage.

But by that time, prudent voices were drowned out by the crowing of the Foundations announcing *urbi et orbi* that the food crisis was definitively licked. The millennium had arrived, man would no longer hunger, and the voice of Lester Brown, Rockefeller consultant and prophet of the Revolution, was heard in our land. And one must admit that on the face of things they had a great deal going for them. Not only could the new HYVs produce more grain per acre—but they could do it with a shorter growing cycle, allowing double or even triple cropping on the same land in a single year. In the space of only seven years (1965–6 to 1972–3) wheat acreage planted in UDCs to HYVs went from not quite 10,000 hectares to over 17 million; rice surface, beginning at 49,000 hectares in 1965, reached nearly 16 million in 1973. During some years as many as 6 million new hectares were added to the total. Beneficiaries of Green Revolution wheat were headed by pioneer Mexico, followed by India, Pakistan, Turkey, in that order; with smaller surfaces planted to HYVs in Afghanistan, Nepal and North Africa. Taiwan, the Philippines, Sri Lanka and again India planted most of the new rice strains. Areas with particularly favorable climates witnessed increases in yields as high as 50 per cent.

What's wrong with that? Nothing, except that as the preceding chapter attempted to demonstrate, no technological innovation consists merely in technology. It also suggested that possibly the worst course a UDC could follow was to purchase technical packages leaving no freedom of choice in combining modern, foreign-supplied inputs with traditional, indigenous elements. Remember that these seeds require inputs—inputs not generally produced in the UDCs themselves—or the whole structure will collapse. These products do not fall like manna from heaven, but must be bought. As all this came to be realized, cries of victory for the 'Green Revolution' began to die down, but not Lester Brown's.* He of course realizes that farmers must "irrigate more frequently and with greater precision. They must use fertilizer in large quantities" (up to four or five times as much as with traditional varieties) and use weed-control chemicals "lest fertilizer be converted into weeds instead of grain." But the extra costs and efforts are worth it since "using purchased inputs and marketing additional production, peasant farmers are drawn into the mainstream of economic life."

*Capsule biography: Formerly resident agronomist/economist for the Overseas Development Council which publishes his books and has "the support of thirty-three business corporations and thirteen foundations," according to the preface written by Eugene Black, former President of the World Bank, for Brown's book about the Green Revolution *Seeds of Change*. Mr. Brown is now President of the Rockefeller-funded Worldwatch Institute.

Rather conveniently, "fertilizer is only one item in the package of new inputs which farmers need in order to realize the full potential of the new seeds. Once it becomes profitable to use modern technology, the demand for all kinds of farm inputs increases rapidly." Into what kind of economic mainstream are UDC farmers likely to be drawn? For Brown, the experience of his own country "provides a useful guide. Supplying farmers' needs can be big business." Agricultural inputs purchased by farmers in the United States in 1965—when US agriculture was *already* heavily mechanized—

. . . totaled $12.5 billion [consisting in] items purchased from the non-farm or industrial sector . . . [ten years later: the figure is about $75 billion]. For each acre of the 300 million acres they cultivate, American farmers spend $42 annually on production inputs and services supplied by the non-farm sector. Expenditures per acre are higher still in countries like Japan which practice more intensive cultivation . . . We can expect a steady rise in expenditure by farmers in poor countries for the same sorts of inputs.

Who is going to supply these inputs, that is, who profits from the Green Revolution?

Brown tells us that *"Only agribusiness firms can supply these new inputs* efficiently. This means that *the multinational corporation has a vested interest in the agricultural revolution* along with the poor countries themselves [emphasis added]." The poor nations, if they want to produce, must implicitly follow the path traced by America where "the institution most responsible for the development and the dissemination of agricultural technology is the private corporation. Its lusty offspring, the multinational corporation, promises to institutionalize the transfer of technology on a global scale." The MNC (shorthand for the multinationals) has been responsible for the take-off of developed countries' farming and there

. . . is good reason to think that the same process will take place in the poorer countries. As increases in farm production *become more dependent on purchased inputs,* and as the proportion of farm production that is marketed rises, *investment in agribusiness becomes more important.* In fact, that investment must grow much faster than agricultural production itself. It is difficult to see how this needed new investment in the poor countries will be found without encouraging the capital and the technical resources of the multinational corporation [emphasis added].

It is, indeed, an admirable system. Not only will poor countries purchase products that alone can make the new seeds work, but by doing so they will finance the expansion of the MNCs so they can sell more inputs *ad infinitum* or *ad nauseam,* as you prefer.

Of course, an occasional snag can occur. For example, Brown reports that Turkey faced a shortage of fertilizer in 1969 (this was long before fertilizer prices quadrupled) while a fair proportion of its wheat acreage was already planted to HYVs. Even though Turkey was prepared to use a major percentage of its foreign-exchange reserves for fertilizer purchases, it could not buy enough. So much for the Turks. Brown recognizes that "the ability of poor countries to produce or buy fertilizer at reasonable prices can affect the future course of the agrarian revolution. However, the ability of the MNCs to transfer technology rapidly and efficiently provides real hope that this problem will be vexing only in the short run." To back his optimism, Brown engages in a bit of prophecy: "The new technologies promise *lower* fertilizer prices in the seventies than prevailed in the sixties."* There is, of course, the alternative of producing one's own fertilizer. Some countries, "facing shortages of foreign exchanges, are also increasing their own fertilizer production capacity, *often with the help of the multinational corporation.*" Such "help" can be illustrated for the case of India. Here is how Brown recounts what happened:

> During the mid 1960s, a number of countries, including India . . . received large loans from USAID to finance imports of sorely needed fertilizer. At the same time, the United States and the World Bank put a great deal of pressure on . . . the Indian government, to encourage multinational corporations to invest in local production capacity. The Indian government changed its policy abruptly . . . to permit these firms to price and distribute their products in India. Joint ventures between Indian and foreign firms were especially encouraged.

Other sources do not give so sanguine a picture of what actually happened. In 1965–6, India was in the throes of yet another famine after a period of drought and dependent on US Food for Peace grain shipments. These shipments, and all USAID contributions, were suddenly placed on a month-to-month basis and threatened with curtailment. During this time the US and the

*This prophecy has, so far, proved wildly inaccurate. See Appendix on "Fertilizers."

World Bank did indeed "put a great deal of pressure" on India. The *New York Times* reported that you could "call them strings, call them conditions" or anything else, India had no choice but to accept America's terms for resuming the Food for Peace program. These conditions consisted largely in greater freedom for US private investment in general and for the American management of India's fertilizer industry in particular. The *Christian Science Monitor* noted that American businessmen insisted on importing all the necessary machines and equipment for fertilizer plants under construction, even though India could have provided some of them. They also insisted on importing liquid ammonia, instead of using plentiful, Indian-produced naphtha as the fertilizer feedstock. Finally, they were able to fix the prices, the distribution circuits and the profit margin.

UDC farmers would be lucky if fertilizer were their only problem in coping with the "benefits" of the Green Revolution. HYVs require pesticides, high-pressure sprayers, mechanical dryers for crops, motorized equipment, etc. Here, too, MNCs are at the ready. Brown tells us that Standard Oil set up "400 agro-service centers in the Philippines for ESSO fertilizer, but also for seeds, pesticides, implements and advice"; they are in fact "one-stop shopping centers for Filipino farmers." Amazingly enough, these centers were "established just as the new varieties were catching on; they are making a strategic contribution to the striking gains in Philippine rice production." Brown leaves his readers to make the connection, if any, between enormous Rockefeller Foundation investments since the war in pushing HYVs, the fact that ESSO also happens to be a major Rockefeller interest and the fact that Brown himself works for a Rockefeller-funded organization. (The best laid plans, even of Rockefellers, gang sometimes aglie—*Business Week* reported that the agro-service stations were closed down in 1970 as not profitable enough. One wonders who is now making a "strategic contribution" in the Philippines.)

It would be a mistake to imagine, however, that the Green Revolution "package" is conveniently delivered all-of-a-piece at the farmer's doorstep at just the right moment in the farming year. The farmer himself usually has to make it up from a variety of sources: this in itself is enough to exclude all but the largest, most literate farmers from GR benefits.

Brown then examines the figures relating to U.S. foreign business investment which has risen from $17 billion in 1930 to

$87 billion in 1966. He laments that "thus far, only a small fraction of the overseas investment of MNCs has been allotted to agribusiness in the poor countries.* *But this amount is increasing . . .* sales of farm inputs and opportunities for new investment and related activities are increasing in the poor countries *in close relation to the acreage planted to HYVs."* Furthermore, "in the 1970s agribusiness investment by private MNCs could far surpass that going into extractive industries," but for this to become the happy case, the reticent poor are going to have to "denationalize" their attitudes to what amounts to foreign control over their farm production and recognize that agribusiness is "an amazingly efficient way of institutionalizing the transfer of technical knowledge . . . The agricultural revolution provides the setting for a more pragmatic approach to a touchy issue [emphasis added]."

Readers may feel I am being unduly hard on Lester Brown,† who is doubtless as kind to his wife and children as the next man. Actually, he is my favorite Green Revolutionary, for without his disarming candor, one would be obliged to sift through any number of sources to compile a description of what the Green Revolution partly is—a complex system for foreign agribusiness domination of how, where and what Third World farms will produce and at what cost.

Other studies also describe the benefits MNCs reap from the Green Revolution. American political scientist Francine Frankel has indicated the harmful effects certain companies are having on rural areas in India like the Punjab where HYVs now occupy nearly all the wheatland. Another scholar, Richard Franke, analyzes her study for what it does and does not say:

Frankel observes that Massey-Ferguson is busy selling tractors to Green Revolution farmers. From her interviews with bank officials,

---

*Robert Heilbroner, in "None of Your Business," *New York Review of Books,* 20 March 1975, explains why it is impossible to compute the amount of direct foreign investments by US companies abroad, but estimates the sum at "well over $100 billion today." This does not include sales value of goods produced abroad by US firms, which amount to "perhaps $125 billion."
†So they deserve to share the good laugh I had when reading the following excerpt from an interview given by Brown at the World Food Conference:
LB: "It is true that agricultural 'experts' (his quotation marks) made a big mistake in favoring the transfer of inadapted technologies to the Third World. But I believe they are beginning to realize this." (*Les Dossiers 'Bis' de Jeune Afrique,* janvier-juin 1975, pp. 96-7: retranslated into English by me.)

Frankel ascertains that over-enthusiasm and "prestige reasons" are attracting many farmers to the new machinery who will never be able to pay back their loans.

These farmers, who belong to the "poorer class" of cultivators, are going to learn the hard way that tractors can be an uneconomic proposition.

One might expect a note of concern following this discovery. Why does the credit program work for the benefit of Massey-Ferguson and to the detriment of poor farmers? Why are tractors being *sold* if they are not justified on economic grounds? Why must "this class of cultivators" learn without leadership and organization that their poverty is going to increase? What will happen to their land when they cannot repay the debt? Such questions are not put.

For richer-class farmers, farm machinery can serve as an effective means of social control. In the beginning, the Green Revolution increased the need for labor: there were fertilizers and pesticides to be spread; moreover, there were two harvests a year. Hired laborers saw the increased yields and increased their wage demands accordingly. Tractors do not present this disadvantage, as wealthy farmers were quick to understand.

In all cases, it is apparent that one of the answers to the question "Who profits from the Green Revolution?" is "the corporations."

Has the expansion of acreage devoted to HYVs—an area multiplied by 568 in seven years—occurred fortuitously? Not at all. As early as 1953, the Rockefeller foundation, through its Agricultural Development Council, was focusing on training foreign "agricultural economists and technocrats" for India. It also joined forces, according to Harry Cleaver, with the USAID Participant Training Program to provide élites who would help "mould the rural economy into forms compatible with technological change and social stability." An Indian author tells how, in 1959, the Ford Foundation sent an expert mission to his country which called for "adequate supplies of fertilizers, pesticides, improved seeds . . ." and other Green-Revolution-type elements; and whose recommendations formed the basis for the Indian government's Intensive Agricultural Districts Program, also called the Package Program, concentrating on the richest, most modern farmers. This network served as a trial run for the Green Revolution. At CIMMYT in Mexico (Rockefeller), at IRRI in the

Philippines (Rockefeller and Ford), in the United States through AID, the Agricultural Development Council and scholarships financed by the foundations, UDC agronomists and rural economists were schooled. They made up "more than a group of highly trained individuals. They made up an international team of experts ready and willing to spread the seeds and the policies of the Green Revolution throughout the Third World." [Cleaver.]

What are the effects of the Green Revolution on nature itself? Ingrid Palmer, author of a study undertaken in the framework of a five-year United Nations Research Institute for Social Development (UNRISD) inquiry into the Green Revolution, is concerned that "many local varieties of food crops are in danger of becoming extinct, so that certain genetic characteristics could be lost forever. Parts of the Near East are being described as genetic disaster areas." She also tells how, at a recent FAO meeting, "the argument for encouraging seed breeding and multiplication to be in the hands of private enterprise . . . was put forcefully by some developed countries." UDC spokespeople objected, pointing out that private corporations would not bother to undertake research for genetically or economically deprived areas; that profitability, not need, would determine who got what seeds, and that consequently "deprived areas would remain deprived." Palmer tries to assess the "potential and likely influence of large-scale private agro-businesses in the determination of crop selection and benefits." Since their obvious tendency is to control inputs and outputs—from seeds to distribution of the resulting crop—she concludes: "The relevant question to ask may not be '*Will* seed sources be monopolized and inputs packaged in formulas?' but 'What is to *stop* large international agro-businesses from monopolizing and packaging the inputs of HYV cultivation?'"

An Australian geneticist concurs. He points out that the areas of the world where the Green Revolution has now nearly taken over the whole farming landscape are exactly those where the greatest diversity of plant characteristics were to be found. (There are virtually *no* "local varieties" left in North America or Europe where every inch is planted to hybrids.) Such genetic properties included resistance to drought, diseases and insects, whereas HYVs are "purified strains and their possibilities for genetic variation are reduced to a minimum." He calls for an internationally coordinated effort to "bank" local varieties before the world's genetic base becomes disastrously narrow.

Impoverishment of the genetic material future scientists will have to work with is already well advanced. When one realizes that several thousand plant species may be necessary for a single screening experiment, this is ecologically alarming.

Geneticists have devoted considerable effort to producing disease-resistant strains of HYVs, but the fact remains that because they are planted over vast areas with no "firebreaks," blights, when they occur, can wipe out whole crop regions. For example, a rice blight in the Philippines in 1971 was so devastating that the country had to resort to imports again.

What are the Green Revolution's effects on peoples' diets? Here again, we turn to Ingrid Palmer whose study for the UNRISD centers on the relationship between the Green Revolution and nutrition. She points out that all the HYV crops are high in carbohydrates and relatively low in protein. Diets in the UDCs have traditionally found their protein supplements in foods like pulses, groundnuts, peas and beans, sometimes including soybeans. But "in all the countries which have introduced the new cereal seeds, government has intervened to make certain facilities and inputs available to farmers willing to adopt the seeds." In other words, to make HYV production attractive, governments have supplied inputs—often at prices below real costs—and have frequently fixed purchase prices artificially high (thereby also raising consumer food prices). This has had the desired, if not the desirable effect: HYV production has gone up; protein-crop production has not kept pace and in several countries has declined. "Against this background, soybean production, once very profitable to Javanese farmers, has become the Cinderella of Javanese agricultural production," says Palmer. ("Poor relation" might be a better metaphor.)

In the light of the very generous credits to Indonesia in the last six years and the active interest of foreign private companies and governments in Indonesia there seems to have been an unwarranted haste in committing the Javanese people to new world records of protein deficiency. Had the Indonesian government been made more fully aware of the appalling nutritional status of the Javanese, they might have bargained harder for the welfare of 60 million people. A more sober look at all the implications of a "rice revolution" might have pressed home wider issues of nutritional standards.

But then again, in the "light of the active interest of foreign private companies in Indonesia," it might not have. Even in Mexico, where HYVs have been implanted longest and with greatest apparent success, "there is little reason," according to Palmer, "to believe that the introduction of HYVs has done much to raise per capita consumption of food." In Mexico the new HYVs of wheat have raised per capita wheat production a great deal, "but the profits accrue to owners of large mechanized farms while the produce itself is exported." The title of one of Palmer's chapters, "The Final Divorce of Agriculture and Nutrition through the Agency of the Green Revolution," more or less sums up what has happened.

What is the Green Revolution doing to research? Since most agronomic research takes place in the developed countries and since the latter have been so dedicated to pushing the Revolution, an inordinate amount of research has been devoted (a) to high-carbohydrate HYVs; (b) to the climatic zones where they can be grown; (c) to fertilizer-sensitive plants that can be protected from disease only by chemicals. Proportionally, and as a corollary, there has been very little research (a) on high-protein crops like peas and beans—although some effort has been given to protein contents of wheat and rice; (b) on non-irrigated areas; (c) on biological, as opposed to chemical, increase of yields and blight prevention.

Since the irrigated areas of the Third World comprise a very small part of its total area, an effort similar to that of CIMMYT and IRRI which produced the HYVs would be necessary to improve yields in areas where rain is the only source of water. The International Crop Research Institute for the Semi-Arid Tropics (ICRISAT) in Hyderabad is a small step in the right direction. Similarly, we have to recognize that poor people will depend on plants, not meat, for their protein for a long time to come. The deliberate down-grading and lack of research on crops that could provide this protein is extremely serious and shortsighted. Much more attention ought also to be devoted to whole *systems* of agriculture: alternate cropping with nitrogen-rich plants (like pulses) which could reduce dependency on chemical nutrients. René Dumont points out that there are about 80,000 known edible plant species—but a mere 50 of them provide 90 per cent of our food. Surely the others have myriad possibilities, if human need rather than foundation/corporate interests redirected the experiments of the world's laboratories.

What has been the social impact of the Green Revolution? If the postulate that technology always has a social effect holds true, then it is logical to assume that the more integrated the technology—the more it makes up a package—the broader its ripple effect on society will be. It would be foolish and inaccurate to pretend the Green Revolution has had no good effects in UDCs: its role in increasing the *marketable* surplus, thus in helping to feed urban consumers, has been very important. Unfortunately, it has also seriously increased inequalities between farmers who can afford it and those who cannot, as well as between more and less favored areas of the same countries. "Green Revolution" is a catch phrase covering a whole concept—even an ethos—of rural development as practised from Mexico to the Philippines, from Afghanistan to India. I had the choice of leaving it out of the book as too complex, or of oversimplifying, and have chosen the second path. Most of the consequences described apply to most Green Revolution areas, but the huge variety of geographical and social structures guarantees that exceptions can be found. There seems little doubt, however, that aside from its contributions to the profit side of MNC business ledgers it has also been viewed by the various American interests pushing it as an *alternative to land reform* and to the social change reform would require. Since land reform is the only *other* way to increase food production, these experts are willing to settle for the lesser of two evils.

Thus even Lester Brown recognizes that the Revolution may create some undesirable social spin-off: "The dramatic gains in income being realized by farmers who are able to use the new seeds abruptly widens the gap in living standards, and the consequent conflicts, between them and those who are still tied to traditional husbandry practices." He does not explain why only a few "have been able" to use the new seeds. He also devotes a few pages of his book on the Revolution to "second-generation problems" which he characteristically sees as mostly technical. Storage, marketing systems and transportation facilities will be overloaded by bountiful harvests; "links between the agricultural hinterland and the world market" will have to be established. (One might think that the "world market" would be the last concern of food-deficit countries). Still, social problems do exist, mostly because the technology is being introduced so rapidly—within a few years rather than gradually throughout the decades it took to bring about the farming revolution in the developed countries. So Brown solemnly asks "a basic question for all mankind: Can we manage progress or not?"

Up to now, "we" haven't been doing very well. We might also ask, "progress for whom?" Mr. Jagjivan Ram, former Minister of Agriculture in India, has been reported as saying that in his country the beneficiaries of the Revolution are not the peasants "who live miserably on a few rupees a month" but the small, privileged stratum of larger landholders. While 22 percent of rural families own no land at all, and 47 per cent own less than an acre, 3 or 4 per cent of the large proprietors with political power and influence are in a position to appropriate for themselves all the resources in inputs, technical assistance and credit put at the disposal of farmers by government agencies. Meanwhile, Indian grain output is still well below the level of self-sufficiency that was supposed, optimistically, to be reached via the Revolution in 1974-5.*

The problem is not confined to India, although Indian examples tend to crop up more than those from other countries. The UNRISD has now completed its five-year research project, *The Social and Economic Implications of Large-Scale Introduction of New Varieties of Foodgrain* of which Palmer's quoted study was a part. I strongly recommend the project summary to anyone who wants to pursue the matter with an informed, balanced study. Here I take the liberty of inventing a dialogue around some of the information it provides concerning the Revolution's social consequences. The characters are a landlord and his tenant, at harvest time. The landlord might be a city man who rarely appears in the neighborhood except to collect his rent (which he may be paid in cash or in kind) or he may farm a sizeable piece of land himself with the help of hired hands. The farmer might be a tenant or a sharecropper; he has only a small piece of land he has always thought of as "his." In any case, the landlord has bought the whole HYV package and has doubled his yield since last year. The farmer couldn't afford the inputs—his harvest is the same.

*India reportedly stockpiled 16-18 million tons of grain in 1976, but this does not mean that all Indians were suddenly well-nourished. Even when food is plentiful, there are millions of people who can't pay for it.

LANDLORD: You owe me a third more rent this year—I'll take it in wheat or in cash.

TENANT: But I can't pay you any more—I didn't even feed my family all year on the last harvest.

LANDLORD: Just look at what my land has produced. You see that it can be done and you ought to be growing more yourself. Your land belongs to me and it isn't bringing in enough profit.

TENANT: It's easy enough for you to talk. I know how you did it—you spread a hundred sacks of fertilizer on the soil and the well is on your property. How am I supposed to buy fertilizer when I already have to buy food? I can't even use the water when I want to.

LANDLORD: Tell you what. I'll give you this money right now and you get off that land. In the bargain, I'll even hire you next year at sowing and harvest time and maybe in between. That's more than you would have got last year, but the land's valuable and I'm generous.

TENANT: But I don't want to get off the land. My father and his father farmed it before me, for your father and his father.

LANDLORD: In that case, I'll loan you the money to buy fertilizer and seeds. That way you can pay me a higher rent when the new crop comes in. The loan will only cost you 5 per cent a month. (Aside: Heh heh, *I* get the money at 8 per cent a year from the bank in town).

TENANT: But I could never pay you back. I already owe money for my daughter's wedding and for the money I had to borrow to buy food last year.

LANDLORD: In that case, consider yourself evicted. I'll farm the land myself. By the way, I still may be needing your services, so stay around. Of course, I won't be able to pay you much. Times aren't *that* good, and if you don't like your wages, there are plenty of others around who'll be glad of a job. Besides, I plan to buy a tractor.

TENANT: But what about my wife and children? What are we to do? In your father's time this could not have happened. He even gave food to tide us over the bad times.

LANDLORD: Sorry about that. Business is business. You might try the city.

If this sounds like melodrama, so be it. It is exactly the kind of conversation that is now taking place all over Asia and Latin America, according to UNRISD. Communal farming arrangements are breaking down everywhere—even paternalism goes by the board as the new entrepreneur farmers squeeze out the marginal ones and landlords get rid of sharecroppers. They join the army of landless rural laborers or the unemployed in town. As yields go up, any human inclination to share goes down: profit in the marketplace becomes the only goal. People who had an umbilical relationship to a piece of ground become proletarians. "Families cut off from traditional village emergency resources experience hunger not as a result of poor harvest but of unemployment." The UNRISD conclusions hold out a hope that may not be entirely to the taste of Western Green Revolutionaries:

> The heightened visibility of the wealth of large landholders can also intensify the sense of deprival of the poor, thus bringing latent conflict to the surface . . . [this group may gain] increasing awareness that the maintenance of livelihood may be better served by collective action than by clinging to a relationship of dependency upon an unwilling patron.

Has the prospect of revolution ever been alluded to more delicately?

That spectre has prompted an Agricultural Development Council official writing in *Foreign Affairs* to wonder whether the Green Revolution is a *Cornucopia or a Pandora's Box*. Mr. Wharton says,

> The quiet, passive peasant is already aware of the modern world—far more than we realize—and he is impatient to gain his share. The Green Revolution offers him the dramatic possibility of achieving his goal through peaceful means. . . . Now is the time to place it [the GR] in its long-range perspective and to engage in contingency planning so that we may respond flexibly and quickly as the Revolution proceeds. Perhaps in this way we can ensure that what we are providing becomes a cornucopia, not a Pandora's box.

Here there is no question of concealing that "we" are doing the providing, so "we" must also supply the response when the going gets rough. But perhaps it is already too late: UNRISD has answered Wharton's query. Western interests introduced the Revolution to sell inputs, but also to promote social stability through increased food production and the strengthening of a middle-class peasantry in nations they saw as threatened by "communism." Now it turns out that everywhere the Green Revolution has been adopted the fact that agriculture is seen not as the means for feeding people but as a "profitable investment . . . sets in motion deep currents of change in the relation between land, labor and capital, between owners, tenants and laborers, between agriculture, commerce and industry, and between town and country."

Some of these changes can be briefly illustrated. In 1969,

according to Indian police reports, for East Bengal alone there were 346 land-grabbing incidents, with many killed and wounded. In Bihar, in 1969, landlords attacked landless peasants with shotguns, killing fifteen and wounding sixteen. Police arrested 740 people. The crime of these peasants: trying to occupy the land they cultivated. In Tamil Nadu (Tanjore, 1968), hired laborers struck for better wages. The Green Revolution had brought higher yields to the land they worked, so this appeared to them normal. To the owners it did not. They attacked the strikers' village. Panic-stricken, the men fled. Forty-two people (thirty-nine women and children, three men) who remained in the village were rounded up by the attackers, and shut up in a hut which was then set on fire. All forty-two burned to death. To date, "the assassins have not been put on trial." Land prices in areas of Pakistan where the Green Revolution has been introduced have increased 500 per cent as landlords compete for land from which tenants have been removed. In 1969, there were 40,000 eviction suits against sharecroppers in Bihar state; 80,000 in Mysore state, India. One could go on and on listing incidents and figures; each one bearing its full measure of human misery.

In the face of such full-scale deprivation, hunger and unemployment, there are two alternatives. One is agrarian reform, land redistribution and curtailment of privilege. The other is repression. At least in India, it seems unlikely that the first will be tried. There has been land reform already in India—on paper. But the rural upper classes also furnish the politicians. Out of 64 Congress Party members in the Punjab Regional Assembly, 45 are large landowners; in Haryana 30 out of 52; "in Madhya Pradesh, 96 Congress parliamentarians out of 220 have landholdings *larger than the limit which they themselves contributed to voting.*"

In late 1974, the *New York Times* reported that "without publicity, the Indian government has increased its police and internal security budgets. A parliamentary report points out that government allocations for the police have doubled in the last five years and have risen by fifty-two times in the last twenty-four years." The Parliament's Public Accounts Committee found this to be "by any standard an alarming increase." The government finds the increase to be necessary because there are riots over food shortages and "communal and political disputes." Some of these security forces have recently been used to "quell agitation" in several of the poorer rural states. The Committee fears that all this is taking place at "the expense of economic and social needs" and is "eroding the resources available for developmental activities." The recent mass arrests of the Congress Party's political opponents indicate that this trend is not likely to be reversed.

Didn't anyone see all this coming? Many people raised their voices against the harmful social consequences of the Green Revolution; they did so in the FAO magazine *Ceres,* among other places. Solon Barraclough warned that the suffering engendered by the Revolution would be greater than its benefits; Mexican agrarian economist Edmundo Flores explained why it would accentuate class conflict and might precipitate violence; Andrew Pearse (who later directed the UNRISD study) said that the introduction of new technology and a generalized market economy would reduce traditional "social security" and intensify hunger. Since the late 1960s there has hardly been an issue of *Ceres* without some mention of the counter-effects of the Revolution. But on the other side was produced an enormous body of work—much of it commissioned by the ubiquitous foundations—which by concentrating only on the Revolution's production/economic aspects managed to convince many well-meaning bureaucrats of the necessity for its adoption. Even today, FAO has not entirely abandoned its official policy, which is to push the HYVs—and hope for the best.

There is, furthermore, evidence to show that the US government, private foundations and MNCs knew exactly what they were about when they introduced the Green Revolution, and they knew it early on. Here is some testimony to the Subcommittee on National Security Policy and Scientific Developments of the House Committee on Foreign Affairs.

Mr. Harrar (President Emeritus of the Rockefeller Foundation): "The expansion of world economies through intensification of agriculture may also provide *major and direct benefits to the developed nations,* particularly in the expansion of cash markets for an ever-broader range of industrial products." (From his deposition, entitled "The Benefits of the Green Revolution," emphasis added).

They were also fully aware of the likely social consequences:

Mr. Carroll (of the Inter-American Development Bank): "The tenants, I think, may become a diminishing breed as they get squeezed out gradually by landlords reclaiming their holdings because agriculture has become profitable . . .Indian farmers are not going to prove to be any more philanthropic as wage bargainers than any farmers anywhere else in the world. . . . (The GR) might make the rich still richer and enable them to capture markets previously served by smaller semi-subsistence producers."

Must the Green Revolution make the rich richer and the poor hungrier? No. The logical outcome of the Revolution under the free market conditions that prevail in most countries where it has been adopted is a landscape of large, commercially operated farms (sometimes growing crops for export) existing alongside fewer and fewer subsistence plots. Hunger and unemployment are part of the social landscape. But *given a different social system* and a concerted effort to make the new technology benefit all the people, the Revolution can be just what it was touted to be—a road towards self-sufficiency and the eradication of hunger. It need not be a poisoned gift.

North Vietnam, which has consistently increased its food production even during the years of bombing, is a case in point. Sorbonne Professor of Geography Yves Lacoste reports on his visit to one of the 500 pilot communes chosen "to put into practice, with their own people and frequently under difficult conditions, the whole body of techniques recommended by North Vietnamese agronomists." These techniques are remarkably akin to all those we have been discussing.

Prior to the 1956 agrarian reform . . . [the commune of] Vu Thang produced about three tons of [unmilled] rice per hectare . . . today production of this cooperative is eleven to twelve tons [both figures for the combined spring and autumn harvests] . . . These spectacular gains . . . progressively attained, are due to the combination of several factors: systematic use of improved seeds and new rice varieties, twice as much fertilizer application as previously, more man-hours of work made possible through the cooperative system, a better division of labor and the use of specialists; regrouping of small plots into large rice fields, and a vastly improved water system which involved the displacement of some 80,000 cubic meters of earth—all done by the local population.

Workers in the commune spend about 250 days a year working on its land. They also have their own individual plots. Vu Thang is a village where 20 per cent of the people—including *all* the members of twenty families—died during the 1945 famine. Now the monthly rice allotment is twenty kilos (forty-four lbs.) per person, to which should be added the production from individual plots. The cooperative has doubled wages in the last ten years, while prices have remained stable. The commune now has its own primary and secondary schools, a twenty-bed dispensary/maternity hospital with five permanent health workers, a theatre/meeting hall and a model pig farm whose 1,500 lucky denizens are also largely fed on *rice*. All of this has been built with income from the cooperative. The members of this and many other cooperatives—though not all of them have reached the stage where they can feed rice to pigs—are living better and eating more because the new technological inputs are being sifted through an equalitarian social structure.

Even limited reforms could do something to improve the people's condition. In India, for example, most water supplies vital for growing HYVs are not publicly or communally owned, but belong to the wealthy farmers. UNRISD notes that here as elsewhere, the "efficiency of [water] arrangements is jeopardized by . . . lack of coordination and cooperation between users and suppliers . . . in most parts of the world cultivators are excessively prodigal with water when they have access to it and ruthless towards neighbors in the struggle to obtain access." In this dog-eat-dog world, governments could begin by concentrating on labor-intensive works to restructure the whole irrigation system and "work towards local cooperation for efficient management within a framework of firm and equitable control exercised by the authority." An official Indian government study cited by UNRISD declares that "if the 40 million hectares of irrigated lands in India could be made to produce three tons per hectare of foodgrains, the country's food needs could be met, leaving much of the remaining 100 million hectares free to be put to more rational and profitable use." UNRISD adds "such a level of productivity could be achieved without difficulty if people and resources could be mobilized to make efficient use of available water."

But are people likely to be mobilized as long as any extra effort on their part is going to profit only the rural bigwigs? These are the people who hold all the cards—from seeds to water to credit to politics. They have frequently been joined, now that HYVs have proved a profitable investment, by city businessmen, retired bureaucrats and other species of absentee landlords, who find it convenient to hire labor-crews glad of any wage and who will not demand a share of the bountiful, marketable, harvest in partial payment.

Where nothing is done to alleviate inequalities, the Green

Revolution is guaranteed to worsen them. Peasants are notoriously the most difficult social group to prod into collective action—not because they are stupider or more lethargic or more inured to their own oppression than city-dwellers—but because their whole lives, not just their jobs, depend on the local feudal powers. The Green Revolution is increasing their misery to what may nevertheless become an intolerable level. The university "development" sociologists and economists on our side of the world have been studying the everyday lives of people benefiting from—in their terms—the Green Revolution, with a view to dealing with them should they express discontent. Meanwhile, the poor have been carrying out research on their own everyday lives and have found them wanting. Even governments which today seem indefectibly bound to Western interests may one day decide—pushed by their own masses—that enough is enough. The least we in the West can do is to understand who is behind this social disaster and attempt to make them stop. Otherwise, the fears—or the hopes—of many will come true, and we shall have a *real* revolution on our hands.

Conclusion to Part Two

In spite of decades of obvious failure to solve the world food crisis, most "experts" continue to proceed as if solutions for it could be purely technical—and Western-sponsored. We have helped to shove pills down the throats of Third World mothers and to vasectomize Third World fathers; we have cultivated entire upper classes so that they will share our ways of thinking; we have assumed in every case that West is Best and consequently we have introduced technology profitable to our own MNCs with brisk and total unconcern for the consequences on other peoples' lives.

We have, in fact, paid attention to every factor except those that could alleviate hunger and misery in the poor world. Some of our more sophisticated institutions are beginning to realize this. In a speech to his Board of Governors, World Bank President Robert McNamara informed the audience that the "possession of land, and hence of *political and economic power*, in the rural areas is concentrated in the hands of a small minority." Furthermore, concentration is moving inexorably ahead. McNamara gives figures to show that millions of peasants are no match for the few powerful landholders and goes on to say,

> Even the use of the land which the small farmer does have is uncertain. Tenancy arrangements are generally insecure and often extortionate. In many countries, tenants have to hand over to the landlord 50–60 per cent of their crop as rent, and yet in spite of this are faced with the constant threat of eviction. The result is that their incentive to become more productive is seriously eroded.

McNamara does *not* go on to say, "Off with their heads." But at least a major, and very conservative, Western-dominated agency like the World Bank now recognizes that the problem is political and social, not technical. Or, as the UN more timidly puts it, "Whatever may be the circumstances of individual countries, all of them need to reexamine their food and agricultural policies to

107

see how to move forward more rapidly towards the elimination of rural poverty."

For it is poverty that is the problem. Many people have tended automatically to ascribe world hunger partly to shiftlessness or stupidity on the part of "backward peasants"—either they won't work or they stubbornly refuse to accept modern farming methods. Neither is true. We have seen that smallholders invariably produce more per hectare than large ones—despite the facts that they have less access to purchased inputs and that the land they do work may often be of poorer quality. We saw in Part One that a distressing number of rural households—doubtless close to 85 per cent in much of Asia—do not manage to feed themselves all year around on the crops they can grow on their limited land and that about half are self-provisioning only half the year at best. This is one reason many small farmers are hesitant to adopt the "modern inputs" like fertilizers and pesticides. They have to pay cash for the inputs (credit is rarely granted by legitimate banks and expensive when it is) but even if they could increase their yields by a third or more, many would *still* not be self-provisioning. Providing an adequate diet for millions of small peasants (not to mention the landless) is not a question of getting them to "work harder" or to "modernize." Under present systems they have the unenviable choices of finding one of the few available off-farm jobs, going deeper into debt, or going hungry. But when a smallholder sees a chance for achieving self-sufficiency, he grabs it. The few field studies done on the subject of self-provisioning show that the farmers already producing enough food for seven to nine months of the year are the most willing to invest in fertilizers, improved seeds, etc. because the extra inputs can help them to attain a year-round supply for their families. But in most cases, as René Dumont has explained,

> The small farmer knows that if he makes an extra effort, most of the income obtained will go to the owners if he is a tenant; to the money-lender if he is in debt; to the trader from whom he must buy dearly, before his next crop comes in, a part of what he had to sell cheaply from his preceding harvest—and if not to all these, then to the more or less corrupt civil-servant.

The problem also exists on the national level, and here again we end with a seemingly ineradicable slate of strikes against the UDCs. They are hindered by the increasing numbers of people they must feed—but these numbers will not decrease *until* a more equitable distribution of national resources comes about. They are dominated from without by long-term strategies to keep them under Western thumbs; either through induced attitudes that propose the consumer society and the free-market system as life's only goals, through technology the West alone can supply and maintain; or through trade terms that discriminate against the only goods they produce.

The old colonial empires are gone but not forgotten. Western interests have had to adjust to changing times. The most intelligent among them are usually way ahead of their critics when it comes to accepting the inevitable and to determining what can most profitably be done under new circumstances. In the following section, I hope to make clear what these adjustments have been and who can use the food crisis to his own economic or political advantage.

* * * *

Dr. Norman Borlaug, one of the Rockeféller Foundation's original bright young geneticists who founded CIMMYT, received the Nobel Peace Prize (Peace, not Biology) in 1970 for his contributions to the development of the Green Revolution. He concluded his acceptance speech to the Nobel Academy with this passage from Isaiah:

> And the desert shall rejoice, and blossom as the rose . . . and the parched ground shall become a pool, and the thirsty land springs of water . . . [35: 1, 7]

Dr. Borlaug did not tell the Academy that the Prophet foresees certain changes as imperative before this blossoming can take place:

> And the eyes of them that see shall not be dim, and the ears of them that hear shall hearken . . . the tongue of the stammerers shall be ready to speak plainly.
>
> The vile person shall no more be called liberal, nor the churl said to be bountiful.
>
> For the vile person will speak villainy and his heart will work iniquity; to practice hypocrisy . . . to make empty the soul of the hungry, and he will cause the drink of the thirsty to fail.
>
> The instruments also of the churl are evil: he deviseth wicked devices to destroy the poor with lying words, even when the needy speaketh right. [32: 3-7]

PART THREE

Getting a Cut on Hunger

6. Planned Scarcity

The fact that food is a basic human necessity does not mean that it is universally thought of as a basic human right. For a limited number of agents in a position to call most of the shots, food is nothing more than a series of commodities on which money can be made (even occasionally lost) exactly like rubber or gold. The powerful traders in wheat or soybeans, sugar or milk, are usually themselves processors, as well as marketers. They have their formal and informal links with governments; together they sustain one of the great myths of modern times: the myth of the market. The market is supposed, with a kind of cybernetic majesty, to "set" prices through the inexorable forces of supply and demand. Our vocabulary conforms to the myth when we say that "prices rise" as if "prices" were the only available subject of the verb "to rise" and as if no human actors could possibly be involved in raising them. These actors exist, however, and although they are not yet always able to put prices up and sustain them at optimum (for them) levels, they are rapidly progressing towards this goal. Their essential concern, as André Udry has aptly summarized it, is: "Beginning with effective demand, what are the best ways of trying to stabilize prices [of food commodities] at the highest possible levels over a prolonged period?"

Pseudo-scarcity induced through trade is not a new phenomenon: a French historian notes that "the great French famines and food shortages of the Middle Ages occurred during periods when foodstuffs were not lacking; they were indeed produced in great quantity and exported. The social system and structure were largely responsible for these deficiencies." At a time when the aristocracy was discovering "the secrets of exquisite cuisine" people were starving to death in France. No one cared much about the misery of the *menu peuple*—the little people—until the eighteenth century. When we speak of scarcity today—and food must be "scarce"; otherwise why would so many hundreds of millions be hungry?—we must place it in the political context of those nations who largely control the world's present food supply and of the huge corporations that dominate the food trade. Today as yesterday nature and sometimes governments' policies may produce abundance, but only man can create scarcity. According to the simplest rule of liberal economics, a vital commodity in short supply will be expensive and he who has some to sell will make money. This basic rule is being applied on a global scale, with considerable success.

In centrally planned social systems, the state and its locally appointed agencies perform the functions of both buyer and seller on the food market, thus controlling prices both for producers and for consumers. We tend to assume—incorrectly—that in a "free" market, these functions are performed by millions of people, expressing their desires in the marketplace through the medium of money—money invested in production or in finished products. In fact, the vast majority of producers and consumers has no say whatsoever in the functioning of the food market.

State intervention plays an important role (especially in states that would be righteously indignant if they were called "socialistic"). Thus,

> . . . if US farm policy over the past half century can be thought of as having a theme, it has been to prevent [farmers'] productivity from driving down prices . . . the tinkering with the market mechanism has been on a scale befitting the world's wealthiest nation. From Soil Bank to Public Law 480 to drowning baby pigs, little that might elevate prices has not been tried.

(This is a professor of international food economics at Cornell University speaking). The Food for Peace Law (PL 480) is discussed in detail in Chapter 8. It has had the desired effect of vastly increasing US commercial markets for food abroad. Keeping food prices high through control of supply is not peculiar, however, to the United States. A former President of the FAO Council, referring to targets for world grain production in the 1950s and 1960s, complained that "as soon as production approached quantities equivalent to *effective demand,* markets became clogged with alleged 'surpluses.' These annoyed governments far more than insufficient food levels did." In the EEC, governments practice "intervention buying" on a broad scale when gluts threaten to drive prices down. They also destroy food by the hundreds of tons to keep it off the market if need be.

One of the best ways of keeping food prices high and under control is not to produce food in the first place. This has been the tactic employed particularly by the major grain-producing nations like the US and Canada. We have already noted how much land they got farmers to take out of production in exchange for subsidies in the late 1960s and early 1970s. This tactic has been reversed only because world food prices are now right. The *Washington Post,* citing a secret US government study, stated that if the United States, Argentina, Canada and Australia had not reduced acreage and had merely maintained a constant rate of cultivation "they would jointly have produced over 90 million more tons of wheat during 1969–72."

The same cycle could be described for rice, on which so many people depend for their chief staple food. During the last five years of the 1960s, rice stocks tripled. Prices began to fall (quite moderately: for an index of 100 in 1963 the world export price was 113 in 1969 and 97 in 1970) so investment and planting were reduced even in some Green Revolution countries. By January 1971 the price was $129 a ton; by January 1974 $538, and it reached an all-time high of $630 a ton in April 1974, making everyone happy, except possibly the hungry.

Most people, including the UN, date present food scarcities from 1972 and tend to cite three major contributing factors: disastrous harvests in 1972 due to bad weather, failure of the high-protein Peruvian anchovy catch creating extra demand for alternate sources of protein like soybeans; and massive grain purchases by the Russians. All these explanations are to some degree mythical. The 1972 harvests were, in fact, just 1 per cent lower than those of the preceding year, and the *second best ever recorded* up to that year (1971 was best). Peruvian anchovies were indeed in short supply, but these shortages had been building up over the preceding years and thus hardly came as a surprise. The Russian deals were well known to the US government (though not yet to the general public) in the summer of 1972. And yet, in the same summer the United States paid farmers to withhold 60 million acres from production—fully 15 per cent of all US cropland. (Fall planting of winter wheat in the US accounts for 75 per cent of its total wheat production.) If the US government had wanted to increase food production, it had all the relevant information pointing to world shortages at hand. It chose, however, not to act. Certain commentators have remarked that 1972 was an election year and that Nixon's coffers were abundantly garnished by agribusinesses who profited from the skyrocketing prices that followed hard upon the US action—or lack of it. According to *Fortune*, one soybean magnate personally gave nearly $122,000 (Dwayne Andreas, President of Archer Daniels Midland) but this may be because Nixon had an honest face.

In spite of drastic rises in food prices of their own making, Western governments, particularly that of America, have managed to convince nearly everyone that worldwide inflation, various scarcities and unemployment are entirely the fault of the OPEC countries. No blame attaches to the deliberate withholding of food-producing land, but we have heard the outraged cries that meet any OPEC suggestion, let alone implementation, of reduced oil production to make prices go up "naturally." OPEC has become such a convenient whipping-boy that unfounded assertions have become unassailable "facts" in the public mind. Even though such sober Western institutions as the OECD have flatly stated that oil price increases have contributed no more than 1–2 per cent to the increased cost of living in the West, and no less a man than the Chairman of the US Council of Economic Advisers has agreed that even "if the oil price were to flatten out and stay flat indefinitely, we probably wouldn't lose more than a small percentage of our current inflation rate," most people still cling to the initial barrage of propaganda and blame OPEC for all their woes. They also accuse the Arabs of being prime movers of increased hunger and starvation in the Third World. OPEC has been particularly damned for high prices and consequent lack of fertilizer in the poorest countries. The crocodile tears shed for the fate of the Third World would be more believable if the richest countries simultaneously re-examined the prices they pay for the poor countries' exports and those they charge for manufactured goods and especially for food. How responsible is OPEC for the current high cost of fertilizer?

During the 1960s, according to *Chemical and Engineering News*, "the world fertilizer industry went on a plant building spree that resulted in massive over-capacity. Prices plummeted and profits disappeared." The small firms obliged to sell out left the big ones in a privileged position. Barry Commoner points out that fertilizer manufacturers blamed oil price increases while simultaneously applying to their own products increases *twenty-three times* as great as the corresponding energy increase: during 1970–74, the cost of *energy* necessary to produce one hundred pounds of anhydrous ammonia went from 47¢ to 70¢. The price for the same quantity of *fertilizer* during the same period rose from $3.79 to $9.15. In other terms, for a 23¢ difference in energy costs the difference for the fertilizer price was $5.36. Prices for all types of fertilizers had *already* increased 100 per cent between June 1972 and September 1973, or well before the December 1973 oil increase. But this situation is now blamed on OPEC. (For a more complete account of how the fertilizer industry plays the planned-scarcity game and maintains what one executive calls a "fine line" between meeting commercial demand and avoiding any excess supply that might cause prices to fall, see the Appendix.)

Still, say skeptics, oil weighs heavy on the balance of payments of the poorest countries. Granted, but not nearly so much as food. Imports of food and fertilizer place a much heavier burden on the poor than does oil. During the worst period of inflated grain prices in 1974, a ton of wheat was selling for three times as much as a ton of oil. Cash outlays for food and fertilizers in 1975 cost the poor nations nearly twice as much as their payments for oil imports and prices for manufactured goods and services flowing from the affluent to the needy world have doubled in the last five years when they have not quadrupled. Aside from that, the only differences are that OPEC is aiding the poor nations proportionally to its GNP far more than the West; and benefits from oil accrue to nations that can themselves be considered developing. In the case of food, fertilizers and manufactured goods, all the return goes to the already rich. There would seem to be a distinct double standard when it comes to outrage.

Most of the world depends on American production of cereals for its food imports, which means in essence that it depends on Cargill, Continental Grain, Central Soya, Archer Daniels, Cook Industries, Bunge, Dreyfus and a handful of smaller corporations. *All* of the US grain exports (including Food for Peace) pass through their hands. These corporations are not merely traders and big operators on the futures markets, although that is their image. A good example is Cargill, still a family company not quoted on the stock exchange, but conservatively estimated (in 1973) to be worth over $5 billion. Since Cargill does not make its financial reports public, there is no way of verifying its current worth, but a partial list of its assets and activities goes a little way.*

Cargill is engaged in buying, cleaning, storing, drying, preserving, loading, hauling, processing and creating consumer markets for grain. It buys soybeans, corn, safflower, flax and other seeds to convert them into oils and other products like livestock feed. It mines salt, operates a fishing fleet and processes fishmeal; it imports and processes raw sugar and molasses; its assets include ocean vessels, tow-boats and barges, a fleet of 1,500 rail cars, plus trucks, elevators and a network of bulk terminals to move 40 million tons of food, fertilizer and other commodities annually towards customers throughout the world. Cargill also manufactures resins, produces seeds and does research on HYVs; it has its own private computerized telegraph system for linking 250 locations in North America and sixty abroad in thirty-six different countries. It markets wheat, corn, oats, barley, sorghum, rice, rye, alfalfa, sugar, soybeans, molasses, edible and industrial oils, poultry breeding stock, animal feeds and salt worldwide. It owned and operated, at last count, some thirty-five animal-feed manufacturing plants in the US and more than twenty abroad. It also breeds animals to which its feeds can be fed. More than a quarter of its capital is invested abroad. This is the company you probably thought was spending all its time bidding up wheat futures ¼¢—if you had heard of it at all.

The other giant grain merchants are also busily increasing their horizontal and vertical expansion and concentration. Through sheer size and diversity, they are in a position to take advantage of every factor influencing the market. They are now, for example, getting information on other nations' potential harvests—probably before the nations in question know themselves—through commercial satellite data firms. Thus *Barron's* financial weekly was able to suggest in early June that 1975 Soviet harvests might be less than predicted: "a big drought-induced headache could be building up in an area . . . normally accounting for about 40–45 per cent of the Soviet Union's spring wheat

*Too late to incorporate in this book, I received a copy of the North American Congress on Latin America's excellent report, *US Grain Arsenal*, which includes a detailed section on Cargill. NACLA's sources include interviews with government and Cargill officials, and it sets the company's current worth at around $9 billion, "making it the largest grain trader in the world." Report available from NACLA, Box 57, Cathedral Station, New York, N.Y. 10025. $1.00 plus postage.

production . . . more than 20 per cent of the total crop could be affected. Quite a hunk. Of course, if rains come within the next two weeks, the crop will be all right." A former NASA scientist, now Vice-President of the Earth Satellite Corp. teledetection firm, writes in the FAO magazine that "satellites now scan the whole planet twice a day. Through them, it is already possible to simulate exactly growing cycles for wheat and maize"; it will soon be possible to "identify and evaluate all the world's important food crops" from satellite data. *Barron's* source was Global Telecommunications System, an outfit that provides paying customers with "instantaneous data around the globe." The big traders certainly know immediately when rain falls in the Volga Valley or elsewhere. They can then take advantage of price flurries when grain purchases like those of the USSR become generally known—they can even, if necessary, create them. Weather as such no longer really exists for the traders. In the world market, there *is* no climate when every variation can be used to turn a profit and to consolidate the system.

The companies' most spectacular coup in recent history has come to be known as the Great American Grain Robbery of the summer of 1972. So much has been written about these Russian sales that I shall simply use the edifying tale to illustrate two points: the grain trade in the US tends to benefit the companies more than the farmers, and the US government and the traders are a good deal more clubby than might be considered strictly ethical.

Many farmers have no on-farm storage facilities, so they sell to those who do—mostly large elevators—or directly to traders. (Cargill alone is capable of storing nearly five million tons of grain). In a typical year, about half the wheat crop is sold by 1 August, and 1972 was no exception. A great many southwestern farmers sold at prices ranging from $1.25 to $1.50 a bushel. Eight weeks later, the same bushel would have brought them a quarter to a third more income—but farmers need cash and cannot afford commercial storage unless they are sure of higher prices later. In 1972, they were *not* sure, because only the biggest traders knew the true magnitude of the Russian deals.

At Congressional hearings on the "robbery," top spokesmen for USDA claimed that even they had no knowledge of how much wheat had been sold to the Russians, prompting one Congressman to exclaim that USDA seemed to be "deliberately denying itself" vital information. "We ask of American citizens in the normal course of the census more information than you are requiring of trading companies involved in sensitive international trading agreements." Agriculture Secretary Butz had previously been quoted as saying that "farmers didn't lose money [because of early sales], they just weren't smart enough to take advantage of the situation." He added at a press conference that "farmers knew precisely as much as we knew. They knew as much as the grain companies. . . . Some money has been made in the deal. Some trading companies have made it. But it's the name of the game." At least part of this statement is accurate, for "some" money was indeed made. Because the US government paid an export subsidy to the traders (equal to the difference between a government-specified target price, i.e., a price close to the world price, and the higher US domestic price) and because it did not modify its subsidy policy even though domestic prices were zooming farther and farther away from the target price, the traders made up to 47¢ in subsidies for every bushel of what they sold to the Russians. By comparison, at the beginning of July, the subsidy was 5¢. During the single week of 25 August–1 September 1972, subsidies costing over $130 million were booked by traders.

As to farmers knowing as much as the traders, representatives of four of the nation's largest farmers' organizations did not agree with Butz. All testified that at no time had their organization received any communication whatever from USDA concerning the sales or the subsidy policy. No grain cooperatives made any sales to the USSR, in spite of the fact that this was the largest single deal in agricultural history. During the period the Russians were negotiating with the private traders, everyone concerned was extremely disciplined. Prices were kept stable and Russia got its wheat at an average of $60 a ton. The firms got not only their subsidies, but were later able to sell to regular domestic and foreign clients at prices that had tripled.

It may well be true, as official after official swore at the hearings, that the traders never told USDA anything—and vice versa.* What is, however, undeniable, is the permanent ballet of personnel that goes on between the bureaucracy and the boardrooms. Butz himself was on the Board of Ralston Purina. The Secretary he replaced *went* to Ralston Purina. When Butz took off on the April 1972 negotiating trip to Russia, he was accompanied

---

*A reporting system on large sales has since been instituted.

by Clarence Palmby, who had, one month *before* this trip, bought an expensive flat in New York using Continental Grain executives as financial references. Yet Palmby assured the Congressional Committee that he had decided only in May to accept the job Continental offered him in March. Not necessarily connected with this switch is the fact that Continental later sold more grain to the Russians than any other firm. Palmby's successor at USDA, Carroll Brunthaver, came from Cook (and has since returned to them). Two other top USDA officials joined Dreyfus and Bunge in 1972, while a Cargill vice-president became the White House Deputy Special Representative for Trade Negotiations (and has since returned to Cargill). The least one·can say is that government and agribusiness are nodding acquaintances, but no misconduct in connection with such moves has ever been proved. Had it been, it is doubtful that it would make much difference to the careers of the men involved. The flaccid Commodities Exchange Authority, until 1975 charged with regulating the grain trade, once put four Cargill men on probation for pushing up wheat futures artificially. One of them testified at the hearings that he "did not know" the dates of his own recent probation, causing an investigating Congressman to remark drily that "little feeling (of) stigma is attached to being found guilty of a violation by those involved."

Cargill was somewhat more sensitive to public opinion than to such token "punishment." Charges of "windfall profits" caused it to call one of the rare press conferences of its highly secretive career in order to explain that during the Russian sales the company had been in "its largest short position in history," meaning that it had sold more wheat than it possessed and had to scramble later to buy enough in a rising market. Figures given at the briefing purported to show that Cargill had taken a *net loss* on the Soviet deal itself. But while "Cargill lost money on the specific sales to Russia, the increased value of farm crops and the increasing marketings of all major grains will benefit all serving American agriculture including an exporter like Cargill," concluded the company's President. The press-conference document makes no references, however, to the number of bushels Cargill may have bought from its own subsidiaries at home or abroad, nor what price the latter may have paid original growers. Might overhead expenses and "trading costs" include fees paid by Cargill to Cargill? These questions are not dealt with (and figures on "cost of sales" are specified as unaudited), so it is difficult to feel much pity for Cargill even if rivals like Continental may have maneuvred more skillfully. What is obvious is that by keeping their mouths shut, the USDA and the traders are capable of freezing "supply and demand" at crucial moments.

Soybeans are another fascinating racket. It has taken a couple of decades to build them up to their present pre-eminent place as top US agricultural export, but the effort has been worth it. A few items: soybeans can be grown only in certain latitudes under specific conditions (day-length at the flowering stage is a major factor). The US, where one acre in 6.5 is now planted to soya, boasts just these conditions. Europe does not. Soybeans are 40 per cent pure protein. Europe is only 2 per cent self-sufficient in plant-protein production. Put them all together, they spell profits—and also total dependence on the US for the major component of animal feed. After the war, Europe introduced American hybrid corn to replace local varieties. This seemed a good idea at the time, because the yields were superior. But the protein content of these hybrids is especially low. A supplementary protein source had to be found for feeding livestock, and soybeans from the US seemed to be a rational and inexpensive solution. It was cheaper—then—to buy US soya-meal feedcakes than to invest in developing local high-protein crops. Soybean meal exports from the US to Europe were only 47,000 tons in 1949, but nearly 5 million in 1972-3. US processors, the obvious front-runners in the industry, soon learned that it was just as profitable—often more so—to ship raw beans to these lucrative markets as to process the feedcakes at home. So they set up crushing mills in Europe. Raw beans imported into Europe now account for another 13 million tons of exports. The upshot of all this is that the entire post-war European livestock industry has been developed on a basis of massive use of low-priced soya, accelerating the industrial production of poultry, pork and to some extent beef. A favorable climate and low prices allowed the US to establish a near-monopoly position for supply not only of Europe but of Japan and other nations: duty on soya and soya products has been kept low or non-existent by all of them. The US vehemently insisted in many an international meeting that it was prepared to supply greater and greater quantities of cheap soya and foreign expansion was undertaken on this basis. For example, the six original EEC countries, during 1961-72, increased their feed-mill capacities from 13 to 38 million tons—an impossible feat without soybeans.

But as exports from the US increased, domestic stocks declined and prices on the Chicago futures market began to creep upwards. US livestock raisers saw prices going up and did not take kindly to an increase of their own costs. Under pressure, the American government slapped an embargo on all soybean exports in June 1973, "in order to examine its protein inventories." The result was pandemonium. Generalized speculative psychosis took hold and soybean prices soared from $2 to $12 a bushel. British farmers slaughtered some of their livestock simply because they could no longer afford to feed it. The embargo was removed three months later. At year's end it became clear that the fever had been unwarranted. There was actually plenty of soya. It never had really been "scarce." France, for example, actually imported *more* soya in 1973 than in 1972. But not at the same price!

Prices are presently (end of 1976) quoted between $6.30-$7 a bushel, and no one expects ever again to see the dear dead $2 soybean. There have been neither public outcry nor Congressional hearings on soybeans, but it is troubling, to say the least, that prices can fluctuate upwards so wildly in such a short space of time. Is this a natural market effect? Isn't it odd that once entire major European and Japanese industries were "hooked" on soya that its price should first sextuple and then "stabilize" at more than triple the previous levels? US government soya-planting quotas have *always* been determined as a function of export possibilities. The Food for Peace law took care to introduce soya oil into countries like Spain and Tunisia that had never before tasted anything but their own olive oil. Even butter-rich Holland now consumes much more imported soya-based margarine than butter. Markets for raw beans, oil and feedcakes can be and are created, and foreign demand can be projected with near total accuracy. But here again, it is the traders who control the physical stocks. Prices on the futures markets in Chicago actually reflect only a small part of the real market, because the major companies like Archer Daniels, Central Soya, Cargill and Ralston Purina can transfer whatever portion of their private stocks they choose directly to their foreign subsidiaries for their own purposes. Far be it from me to suggest collusion I can't prove, but it is at least evident who profits from higher prices and who suffers. A futures market in soya meal was opened in London in April 1975 as a measure that might check price fluctuations. *The Times* re-marked on opening day that "the international community has a right to expect that [soya] will be available at a reasonable price. The opening of a soya-bean meal futures market in London is a firm indication by European producers and consumers of their interest in expanding trading opportunities." One wishes them luck. They may trade away and get a small piece of what is known as the action—but their countries still do not produce the soybeans, nor any substitute protein crop.

There is one factor militating in favor of slightly reduced prices and which explains why 1973 and 1974 price levels cannot be sustained. *Alternate sources of production must not be stimulated by exaggerated US prices.* For instance, France must not be encouraged to raise the extra quantities of wheat it could quite easily grow. Soybean processors are already screaming that African palm oil is cutting into their market. They are also furious that the EEC intends to substitute some of its surplus dried milk for soya meal in animal feeds. The US government has threatened reprisals for this move.

Now that the livestock-feed market is pretty well sewn up, US firms are concentrating on extending the use of soya from animals to humans and on controlling any future sources of supply. We have already noted how the big US firms have taken over processing and marketing of soya in Brazil; they are beginning to do the same in India. Since they control the technology, their hegemony in the field should remain complete. This will also be the case for textured vegetable protein (TVP)—the name for a new series of processes (most of them already patented by Archer Daniels Midland: "TVP" is itself a registered trademark of ADM) that can make soya directly digestible for people. With artificial flavorings added it can become a food-stretcher for meat and other human food. TVP will undoubtedly be the biggest marketing breakthrough for the MNCs since they captured the European livestock industry. An entire international conference held in Munich was devoted to the subject in November 1973; the roster of those attending was a who's who of the biggest soybean interests: Archer Daniels, Cargill, Unilever, ITT (through Continental. Baking), Central Soya, Swift, General Mills, Ralston Purina, Soypro International, etc., plus the requisite number of USDA officials, Europeans and a smattering of academics, nutritionists and researchers. Earl Butz led the American delegation.

He announced once again that the US would be a "loyal" seller of soybeans, but on the condition that American producers and exporters could be assured of a "free market," particularly inside the EEC. He explained that TVP had enormous commercial possibilities and asked "the other countries represented at this conference to help us eliminate obstacles to the expansion of markets." He even went so far as to give the Europeans instructions on how to handle upcoming tariff negotiations on soybeans for human consumption and asked that they be kept in the category ETN 35.04 (are you taking notes, gentlemen?) rather than in a higher tariff bracket. The conference nominally concerned nutritional and technical aspects of soybean proteins. But Americans presented 24 out of the 38 papers (including 13 by agribusiness representatives and 10 by USDA people). Only one was given by a nutritionist. Hubert Humphrey was also there. He reminded the Conference of his country's agripower: "Food is a new form of power. Food is wealth. Food is an extra dimension in our diplomacy." Butz's directives, Humphrey's pointed remarks and the commercial onslaught showed that the real concern of the Munich Conference was to pave the way for a new type of market for US soya. One sees absolutely no alternative to continued US MNC control of the world plant-protein production and prices. It appears highly unlikely at this juncture that dependent countries will embark on crash programs to make themselves self-sufficient. They will pay the prices set by the MNCs who control the processing, the exports and the technology. As consumers, so will we.

The only rational way to offset price and foodstock manipulations by the giant traders would be to have grain stocks held in government hands, to be released or held back as the market situation demanded. The FAO has long been proposing the establishment of internationally managed world grain stocks, and sets the "safe" level at 230 million tons: 160 as a working stock and the extra 70 million as famine insurance against crop failures. Stocks fell below 96 million tons in 1974. The grain-trade firms are frantically opposed to any reserve system in the present world context—if there is to be one, "Private trade is the vehicle to handle it," they say. But should America again begin to accumulate stocks as it did in the 1950s and 1960s, the tune will change. In the present scarcity context of low stocks, the US Senate Select Committee on Nutrition and Human Needs, chaired by Senator McGovern, made a brave and unpopular move when it decided to recommend a policy of government-held stocks to the American delegation to the World Food Conference. Its advice naturally went unheeded by this delegation; the Committee's reasoning is nonetheless interesting. Grain stocks, it said, cannot be maintained in private hands, as the traders would like, because

> . . . the contention that the world can have reserves held in private hands is fallacious on its face. Private traders are in business to turn investment into profit as rapidly as possible. To expect that a multiplicity of private traders would or should manage the acquisition and release of food and feed grains in a manner which will meet the goals of a conscious reserve policy—to flatten the widest upward and downward fluctuations in market prices and to maintain a steady supply against times of shortage—would be contradictory. . . . In reality, a reserve in private hands is no reserve at all. . . . It is indeed precisely the same market mechanism which has produced the situation we face today. [Preface by Sen. McGovern to the Select Committee's Report.]

This is the gospel truth, but "nutrition and human needs" is not, as ex-Secretary Butz might say, the name of the game.

In the free market countries, we do not have state agencies for buying and selling food at fixed prices, and we do not generally have government-held stocks for regulating the market (these do exist to some extent in the EEC.) What do we have? Commodity futures markets and speculation. Futures markets had to be invented in market economy countries for the simple reason that a crop is harvested all at once, but can't be used all at once. Nobody, figuratively, is going to make his 365 loaves of bread for the year on 1 August. So there was a need for a mechanism that would add the *time-and-location* dimensions to the more usual quantity-and-quality dimensions of supply and demand. The volume of futures trading has gone up dramatically in the last couple of years as sluggish, depressed stock markets have become unattractive targets for investment and it has dawned on many speculators that food is expensive and a good place to make money. According to Harvard Business School Professor Goldberg, "At present US private enterprise has $300 billion in transactions on the futures markets. This volume is expected to rise because of the growing volatility of prices of most commodities all over the world."

Anyone who wants to try his hand at futures speculation will get more information from any broker than from me, but to put it very simplistically, the markets operate through what are known in the trade as hedges. The point of hedging is to try to eliminate for oneself, to the maximum degree, the risk of price movements. A Cargill executive explained this very sophisticated game to another Senate Committee in 1974: for a trader the ideal hedge is

> ... for example, in the case of a cash sale of 50,000 bushels of hard winter wheat for delivery in Kansas City in December, the ideal hedge would be a *purchase* of 50,000 bushels of hard winter wheat to be delivered in Kansas City in December. In other words, the ideal hedge would be cash transactions offsetting effect of type of commodity, quantity, location and time. ... Merchants use futures markets to offset not only commodity and quantity but also location and time whenever possible.

He says that this system "smooths out the harvest rush into a steady, reliable stream to consumers' tables." As we have seen, it also assures a steady, reliable stream into the traders' pockets, but in the US, at least, futures market prices and government policies (i.e. subsidies or lack of same) are the only guides the farmer has as to how much of which crop to plant next time.

This system, as has been indicated for the case of soybeans, is not always even a reliable guide to the true state of the market. It can also promote anarchy. As *Fortune* explains,

> It is a fact of the world's agricultural economy that a relatively small change in output and trade can generate a relatively large change in price. The reason is that a shortfall in production means that additional supplies must come from reserves and world reserves for most foods are badly distributed.

Translated, "badly distributed" means that the US and to a lesser extent Canada—which is to say the traders—control almost all the world's grains. When food prices are low, traders—and even nations like Japan—"load up" (*Fortune*'s phrase) on supplies. "Loading up" is again a polite way of saying "speculating." USDA economists who "attempt to determine the price consequences of various demand and supply conditions were able to account for only one half to two thirds of last year's (1973) sudden price rise in foods. 'The rest,' they say, 'is psychological and speculative activity and these are not in our models.' " So when wheat production fell off by less than 5 per cent—owing to this "activity" the USDA says it cannot account for—wheat prices went up 300 per cent and soybean prices went up 600 per cent with *no* decline in production whatsoever—the threat of one was enough. Dwayne Andreas, President of Archer Daniels Midland, has a suggestion: "The only cure for high prices is higher prices," because this, he says, is the only way to elicit greater productivity.

Up to now we have spoken mostly about the planned scarcity of cereals. Grain is the most important element in mankind's diet and accounts therefore for a disproportionate amount of world trade. But requirements for other foods are going to go up just as sharply as cereal needs, and all of them will have to be paid for. The UN compares consumption in 1970 with projected demand in 1985 and estimates that the world's farms will need to provide *per year,*

> An additional output of nearly 40 million more tons of sugar; an additional 110 tons of vegetables and 90 million tons of fruits, a further 60 million tons of meat and 140 million tons of milk, together with the [livestock feeds] to sustain these increases. The total requirements of cereals in 1985 . . . would be of the order of 520 million tons more than in 1970; an increase of 43 per cent in 15 years.

All these figures reflect, as usual, projected *commercial* demand, not human needs. Someone is going to get his cut on each of these extra tons of food produced (always assuming they *are* produced). No one expects prices for grain or any other important commodity to decline. Not all of the food industries have reached the point of hegemony of, say, the soybean processors and marketers, but all of them are working towards this goal. The aim is to concentrate, integrate, control the technology, reduce the possible number of suppliers, and then—openly or secretively—set prices for each commodity on the world market and keep them set.

During the World Food Conference, where delegate after delegate spoke of imminent disaster, an article was published in *Business Week* entitled, "Sugar Shortage: Sweeter Profits for Amstar" (the American Sugar Refining Co.). The gist of it is that Amstar is delighted. Inventories are way down and prices have skyrocketed. In fact, Amstar itself has raised them "19 times in 11 months, from $15.65 per 100 lb to $56.20." Its earnings per share are up 420 per cent for this same period and sugar prices on the futures market for March 1976 are "at an all time high." Amstar owns its own farms and sells its sugar by-products as beef-fatteners. It also owns warehouses which allow it to hold sugar off the market for "a more attractive price." The big, industrialized US sugar-cane and sugar-beet producers are also happy (they include, naturally, Amstar itself): "US cane growers are getting the bulk of the sugar dollar even while they continue to receive federal subsidies. Because US beet farmers, also subsidized, split profits with producers of refined beet sugar at spot prices on a 55-45 per cent basis, they and the producers also share in the bonanza."

Those who do not share in the bonanza are the US sugar workers. The International Union of Food-workers reported early in 1975 that despite record industry profits, workers in Louisiana are making $2.30 an hour. They may work up to 70 hours a week, but get no overtime pay. Average earnings are about $3,500 annually—below the US poverty line. The IUF says that "many sugar field workers live on plantations in incredibly primitive shacks and are in debt to the company throughout their lives as a result of their low wages and the exhorbitant prices charged by the company store. Unless legislation is enacted to insure fair wages, workers are threatened with wage cuts for next year."

Since the 1974 peak, sugar prices have gone into a tailspin. Euphoric industry leaders who were crowing that "sugar prices have nowhere to go but up" and "we can look for tight supplies and high prices of sugar in the US through the rest of the decade" are now singing a pessimistic tune and complaining about "cutthroat competition." But their own greediness is largely responsible for their current fate: they made the fatal mistake of encouraging increased production through unrealistically high prices. By 1976, the world was producing about 83 million tons of sugar—and consuming only 80 million of them. Most of these producers are Third World countries who will again learn the hard way the dangers of hitching one's economic wagon to fluctuating world markets for cash crops. As the *Wall Street Journal* reported in late 1976, "The decline of sugar prices on the world market is straining the already weak economies of the developing nations that grow it. From a record 65.5¢ a pound in November 1974, the price of raw sugar has fallen to 7.05¢. That's far below production costs in most sugar growing countries." The US has, moreover, reacted to increased UDC sugar exports by tripling import duties and is expected in many quarters to reduce drastically the present sugar import quota from seven million tons to about four.

The Amstars of this world have also brought upon themselves

competition from US corn-syrup producers: "Sweeteners derived from corn are invading the market for sweeteners taken from sugar cane and sugar beets. And whatever the outcome, a very major segment of the food business may never be the same," declares the *WSJ*. (Don't weep for Amstar, however. It also owns a corn-syrup plant . . .).

Silver lining department: The bonanza has now shifted to the bakery and soft drink industries. As the President of the American Sugar Cane League complained in *Business Week*, this is the group that "really will clean up." "The industrial users (who consume 75% of all sugar produced in the US) are paying six times less for sugar than they were in November 1974 and their prices haven't come down. And something ought to be coming down." What ought, perhaps, to be coming down is consumer tolerance for the pricing practices of the food industry.

The IUF also held a conference of dairy workers in response to broad-scale firings of workers due to what the industry calls a "crisis of overproduction." As usual, there is no overproduction— just a price policy that puts dairy products beyond the reach of those who most need to be able to consume milk, butter and cheese. The conference found for the dairy industry the same *leitmotif* we have been singing elsewhere:

The world dairy economy continues to be subjected to the influence and intervention of major multinational corporations who were taking advantage of their control of the industry in the temperate zone to plan production and distribution on the basis of maximizing their profits. This was illustrated by the trend, noted in several . . . corporations such as Unilever and Nestles, to withdraw from the fluid milk industry and semi-processed products and to concentrate instead on highly processed and sophisticated dairy products which are more profitable but do not meet the basic nutritional needs of the world population.

As the IUF (like the hapless Senator McGovern) perfectly well realizes, "the nutritional needs of the world population" are not the point.

The IUF Conference also stressed that the technical and marketing superiority of the major dairy corporations (Beatrice Foods, Borden, Kraftco, BSN-Gervais-Danone, Carnation, Foremost-McKesson, Nestles, Unigate, Unilever) were preventing indigenous milk-processing industries from arising in many countries and that they invariably displaced inexpensive, labor-intensive technologies in favor of imported, labor-saving machinery.

Not every food industry can be tightly controlled by government/corporation cooperation. Meat producers, for example, are not concentrated enough worldwide. They depend on the feedgrain people who are—and thus they are not making much money at present. Small producers still provide the bulk of our fruits and vegetables. But the corporations are not going to stop at wheat, soybeans or dairy products. In the next chapter we will see how agribusiness is moving into the lucrative field of Third World agriculture, in order to make, perhaps, a new improved contribution to planned scarcity.

7. There's No Business Like Agribusiness

The word "agribusiness" entered the language about fifteen years ago and coincides with the switch to vertical organization on the part of certain giant companies able to control the whole food chain from field to table. These big boys have what they like to call the "total market concept" and they are applying it both in the affluent and in the underdeveloped countries. Harvard Business School Professor Ray A. Goldberg coined the word agribusiness" for his specialty. He defines it as "all production and distribution of farm supplies, production operations on farms, and the storage, processing and distribution of farm commodities and processed foods."

Some of the companies loosely included under the term are thus single-input producers—fertilizer and pesticide manufacturers or tractor firms. Most of them are attempting to adapt their production and distribution techniques to new markets opening up in poor countries—especially those where US government effort has paved their way. As one fertilizer company executive told a Congressional committee,

> I must emphasize that there would be scarcely any investment if it were not for the infrastructure, the education, the training and the support provided by our [US government] aid programs. We certainly would not be in India and very few investors would be in any of the underdeveloped countries were it not for our effort at economic assistance.

Some of them were at first hesitant to expand into UDCs but have now changed their minds. For example a vice-president of Massey-Ferguson explained at an agro-industry meeting that his company had once been reluctant to launch operations in Brazil, which are now among its most profitable. But these input

132

producers are just following the lead of other MNCs that are profitably building, manufacturing and selling abroad from Afghanistan to Zambia.

The agribusinesses that concern us more in the context of the world hunger crisis are the ones that use a "host" country's land and labor for producing food—rarely to satisfy local needs, almost always for export to the developed countries' markets that will pay the most for their produce. They can be compared to mining enterprises because they are truly "extractive industries" which need not, however, fear depletion of their reserves.

Despite all the recent hue and cry over MNCs, and the avalanche of literature concerning them, most readers—and most writers for that matter—have very little grasp of the fact that while investment in manufacturing abroad is gradually becoming less profitable, new world food prices make investment in agriculture in the UDCs a very attractive proposition. Even in a world rife with economic crisis, food is essential, while transistor radios are not. Public opinion is much slower to smell the sweet odor of a new and relatively unexploited field for profits than the quivering and alert noses of the MNCs. The kind of penetration of UDC agriculture we are currently witnessing—and which is bound to increase—could make the green of the Green Revolution seem a very pale olive color by comparison. If the Green Revolution has been a social disaster, the effects we can legitimately expect from direct Western agribusiness intrusion into traditional rural societies may be nothing short of catastrophic. There is already plenty of evidence to suggest that agribusiness is capable of destroying everything it touches: local employment patterns, local food-crop production, consumer tastes, even village and traditional family structures.

This is not, of course, the way the agribusinesses view their own activities. In two words, they see themselves as the world's salvation. They alone will be capable of solving the problem of world hunger, for the "profit-oriented approach to increasing food production in the less developed countries provides the only mechanism for real progress and decisive action." This homily comes from a 1967 speech by Louis Lundborg, then Chairman of the Bank of America, titled "The Agribusiness Approach." He says his motives for this approach are (1) humanitarian (which he disposes of rather quickly), (2) political, because increasing poverty could lead to a global confrontation between the rich and poor nations and, finally, getting down to business, (3) "self-interest and profit." "There is money to be made in agribusiness around the world—profits for both the US and the host country's agribusiness enterprises and for indigenous farmers and entrepreneurs." But even the messianic Lundborg admits that "private business can attack malnutrition, not starvation." To begin doing so, agribusiness must "zero in" on land where "potential productivity is relatively high" (which means the best land the poor country has) and "invest in areas where immediate results will be conspicuous" so that "farmers will be prepared to enter into productive enterprises with [agribusiness] for mutual and adequate profit." He feels that the US government (through USAID) and the World Bank (through its affiliate the International Finance Corporation) should help agribusiness get set up in the initial stages abroad, but private banks will also have a role to play. Lundborg's own, Bankamerica, intends to "assume a catalyst role in launching a US effort to help increase food production abroad. We believe [the profit motive] is the only inducement that can get the job of feeding the world done in the shortest period of time." Naturally, the host country government will be expected to do its bit: "All our efforts will be channeled to those nations which are willing to take the tangible—and often politically unpopular and difficult—steps to assure the proper climate for investment."

Harvard's Mr. Goldberg shares the opinion that the US government should be active in supporting agribusiness abroad, and he too points out that a basic condition for agro-investment is a "stable political and social structure." What is more, he seems to have done something about it, for he appears to have been the instigator of a meeting between government and agribusiness leaders that took place at Harvard in May 1966. At this meeting, "the recognition of the necessity for effective government-industry partnership in the world agribusiness market was underscored by the high caliber of committee members" who included top officers of Ralston Purina, Quaker Oats, Corn Products (now CPC), General Mills and General Foods among others; along with USDA and USAID VIPs. This exclusive club took stock of the fact that "US world food policy is actively in the process of change with increasing emphasis on an integrated package of self-help programs" (see Chapter 8 on Food for Peace). "This has provided a new climate for expansion in every segment of international agribusiness." It would appear that "self-help programs" for the poor involve one part "self" for several parts "international agribusiness": the decisions of the meeting, as reported by Goldberg, support this conclusion. The companies and the government representatives affirmed that US agribusiness should "employ the resources of its local economy as fully as possible" (i.e., land and cheap labor) and that business should stand ready to move into whatever vacuums might offer themselves: "Production and marketing sophistication of private companies is indispensable to the success of a world food program. In a number of developing countries, the local governments are often ineffective in their own rural areas and nongovernment centers are necessary to get the job done." Everything will be for the poor's own good. In fact, "To the fullest extent feasible," the meeting decided, "products should be within the commercial price range of low income consumers." We shall shortly discover whether or not this has been feasible.

While agribusiness is all for the profit motive, it is less enthusiastic about taking commercial risks in the "most underdeveloped countries." For instance, "government could perhaps take a majority of the risk and let private companies receive management fees and options to purchase the government's interest over time." Ralston Purina is a perfect example of this sort of technique: in Colombia (certainly not one of the "most underdeveloped countries") it obtained the cooperation of the Colombian government and of USAID for building a feedmill. This mill for producing livestock feed absorbed corn formerly eaten by people, something which apparently had not occurred to Ralston Purina. The production base was changed after some time, and "furthermore, company officials provided consumer education services for their food products" and even retailed these products to Colombian consumers. Poor Quaker Oats has not been so fortunate. It received licences to produce and market its high-protein product Incaparina in seven Central and South American countries. But Incaparina didn't sell, for, according to Goldberg, "even though there is unanimous agreement as to the excellent nutritional value of Incaparina, some food experts claim that the product must also look, taste, and smell good, and Incaparina, they say, does not have this type of consumer appeal." This is not entirely surprising, as the product was made largely of cottonseed (people less finicky than Goldberg's "food experts" describe Incaparina's overall olfactory impact as "wet dog"). At the time of Goldberg's article, Quaker Oats was still hoping for government subsidies during the "demand-creating stage." The retail price of Incaparina in Guatemala is four times as much as the corn meal it replaces. At a time when per capita income in Guatemala was 86¢ a day, Incaparina cost 20¢ a pound.

Government subsidies were requested and received by agribusinesses when Goldberg's quoted article appeared (1966), but giving agribusiness *extra* money now would just be putting more caviar on their toast. Orville Freeman (former US Secretary of Agriculture, now President of Business International, an information and servicing outfit for MNCs) says that "the fact is that well-run agribusiness projects in some developing countries have returned as much as *30 per cent a year* on investment . . . and aggressive, imaginative international companies always respond to an opportunity that makes profitable use of their abilities."*

Some of the agribusinesses clothe their projects with a rhetoric of development and social uplift. The best example is probably the International Basic Economy Corporation (IBEC), a Rockefeller enterprise that operates mainly in Latin America. *Newsweek* says it is a company "dedicated to the then [in 1948] unheard-of idea that private enterprise could help improve economic conditions in less developed countries and make money in the process." Although profits were modest for the first twenty years of IBEC's existence, they have increased substantially since the late 1960s—up, for example, by 14 per cent from 1968 to 1969. Company spokesmen say quite frankly, "We have made money by meeting human needs in an efficient, businesslike way . . . over the past ten years our total revenue has nearly tripled and our stockholders' equity more than doubled." Chairman Donald Meads feels that "many American firms are quite insular and have little idea of the opportunities in the underdeveloped world. This is the universe from which we pick most of our projects. It's a great opportunity for us."

Rodman Rockefeller (Nelson's son) considers IBEC public-

---

*Freeman's enthusiasm is, from his point of view, comprehensible. As he told *Fortune:* "I have been in places [in tropical countries] where test plots with multiple crops will produce three, four and five times as much as the best land in the US. When you have 360 days of sunshine to work in and you know what you are doing, then new seeds, pesticides, chemicals and fertilizers can give you an explosion of production."

spirited: "We have long operated in economic sectors such as agribusiness where demand and supply are political as well as economic questions, with the result that public needs become an important part of the decision-making process." He suggests that "in the future, business will profit by assuming a more aggressive leadership role as an innovative force capable of exercising social judgement, consciously initiating change and shaping the overall environment." Even the "social-uplift" company assumes it has a right to make any change it cares to, and that shaping the overall environment is its own concern, not that of the host country.

One of IBEC's money makers is the CADA supermarket chain in Venezuela, where the Rockefeller family has other major interests. IBEC claims that the chain has reduced food prices to urban consumers by 10 per cent while ensuring local suppliers of a permanent outlet for their produce.* IBEC served as a catalyst for creating the dairy industry in Venezuela by upgrading herds. Previously, the country imported milk in powdered form. In Argentina, the IBEC subsidiary Arbor Acres Farms is producing chickens in 8½ weeks instead of 13 at a third of the former cost and egg production has risen. Some of these IBEC-created products stay within the country of investment, and thus may marginally benefit some middle-class, urban consumers. Elsewhere, IBEC follows the usual agribusiness pattern of export to the best-fed countries. It processes sea-food and coffee in Latin America for export to the US. And however much it may, in Chairman Meads' phrase, "uplift the world," the fact remains that it is foreign-based and foreign-owned, and the countries uplifted have nothing to say about where future investments should be made or how products should be distributed within the framework of an overall national development plan. The fact that IBEC's investments exist chiefly in the better-off Latin American countries with a substantial middle class able to compete with rich Westerners in the global shopping center is no accident. The day IBEC starts uplifting, say, the Indian population of Bolivia which is starving and almost totally outside the money economy, I shall be glad to eat my words.

---

*In 1976, IBEC preferred to sell the chain to a Venezuelan company because new legislation obliges foreign retailers to reduce their share of local operations to 20%.

As we did for the Green Revolution, let us now proceed with some pointed questions,

(1) Is agribusiness beneficial to the affluent nations where it is based, and especially to average consumers?

The vertical-integration concept has gone farthest in the US, so the answer to this question for America should also give us an idea as to whether or not agribusiness should become a worldwide model. Agribusiness at the farm level is encouraging and hastening hyper-concentration. Small farms are failing at an appalling rate (2,000 a week in 1971). "Agribusiness prospers at the expense of the great mass of American farmers . . . half the farms in America had gone out of business by World War II . . . the USDA admits that the number of American farms remaining in 1980 may be one tenth of those existing in 1972." Even if one is willing to give agribusiness the benefit of the doubt, when such concentration in food production comes, can price fixing be far behind?

Consumers are also at the mercy of the agribusiness giants. The first thing to understand about the food industry is that small firms don't survive—and big ones prosper through sheer size. The second and complementary thing to know is that since food-processing technology is relatively uncomplicated, and the same for all the companies, the only way to get ahead is through marketing and packaging techniques and "product differentiation." This requires huge advertising budgets and eliminates competition from small companies who haven't the means to flood the market with sales messages.

You have to be big to stay afloat in the food-processing industry, because bigness insures your access to bankers, raw-material suppliers and sales outlets. But size really becomes crucial when it comes to promotion. A *Standard and Poor* study notes that "an unusually large proportion of operating expenses of marketers of packaged foods and of canners represents promotional outlays, and changes in advertising policies may have a significant effect on earnings." To choose only one example—the breakfast-food industry—as early as 1964 the top four companies (in the US) controlled 85 per cent of the market. Their outlays were: Salaries and production 38 per cent; raw materials 20 per cent; marketing, advertising and sales commissions 28 per cent; packaging 14 per cent. While advertising and packaging here get 42 per cent of the pie, research and development always come in last. According to the National Science Foundation, "In 1969, the food and beverage industry spent only 0.4 per cent of its sales [revenues] on Research and Development, which compares rather unfavorably with the 4 per cent average for all manufacturing industries." One tenth is a "rather unfavorable" ratio and demonstrates that in the agribusiness world, they care very little *what* you eat so long as they can persuade you to buy it. R&D expenditures on food actually *decrease* proportionally to sales while advertising increases. This is, perhaps, not altogether a bad thing, for in this very peculiar industry, "R&D" usually means "What new chemicals can we add?" If the most profitable foods agribusiness makes are the most highly processed, this is no accident. They *have* to be to sustain the vertical integration that includes nationwide distribution and long storage periods. Five hundred million dollars were spent in 1969 by agribusiness (and passed along to the consumer) on food additives that "make stabilization of color, texture and other illusions of freshness possible." The author of the article giving this data confirms that the "food industry spends more on advertising and less on research than any other industry in America." It seems fair to conclude that agribusiness is not the most thrifty and wholesome way that could be found to feed people, nor to protect the interests of the majority of small farmers—those who are left—against the interests of huge corporate processors.

Furthermore, big food firms are integrating backwards, forwards and sideways; they are merging, diversifying, extending, concentrating and conglomerating; food companies are moving into non-food as non-food companies move into food. They are not merely taking over farming itself, but are producing the cardboard boxes and cans to put their products in, producing their own TV ads, snapping up whole supermarket chains and devouring small competitors who never had a chance. The US Federal Trade Commission's 1968 report on large mergers (those over $10 million) says that for the 1961–7 period, "approximately 50 percent of total mergers were acquisitions of food and beverage manufacturers by firms outside the food industries" while "over 30 percent of total mergers in 1961–7 were acquisitions by food and beverage manufacturing companies of non-food firms." In the study on "Conglomeration in the Food Industries" where these figures are cited, the author explains that it is quite possible for these huge firms to raise their prices to consumers "without attracting other competition." Here again the free market ceases to function. This is hardly astounding for an industry where the top few companies consistently control production, manufacturing and distribution (field, factory, shop). Their considerable profits are not used to lower prices, but to buy up more firms and so to increase conglomeration itself. As early as 1963, out of about 30,000 food firms in the US, the 41 largest made over half the total profits. Borden Milk completed twenty-nine mergers during 1959–69, Foremost-McKesson multiplied its assets by sixty in 1947–70; Hunt Foods, which now does well over a billion dollars of business annually, multiplied itself by ten in twenty years; while Consolidated Foods made forty new acquisitions during 1945–65 and another forty during 1965–70. And so it goes.*

With this kind of power, it is inevitable that these companies will influence the behavior of all of us—partly because they leave us no choice. A housewife who asks for 10 pounds of flour out of a barrel or a pint of cream out of a jug is not going to contribute appreciably to anyone's profits. She must first be divested of her antiquated ideas and must be encouraged to believe that this flour and that cream are distinguishable from some other kind. She should then, whenever feasible, be discouraged from buying flour or cream at all since such purchases prove that she harbors the reprehensible intention of cooking, rather than of using the far more profitable, highly processed convenience foods (like cake mixes or aerosol whipped cream) the companies are only too pleased to supply.

American consumers are supposed to be the richest in the world, but if the quality of what they eat is any indication of wealth, then they are poor indeed—although the same cannot be said of the firms that feed them. According to USDA figures, during 1959–70, consumption of milk dropped 20 per cent while that of soft-drinks went up 79 per cent. Fruits, melons, vegetables and potatoes on American tables all declined by more than a fifth, while junk foods enjoyed spectacular gains: unenriched commercial bakery products went up 67 per cent, potato chips 85 per cent, ice cream 29 per cent and fruit (i.e., artificially flavored) punch no less than 750 per cent. A small sampling of food-company profits in *Business Week*, comparing the last three months of 1972 with

---

*And so it went in 1976: Merger activity for the first six months was up 30% over the previous year and "most of the action, as it normally is, was in food," according to *Business Week*. ARA Services bought five companies during this period, while McDonald's, National Can, and Beatrice Foods bought four each.

the same period in 1971, shows that the deterioration of the American national diet is splendid news in the boardrooms: Kraftco's profits were up 27 per cent, Beatrice Foods' 25 per cent, General Foods' 27 per cent, Campbells' 60 per cent, Quaker Oats' 44 per cent, General Mills' 21 per cent.

Let us not make the mistake of believing that such phenomena are of concern only to American consumers. It is probably much later than the rest of the world thinks. According to a survey of eleven multinational agribusiness corporations made by the US Senate Emergency Committee on American Trade, these companies put over a quarter of their total investments into food processing plants *abroad* during 1960–70. By 1970, the overseas operations of these companies accounted for a quarter of their total sales. It was learned that their foreign sales had been growing at an average *annual* rate of 50 per cent throughout the 1960s.

Processed-foods purveyors pick their markets carefully. They also invest in local production in countries with relatively high per capita incomes where consumers can be taught to pick convenience foods over raw foodstuffs. These consumers must thus be able to receive advertising messages, which implies literacy and a certain number of television sets. Thus the top markets for US food processors abroad are Canada, the UK, West Germany, Mexico and Brazil. In Britain, American interests control 50 per cent or more of the market in the fields of custards, baby foods, breakfast cereals, potato chips, cake mixes, pet food and canned milk.

Agribusiness is harmful to small, family-type farms and to consumers in the affluent countries, but it is no less harmful to ordinary working people who happen to get in the way of corporate "rationalization of production" or the "free flow of capital." It is not "rational," for instance, to produce pineapple in Hawaii if cannery workers are going to make unreasonable demands—like being paid half as much as workers in other US industries. So Del Monte and Dole have shifted part of their pineapple growing to the Philippines and to Thailand where a worker gets $1.20 a day for eight hours work. This does not mean that the price of a can of pineapple goes down.*

*Since this was written, NACLA has done its usual thorough investigating job on Del Monte: *Del Monte: Bitter Fruits,* September 1976, $1.25 plus postage, address pp. 118.

If tomorrow the agribusinesses decide it is cheaper to process their production in the UDCs rather than in America, Britain or France, their workers will have no choice in the matter. The companies are flexible and cost-conscious; their multinational status allows them to play with variables around the globe; to divest themselves of unprofitable operations and to jettison labor as the situation dictates. In an April 1974 article titled "A Multinational's New Road to Profits," *Business Week* recounted how Unilever, the world's largest food company, had recently sacked 11,000 people, mostly in Britain.* The road to profits for the one and the road to the unemployment bureau for the others is often the same.

(2) Does agribusiness benefit the Third World, and particularly the least well off in the poor countries?

We have seen how the processors pick their markets and sell, to Britain, for example, everything from ketchup to dog food.

If that is what the British want, then at least one can hope they can afford it. This is, unfortunately, not always the case in Brazil or Mexico where the major market thrust of the companies has predictably been in "gelatine deserts, candy, soft drinks, chewing gum, ice cream" and what the trade calls specialty (i.e., junk) foods with little or no nutritional value. A Mexican rural sociologist did a study on changes in dietary habits in Mexican villages and discovered that "the two products which peasants want and buy the moment they come into contact with the advertising message are white bread and soft drinks." As one food company executive freely admitted, "If we could obtain the ingredients for nothing, market and distribute them for nothing and made no profit (because of packaging costs), they would still be too expensive for the multitudes who need them most." Interviews of foreign food firm heads in India showed that their products were invariably aimed at upper-income-level consumers. An official of one of them said, "It is a sad fact that the most nutritional food products marketed by commercial firms are aimed at the segment of society least in need of them." The poor

---

*"If our profits continued to grow at their present rate, we'd wipe out the world," *BW* reported a Unilever executive "gloating." The world had better hang on tight. A *Dow Jones* dispatch concerning the company's performance during the first half of '76 is headlined "Unilever Profits Soar 227% But Margins Said Not Enough."

buy all the same because they are influenced by the companies' barrage of advertising. The same study on India showed that food advertising had increased 300 per cent in New Delhi's four highest-circulation papers in two years, and the author believes that "such advertising can convince low-income purchasers that they *must* buy certain high-priced nutritious products to keep their children well and alert . . . People in West Bengal were buying processed baby foods on the black market at outrageous prices when they could have bought cow's milk much cheaper."

"It is not uncommon in Mexico [doctors who work in rural villages report] for a family to sell the few eggs and chickens it raises to buy Coke for the father while the children waste away for lack of protein." The result of teaching the people that their traditional foods are somehow inferior is what one nutritionist has called "commerciogenic malnutrition." If a profit is to be made, one cannot stop to consider at whose expense this will be the case. If an already undernourished person can be made to want junk food, this is not the companies' problem.

Here is the rather admirably cynical view of the Board Chairman of International Flavors and Fragrances in an article on how to market successfully in UDCs:

> How often we see in developing countries that the poorer the economic outlook, the more important the small luxury of a flavored soft drink or smoke . . . to the dismay of many would-be benefactors, the poorer the malnourished are, the more likely they are to spend a disproportionate amount of whatever they have on some luxury rather than on what they need . . . Observe, study, learn [how to sell in rapidly changing rural societies]. We try to do it at IFF. It seems to pay off for us. Perhaps it will for you too.

As the International Organization of Consumers Unions reminded the World Food Conference, the "new consumers" of the developing world,

> . . . passing from agrarian subsistence into the market place, are frequently pressured into dietary tastes and habits whose high cost is related less to nutritive value than to the promotion, packaging and profits of foreign brand owners . . . the market dominance of multinationals in some countries makes it less and less possible for alternative high nutrient foods to be produced and sold at accessible prices.

This changing of peoples' diets happens everywhere the MNCs go—as we shall shortly see in a particularly horrible example in Africa.

They also change local societies by the way the "zero in" on the land. Plantation-owning agribusiness left over from colonial days is going out of fashion in some areas of the world in favor of more sophisticated types of control. The archetype of agribusiness used to be *"El Pulpo"*— the "octopus" United Fruit (now United Brands) that could and did make and unmake governments in the "banana republics." The best candidates for neocolonial plantation farming are still bananas, pineapple, sugar, oils, tea, and now ranching. Outright ownership of land is now not necessarily desirable, although as Samuel Gordon, President of Del Monte Banana Co., explains, "the only way to be in the market 52 weeks a year is to control your production." But there are more ways than one to skin a banana. If you get rid of land ownership, you can also eliminate a lot of fiscal, labor and political problems in one fell swoop—as well as the fear of nationalization. United Fruit used to own nearly a million and a half hectares in Latin America. Now it holds much less land directly, but has lost no control over the vital aspects of marketing and distribution. In the Philippines, Del Monte and Dole "own" relatively little land—Del Monte only owns 107 hectares—but through complicated joint-venture arrangements with the Filipino National Development Company, they really control 18,000 and 9,000 hectares respectively. The Ivory Coast and Indonesia also have supposedly national agencies whose sole function would appear to be the returning of land control to former colonialist powers, with some new ones thrown in.

One of the more fascinating national-government/MNC giveaway schemes is now in full swing in Brazil. Enormous tracts of Amazonia are being literally handed over to the MNCs through tax-break incentives to "develop" certain areas of the country. Any firm can avoid 50 per cent of its taxes—and can obtain a basketful of other advantages—if it consents to invest the tax rebate in certain locations. If you are Nestles, you build a new milk plant in Bélem almost for free. If you are Volkswagen, Goodyear, Anderson-Clayton, Mitsubishi, Swift & Armour, Borden or Italian Liquigas, you take your pick of several tens-of-thousand hectare tracts to start a ranch through the kind offices of a Brazilian national corporation. I happen to know that Goodyear has elsewhere consistently refused to invest in anything besides rubber and related chemical synthetic areas—for them to go into meat means that the Brazilian government's inducements must really be attractive. Even if the cattle they raise all have three legs and hoof and mouth disease, it is hard to see how these MNCs can go wrong: land prices in Amazonia have appreciated more than 1,000 per cent in eight years and are still climbing.

Elsewhere, where governments are not so openly freehanded, the more sophisticated agribusinesses prefer to establish "satellite farms" around the nucleus of the company's technical, processing and management center. Some of these projects have been established with UN agency or World Bank cooperation and we will look at them in more detail later. Essentially, the system calls for contracts with satellite farmers who are to produce perishable goods to company specifications in exchange for payment (for top-quality produce only) at a fixed price. The company handles both inputs and distribution; the farmer himself is left to cope with such boring details as the weather and other unpredictable elements of farming.

Agribusiness can adapt to any number of land-use systems. One good example is Brooke-Bond Liebig, which had outright ownership of only about 1 per cent of the tea plantations in Sri Lanka (formerly Ceylon), but is still able to control about a third of the country's tea exports—and that is where the money is to be made. In 1973, BBL reportedly made £228,000 on its Sri Lanka operations. It seems academic to make fine distinctions about which country is more dominated—Brazil with its giveaways, or Sri Lanka whose entire foreign exchange resources are controlled by the British companies that monopolize the marketing of tea— even though Sri Lanka has far more radical internal politics than Brazil. In both cases the MNCs hold all the trumps. As a Sri Lankan publication points out, it is a serious mistake to believe that nationalization alone can change the future of the country very much for the better, for the simple reason that the tea companies control distribution.

One can only foresee the danger to the Ceylonese tea industry from any large-scale divestment of British capital here and its use to expand the industry in East Africa or India. Having no further interest in the Ceylonese industry, there will be every inducement for those controlling the world's trade in tea to promote and foster the African and Indian industries . . . These calculations [concerning nationalization] for a brighter future have all been based on the restrictive assumption that there are and will be no obstacles to the free marketing of tea.

In other words, the more control Sri Lanka may gain over the land itself, the less influence it may have in the marketing of its major marketable crop.

Agribusiness is basically antagonistic to national control over local food production and marketing; thus governments that welcome it should do so in the full knowledge that what is raised will be largely exported to paying customers, with only a small residue left out for the local middle class. For example, only 10 percent of what Del Monte and Dole produce

... is sold in the Phillipines, including those canned goods which will not meet foreign health specifications, according to a Dole cannery official. In addition to canned goods, both corporations ship fresh pineapple to the Japanese market. In Tokyo, a Del Monte or Dole pineapple costs the equivalent of $1.50, compared with 8¢ at the plantation . . .

About fifty-five per cent of the entire Philippine farming acreage is used for export crops—sugar, coconuts, bananas, rubber, pineapple, coffee and cocoa—much of it directly controlled by foreign interests in cooperation with a tiny local élite. Meanwhile, according to FAO figures, the average Filipino is eating just 100 calories more a day than the average inhabitant of Bangladesh (1,940 versus 1,840 calories).

Because the whole agribusiness system is based on profitability, it is not surprising that "in Colombia, a hectare devoted to the raising of carnations brings a million pesos a year, while wheat or corn brings only 12,500 pesos. As a result, Colombia, like most other poor countries in Latin America, must use scarce foreign exchange to import basic foodstuffs." Rich sources of protein like fishmeal, which could perfectly well be used for human food, are processed and exported by agribusinesses like General Foods, Ralston Purina, Quaker Oats, or Swift & Armour to feed America's 35 million dogs and its 30 million cats. The Pet Food Institute, the trade association of dog- and cat-food manufacturers, estimated the 1974 US grocery bill for pet food at $2.1 billion. . . Any rich mongrel or pampered puss is a better customer for agribusiness than a poor human being. Little has changed since William Hazlitt, replying to Parson Malthus in 1807, stated that the dogs and horses of the rich "eat up the food of the children of the poor."

More and more land in the UDCs is devoted to greater and greater quantities of luxury food products that fewer and fewer people, proportionally, can afford. Africa is now supplying not only its traditional palm, peanut and copra oils to Europe, but fruits, vegetables and even beef. The beef mostly comes from the Sahel nations! Mexico and South America are purveyors of luxury foods like strawberries and asparagus to the US, while South Asia takes care of the affluent Japanese market. An increasing amount of the grain produced in the UDCs is now being promptly sent to feedmills, from whence it goes to fattening poultry and animals whose meat most local consumers cannot afford. For example, Costa Rica has increased its beef exports to North America by 92 per cent in recent years. This has been accompanied by a 26 per cent *decline* in local meat consumption.

We have seen how the recent introduction of soybean cultivation to Brazil has downgraded the quality of the local diet by occupying formerly food-producing land and causing prices to rise. This classic pattern is being copied in the Dominican Republic where American conglomerate Gulf & Western owns 275,000 acres (sugar plantations and cattle ranches) and the world's largest sugar mill. The overall picture in the Dominican Republic is approximately this: in the past twenty years, the amount of land under sugar cane has doubled, and now stands at about 25 per cent of the total acreage; while food production per capita has decreased. Food prices are twice as high as ten years ago, and many Dominican families are now eating only one meal a day. A 1969 study by a Colombia University doctor showed over half the sample of 5,500 Dominicans were anaemic and "showed chronic malnutrition since birth." Dominican Republic exports are not limited to sugar (which represents over 50 per cent) but also include tomatoes, cucumbers, onions, peppers, avocados, vegetable oils and beef.

And G&W's contribution to this general state of affairs? It now directly controls at least 8 per cent of all the cultivated land in the country, although it entered the Dominican Republic only in 1967. To increase its production surface, it contracts with local farmers and these contracts oblige the farmer to plant every inch in cane—nothing is left for his subsistence. Coercion is not unknown if persuasion fails. In March 1974 the people of a village near G&W's sugar mill seized a few hundred acres that were about to be planted with cane. Sympathetic merchants provided tractors and seeds and the people planted food for themselves and demanded that the government keep its legal promise to turn over land to the poor. Because powerful land-owners wanted to plant cane to sell to Gulf & Western, the army was called in and the people's food crops were ploughed under. Such tactics are only to be expected in a nation where the President, Mr. Balaguer, can make a statement like this one: "Central Romana [the name of the G&W sugar mill] has a contract and provisions of contracts supersede [*"derogan"*] national law. This is a legal principle [Bosch] should know." (Ex-president Bosch had supported the sharecroppers' movement.)

The IUF says that the once powerful cane cutters' trade union has had its back broken. On the G&W plantations, a cutter is not paid by the hour but by the ton. He can make at most $3 a day. Workers in the mill get 30–40¢ an hour. The company buys almost no supplies on the local market; even most of the workers are Haitians, not Dominicans. "If they have worked for Gulf & Western for at least 48 years [the workers become] eligible for pensions of US $6 a month. The Chairman of Gulf & Western, Mr. Charles Bluhdorn, receives an annual salary of $272,00; his retirement pay will be $74,829 yearly," if we are to believe the IUF.

Although G&W is a huge conglomerate with relatively small investments in agribusiness, "Bluhdorn, reflecting his early career as a commodities trader, takes an especially active interest in the food and agricultural products group whose principle product is sugar . . ."

Not even the Brazilian ranches in Amazonia have been created from unoccupied virgin territory. Several thousand peasant families have been expelled from their subsistence farms to make way for the the tax-haven cattle farmers. These people provide a convenient labor force for the preparation of pasture land. To keep their wages low, they are joined by thousands of other jobless people—one of Brazil's richest resources—sometimes transported from hundreds of miles away. The ranching MNCs turn their employment problems over to *gatos,* as the labor brokers are called. These "cats" recruit workers for about $2 a day, retaining half this sum for food and for their own commissions. Since many workers must also pay back exorbitant costs of transportation to the job site, the *peões* live in conditions of "semi-slavery and are guarded by armed militias." Since no semi-slaves are directly employed by the ranching companies, but are provided by the *gatos,* the MNCs need not consider themselves responsible for the appalling state of the *peões.*

The World Bank announced a $60 million loan to Brazil in 1974 for the improvement of its cattle-raising industry. The loan, we may safely assume, will contribute to increasing the growing beef-export business, largely foreign controlled.

Plantation workers do not appear to be entirely content in the Philippines either. According to the *Far Eastern Economic Review,* neither Del Monte nor Dole pays beginning workers the legal minimum wage, and Del Monte pays even less than Dole. Still, for the workers, it's a toss-up, for at Del Monte they stand a better chance of becoming "regulars" eligible for housing benefits and better wages. At Dole, 70 per cent of the workers are "casuals" with every chance of remaining so. "Plantation workers at Dole are annoyed with the management because they are kept as casuals [without any rights or benefits] and because of the absence of a union. Stories are told of field workers sending to the cannery pineapples which have been carefully filled with debris or faeces or angry notes."

Since even foreign labor can grow restive, many agribusinesses opt for the same kind of capital-intensive, high-energy farming that has become so profitable in the West. This means all the Green Revolution type inputs and a high degree of mechanization, including mechanical harvesting. Modern farming means controlling one's land (not necessarily through ownership) but especially the incoming technology, marketing, transportation and the primary manufacturing industries set up either in the home or in the host country. With this system, agribusiness pockets the maximum margin at every stage of the game. We have noted the case of bananas, where only 11 per cent of the final value of the product remains inside the producing countries. An interesting example of control of incoming technology is provided, again, by Brazil, where a research center originally set up by IBEC, and now financed by USAID, is examining the problems of tropical soils.

The selection criteria are the reactions of various plant strains to chemical fertilizers, whereas it would have been much more useful to choose criteria related to plant varieties' resistance to drought and adaptability to soil deficiencies. However, one must understand that Brazil depends on American firms for 70% of its fertilizer imports.

Agribusiness has incentives other than cheap labor and high margins for moving into the Third World. Their overall taxes are often substantially reduced for operations in host countries. As Charles Ray Barrett of Fresno (feedlot beef, in Ethiopia and other countries) explains, investment profits in UDCs, if left productively employed for ten years, allowing profit to accrue, can then be repatriated and taxed as capital gains, or "next to nothing in taxes," if we are to believe Mr. Barrett. Foreign subsidiaries are consistently taxed at lower rates than identical operations in the US; for example at a flat 34 per cent for businesses with operations in North, Central and South America rather than at 48 per cent. If profits are not repatriated, there is not much the Internal Revenue Service can do about it.

There is no doubt that the governments of host countries are usually eager to cooperate. Frances Fitzgerald, back from Iran, reported,

> Over the past few years, the government has leased hundreds of thousands of acres of productive land to multinational agribusiness. In the Khuzestan region . . . Shellcott, Hawaiian Agronomics and other multinationals have taken over huge tracts of newly irrigated land to develop with foreign technicians and modern farming machinery imported tax free. The productivity of these businesses, which have displaced some 17,000 Iranians from their land, is far lower than predicted (according to one expert, it is lower than that of medium sized Iranian farms in irrigated areas) but it is easier for the government to rent land to foreigners than to help out its own small farmers.

Despite oil revenues, the average daily calorie intake of the average Iranian, according to FAO, is only 150 calories higher than that of an Indian or a Pakistani (protein intake is the same). Fitzgerald tells us that the Iranian government is "hoping to attract more agribusiness." A look at other sources shows it has succeeded. Among US partners in Iran are Foremost McKesson (dairying) and California almond growers like Naraghi. A spokesman for one of these growers says, "They develop the water first and we come in and farm it. It's an attractive arrangement." Feedlot-beef technology is being developed near Teheran by FMC and even World Airways is getting into the act through a contract to airlift 250,000 pregnant cows to Iran by 1979.

Throughout the world, agribusiness is "zeroing in," as Bankamerica President Lundborg suggested years ago, on the best land and the cheapest labor in the UDCs. Speaking of his company's new thrust towards overseas production (in Guatemala, Iran, Indonesia, etc.) Murray Stewart, President of C. Brewer and Co.

(which controls 265,000 acres in Hawaii already) says, "We've been in this business longer than almost anybody else, so we're interested in anything that can be grown profitably." *Duns Magazine* praises Stewart for having "lost no time in planning how to take advantage of the sudden spurt in food prices last fall [1973]. He immediately diverted the company's major thrust from land development to all phases of its agriculture business and is now expanding as fast as possible to take advantage of the boom."*

Mr. Lundborg (or his successors), true to his word, has put Bankamerica money into the Latin American Agribusiness Development Corporation (LAAD) which loans to "deserving farmers and businessmen." The undeserving are presumably taking care of themselves. LAAD (whose membership also includes Borden, Cargill, Caterpillar and Deere tractors, Dow Chemical, Gerbers Baby Food, Ralston Purina, Goodyear and Standard Fruit and Steamship) is not the only consortium of companies and banks backing agribusiness investments in the underdeveloped world. Another group called ADELA is also active— although not exclusively so—in investments in Latin American farming. When it was founded (1968), it had nothing but stars on its board: Eli Black, then President of United Brands; Emilio Collado, former US Executive Director of the World Bank and later chief executive of Standard Oil; IBM's Jacques Maisonrouge; Fiat's Agnelli and Rudolph Peterson who succeeded Lundborg at Bank of America. Black jumped out of a forty-fourth story window in February 1975 when the scandal of his bribe of Honduras President Lopez Arellano to reduce the banana export tax was about to break; but Peterson has gone on to become the head of the United Nations Development Program. PICA is the private investment consortium for Asia, counterpart to ADELA. It also places emphasis on medium-sized private enterprises in "manufacturing, distribution, services, transportation and processing of forest, farm and fishing products." The handful of really important people who run American agribusiness can also meet through the auspices of the Agribusiness Council, founded in 1967 when "Business, university, foundation and government

*It is possible to be too smart an agribusinessman: Stewart's company was bought up against his will in 1975 by the Philadelphia conglomerate IU. Stewart resigned and has joined Alexander and Baldwin, another Hawaiian food firm, as an "international agribusiness consultant."

leaders met to discuss the ways in which private investment and government cooperation could help resolve some of the world's food problems *through using the skill and resources of private business"* [their emphasis]. The Agribusiness Council helps identify investment opportunities and does detailed studies on countries providing a welcoming climate for agribusiness. It also "administers an important program for USAID. This program provides funds for reconnaissance and feasibility studies of American firms interested in development oriented agribusiness abroad." The banks, the corporations, the government and the multilateral aid institutions are virtually indistinguishable and thoroughly intermingled when one reaches the highest echelons of agripower.

There is a good deal of competition for the title of World's Worst Agribusiness Firm. United Brands, Ralston Purina, Del Monte and Unilever* are all strong contenders. My own first prize, after careful consideration, goes to Nestles, whose advertising policies have evidently contributed to increasing infant malnutrition in Africa. Nestles also makes a good showing in the minor award categories of labor disputes and contracts prejudicial to the interests of host countries.

The *New Internationalist* must be credited with publishing the first news about the Nestles baby-food scandal in 1973. Its article took the form of an interview with two professors of child health with over thirty years of experience dealing with infant malnutrition in several African countries between them. These doctors cite Nestles specifically as a company encouraging African mothers to abandon breast feeding of their children in favor of formula-milk feeding. The fact that mother's milk is unquestionably the best baby food (even providing immunizations) is only one aspect of the issue. In Western countries, mothers who do not breast feed at least have pure water, sterilization equipment—and money to buy formula. African mothers usually have none of these things. But because they have been convinced through advertising that Nestles equals healthy baby, they buy formula. Then, because they have primitive cooking equipment, they mix it with unboiled water in an unsterilized bottle. One of the doctors says,

---

*I exclude Unilever from the sweepstakes because the Counter Information Service has already done a magnificent exposé in its 100 page "antireport": *Unilever's World* available through CIS, 52 Shaftesbury Avenue, London W1. (£1 plus 15p postage.)

A quarter or a third of a husband's salary goes on just feeding this one infant with artificial milk. This is clearly impossible to sustain. So in fact they still buy the milk [their breast milk has dried up] but they don't buy adequate quantities . . . probably less than 10% of the mothers buy sufficient milk to really adequately feed their babies.

Nestles, and the other formula-milk companies like Unigate, use posters, radio advertisements and loudspeaker vans to push their products. They also use saleswomen, *dressed as nurses*—and who may even *be* nurses—to go around maternity hospitals and clinics to demonstrate the use of Nestles products. "The mothers are not to know that they are not paid by the government. They go into the clinics and try and sell their products." In some hospitals, every mother is given a free tin of milk and a feeding bottle before she leaves for home with her new baby. Both these doctors report increasing malnutrition—marasmus, kwashiorkor, gastroenteritis—in Africa, and although they are cautious scientists, they do not hesitate to say that "undoubtedly, the increase of malnutrition in the young baby and the many deaths which occur from this must have some relationship to the increased misuse of artificial feeding."

Some African governments—Nigeria in particular—now oblige all milk companies to preface their advertisements with a phrase like, "Breast feeding is always best for your baby, but if for some reason you cannot breast feed, then use *x*." Other governments have instructed rural health workers to destroy formula ads wherever they find them. Others should follow suit. The *New Internationalist*, since its first article, has received confirmation of the above facts from doctors and nurses all over Africa. One medical volunteer in Zambia wrote to tell the story of a mother with twins—both of whom died after a few months of watery milk diet adopted in spite of the health worker's advice. "So widespread is this cycle [of malnutrition] that babies in some African hospitals are in beds marked "Lactogen Syndrome" after the [Nestles] babyfood of that name."

The companies can and do justly claim that there is nothing wrong with their milk and particularly stress that the quality of the product bought by an African and a Swiss mother is exactly the same. This is entirely true—and it is part of the problem. The prestige of Western foods is high; still the companies consider that what may happen as a result of their products is not their concern. Yet as one of the *New Internationalist* doctors says,

"There is enough evidence now to make anybody sitting on a company board sit up and take note of what their sales promotion campaigns may be doing."*

Dr. Henri Dupin who has spent much of his career teaching public health in Africa was amazed in 1970 to see mothers in the Ivory Coast giving Nescafé to 19/20-month-old toddlers. His students explained that the following message was broadcast thrice daily over the national radio: "Nescafé makes men stronger, women more joyful and children more intelligent." These African mothers were simply putting this "advice" into practice. Dr. Dupin sometimes feels he is waging a losing battle—Nestles' advertising budget is far greater than the total annual budget of the World Health Organization.

Nestles is the world's second largest agribusiness (Unilever is first); and its labor record is no better than it should be. The International Union of Foodworkers now devotes a whole periodical just to news about Nestles around the globe—a difficult enough task, as the company, at last count, had seventy-seven plants in the UDCs, with the heaviest proportion in Latin America. The IUF has had some success in international labor organizing against the firm. International solidarity it helped to coordinate allowed Peruvian Nestles workers to hang on during a long strike and finally to obtain satisfaction.

Another tidbit for Nestles-watchers is the tale of its Greek milk-processing factory agreed to under a contract drawn up with the colonel's regime in October 1972. Now that freedom has returned to Greece, the terms of the contract have become known, and the whole Greek press—left, right and center—has raised an uproar. Headlines like "Nestles Monopoly of Greek Milk" and "The Confidence of a Colonialist Imposing its Rule on Savages" were common occurrences early in 1975. A parliamentary commission has been appointed to re-examine the conditions of the contract.

This is what has come out: When Greece decided to build a milk-processing factory, an appeal for bids was tendered. Shortly afterwards, the Ministry of Agriculture suspended bids and opened negotiations with Nestles, though it has since been learned that a Dutch company had made a more favorable offer. Nestles got 51 per cent of the capital, six out of nine places and the

---

*A code of advertising has been adopted since this writing by eight milk MNCs operating in Third World countries, including Nestles. This proves that *pressure pays.*

Presidency and Vice-Presidency on the Board; and Greece, under the terms of the contract, *was not allowed to authorize the creation of a similar plant for twenty-five years,* thereby giving Nestles an effective monopoly over all milk processing in the country. Furthermore, Nestles got "start-up" subsidies from the government, royalties amounting to 5 per cent on cost of sales for a thirty-year period, protection via tariffs against imported milk products, bank loans at a preferential interest rate, and no sanctions to be applied in case they did not live up to the few obligations imposed upon them in the contract. Greek financial experts, now freed from the colonels' tutelage, claim that Greek milk prices will go up about 30 per cent if the terms of the contract are allowed to stand. Nestles' reaction? It says, "As a result of circumstances, Greece wishes to renegotiate. There is no question of imposing our point of view, but we think ourselves justified in demanding that the agreements be respected; we will not lend ourselves to any negotiations which would call them into doubt [*Tribune de Genève*]."

I could go on and on giving examples of agribusiness and all its works, but I am afraid readers may already feel like the little girl who, asked to submit a book report, wrote, "This book told me more about penguins than I wanted to know." Agribusiness is everywhere it is allowed to be—which means most of the Third World—and is even making some headway in the socialist nations. United Brands was recently reported to be negotiating banana-marketing rights with the USSR and the Eastern European governments, although it has not yet taken over any kolkhozes. As long as food prices stay high—and no one expects them to do anything else—this investment trend will swell, and all those friendly multinationals you can meet every day at the supermarket and on your television screen will be fruitful and multiply.

(3) *Given all this, can agribusiness still feed the world?*

As a Sunday School teacher of mine never wearied of repeating to her charges, "If you have a kind word to say, say it now." This is what I propose to do for agribusiness, because in the course of my search, I have found one example for which I can find nothing whatsoever to carp at. Granted, I have only the company's word for it, and no news from the Kenyans involved; but on the face of it, it appears to be an excellent specimen of the contributions business *could* make to development if *social goals*, not merely profitability, were present in the project from the drawing board to the actual operation. This example is the Mumias sugar complex in Western Kenya, set up through the cooperation of the Kenyan government and the UK firm Booker McConnell, with assistance from UK overseas development aid funds and extra capital from the World Bank and the East African Development Bank. Bookers holds 5 per cent of the equity and its management and technical fees are indexed to the profitability of Mumias for the Kenyan economy as a whole.

The Mumias area is densely settled with a very high population growth rate (4 per cent a year) and the people traditionally depended on subsistence farming alone for their livelihood. There was no local industry, the farmlands were generally underutilized (people raised just enough for their own consumption because there was no access to a market anywhere else); and as a result there was considerable urban drift towards Nairobi. Average farm size is about ten acres, but "farm" is a misnomer, because much of the land was either swampy and not drained or consisted of bush and scrub.

Two other sugar plants existed in Kenya, but they had never been able to produce more than about half of the country's requirements, which meant a serious drain on foreign exchange for sugar imports. Thus the Kenyan government fixed the goal of sugar self-sufficiency and approached Bookers to help them achieve it.

There are two basic problems in an enterprise like this: how to grow the cane itself, then how to turn it into sugar. Although it might have been preferable from a narrow economic point of view to have all the cane grown on a large estate, expropriating land and hiring labor to cultivate it, this course was not chosen because one of the government's main objectives was to provide cash incomes for small farmers. The satellite-farm, or outgrowers, system was adopted. The average plot farmers devote to cane growing is four acres (usually not previously utilized at all) leaving them ample land to continue raising food for themselves and their families. In fact, no farmer is allowed to put more than half his land under cane so that he will not become dependent on it and lose his food source. In 1976–7, with the operation in full swing, there will be 5,000 outgrowers. Neighbors have been encouraged to regroup their lands so as to make more easily harvested stands of cane of about fifteen acres minimum, but each farmer retains ownership of his own land so this has not presented a real problem. The company does the hardest operations for the farmers with machinery—ploughing, furrowing and cane loading—since this helps to maximize the farmer's individual income—but the cane is cut by teams. Any farmer who wants to supplement his cane-sale income by working with a cutting team has priority for employment. The company provides seed cane and fertilizer under a state-supervised credit system; it gives free technical advice and maintains a laboratory for research on improved cane varieties, disease resistance, etc. At harvest time, each farmer's cane is weighed individually before mechanical loading—the most exhausting job of all in sugar raising if it has to be done by hand. Besides the outgrowers themselves, about 30,000 dependents are estimated to be benefiting from the project. All sugar and molasses are sold directly to the Kenyan government and the farmer makes about K.Sh 500 per acre per year (at 1974 cane prices) or about £168 per year for a five-acre plot. He can supplement this with cane-cutting wages and with his own garden produce.

The plant itself, set up as the nucleus of the cane fields, employs 2,500 people, sixty of them foreigners. As a result of comprehensive training courses supplied by Bookers (and begun well before the plant was operational) there should be no more than six foreigners employed by 1980. All foreign personnel are given incentives to train Kenyans and to "work themselves out of the job." The company lays considerable stress on training because a great many employees at Mumias have never held any paid employment in their lives. They are now "achieving standards of performance in a wide range of jobs comparable with those in other parts of the world." Costly labor-saving devices in the plant were avoided and labor-intensive technologies employed whereever feasible. The plant can produce 45,000 tons (1974) and can easily expand production to 70,000 tons, the figure expected for 1976. It has proved profitable in its first year of operation. Foreign-exchange costs for plant equipment were already amortized in 1974 and future hard-currency savings will be at least £1.8 million a year—much more if world sugar prices stay high. With government help, an extra one-hundred miles of market-access roads have been built, and the company has provided housing for 1,250 employees. The houses all have running water, most have toilets, and they were not built in a company "ghetto" but integrated into four different existing communities. A free clinic, social and recreational facilities have also been furnished. There is an active branch of the Kenya Union of Sugar Plantation Workers on site with which the company says "relations are good and regular consultations take place with the branch officials and shop stewards." Bookers does not state the terms of its own contract with the Kenyan government, but presumably there is a "fade-out" arrangement as more and more Kenyans are trained to supply skilled management. Bookers will probably retain its 5 per cent equity, although this is not specified either. Besides the 7,500 people directly employed either in growing or milling, a whole local commercial/artisan sector has sprung up around Mumias in response to the cash incomes the project has generated. Drift towards Nairobi has been halted, and many natives of the Mumias area have come home. The *Financial Times* reports that Bookers is moving on towards Mumias II, another joint venture with the government, which will be run along the same lines and produce twice as much sugar as Mumias I.*

You may well ask what a project like Mumias is doing in a chapter on agri*business*. It is, of course, highly doubtful that, without the World Bank, UK overseas development funds and especially the strict attitude of the government insisting that social goals be placed first, Mumias would have turned out to be anything other than a classic sugar plantation on the model of many that Booker McConnell manages and/or owns in other parts of the world. In the absence of such outside influences, there is nothing to prevent a company from aiming for the most economically profitable method of production. As Bookers itself says, normally, "to ensure full utilization of capacity, it makes good sense, in terms of organizational efficiency, to have all cane requirements grown on a single large estate and to put the whole scheme under one management so that field production matches factory capacity as closely as possible . . . However . . " and then follow the special conditions placed on this particular enterprise. In another sense, the success of Mumias is a further argument that multinational agribusiness must be controlled, for when it is, it has a contribution to make.

*The Chairman of Booker's wrote me shortly after publication of the British edition of this book to say that "the project has more than fulfilled its social and economic objectives. It is now being doubled in size and by 1979 some 12,000 small holders will be growing cane as a cash crop, in addition to other food crops."

There is another type of agribusiness that has helped UDCs make real strides towards better nutrition for their populations, and this is the food-processing machinery industry. Here it is important to note that the companies that have proved most useful are those that have no stake in *selling* the finished product, nor in providing the *raw materials* to manufacture it. In other words, the only good agribusiness, from a UDC point of view, is the *non*-integrated agribusiness that cannot, or does not want to, control the whole food chain from the producer to the consumer. (A company like Booker McConnell, under normal conditions, is fully integrated. It raises its chosen crop on land it controls, processes it in its own plants and ships it in its own vessels to the customers of its choice; it markets the finished product under its own brand names in its own supermarkets.) Two good examples of processing-machinery companies are Sweden's Alfa-Laval and Switzerland's Buhler. Both have cooperated with UN agencies like UNICEF, WHO, FAO and the development assistance programs of their own governments. Buhler specializes in designing machinery for processing UDC crops in order to transform them into low-priced, highly nutritious foods for the local population. It designed and provided the plant for the production of Superamin—a low-starch, high-protein, cheap Algerian baby food—in cooperation with the UN and the Algerian government. It also concentrates on corn, wheat and pulses milling plants from Venezuela to the Sudan. Other Buhler processes provide improved grain loading and storage facilities in countries where a tragic proportion of the harvest is traditionally lost during these stages; it has also designed plants for transforming garbage into compost fertilizer. These are now being used in Morocco and Algeria, and Buhler foresees increased use of the technique as chemical fertilizer prices climb. Alfa-Laval does approximately the same kind of work in milk, oils and fruit-juice processing and is currently experimenting with techniques of protein extraction from portions of green plants that are usually thrown away. It concentrates on maximum use of raw materials through improved processing and the recycling of wastes.

Both these companies have become involved in the field of development through their cooperative activities with national or international agencies and both have comprehensive training programs for local technicians. One problem both point to in their development literature is that UDC consumers behave exactly like Western consumers. They are perhaps even more easily influenced by Western advertising techniques and are more than likely to assume that the high-priced, imported food product is automatically "better" than its locally produced and processed, far less expensive, and nearly always more healthful competitor. This holds true even and especially when these poor consumers cannot afford the imported product. The only solution would appear to be that UDCs that have developed useful foods (like Superamin) ruthlessly outlaw imports of substitute foreign foods. Otherwise, they are going to have to devote disproportionate and precious resources to promotion campaigns to counteract the effective and costly advertising of the integrated agribusinesses that have gained a foothold, or a stranglehold, in their nations.

UDCs must measure the real costs of imported technology. For vital food products, it is probably better to bear the cost of importing processing machinery for three reasons. The first is obviously better nutrition right now for the local people, *when* the government has a coherent policy with this aim. The second is that processing of local agricultural raw materials is the only thing that can add value to these products and thus obtain a better price on the world market, *when* Western nations accept such processed imports. There is every reason why chocolate should be manufactured in Africa from African cocoa beans and instant coffee from Latin American coffee beans—but UDCs that try will invariably have a fight on their hands. General Foods (Maxwell House) single-handedly prevented US imports of Brazilian instant coffee. Finally, it is unrealistic to assume that each UDC government can or will behave like the Chinese and invent processing technology of its own with little or no recourse to outside suppliers. Food is an emergency area and existing processes that can be usefully adapted to local specifications must be used now, however much we would like to see the UDCs self-sufficient in the future.

Companies like Buhler and Alfa-Laval furnish plants, train people and leave. Other processors, unfortunately, move in their machines and stay. Thus in Senegal, the French MNC Les Grands Moulins has not wanted to be bothered incorporating local food grains (sorghum and millet) into its flour mills because it would be obliged to re-tool its machinery. And because local sources of supply can fluctuate, it also prefers to import wheat because it knows the boat will arrive on time with the right quantity. Since 1960, doctors have been encouraging Senegal to use sorghum and millet in bread to combat malnutrition, but there is no law obliging the major flour processor to do so, thus no encouragement for local crops.

In spite of a few counter-examples which took some perseverance to unearth, the best answer to the final question (*Can agribusiness feed the world?*) has been given by the International Union of Foodworkers which groups 125 national unions and has a total membership of 2.2 million. IUF's answer is not only that agribusiness can't feed the world—it can't, or won't, even feed its own workers. Here is part of a document prepared by the IUF for the World Food Conference:

Agribusiness bears a special responsibility for the present food crisis. While food deficits and malnutrition have grown worse during the past ten years, the accelerated growth rate and prosperity of the multinational firms during the same period has been inversely proportional to the increase of scarcity.

This phenomenon is only paradoxical on the surface; the goal of agribusiness is not to increase food resources, nor to contribute to their equitable distribution, nor yet to adapt existing technology to the conditions of particular countries. Their goal is first and foremost to increase their markets and their commercial outlets, to realize maximum production-costs reduction and to increase their profits. This is a truism, but should be made clear, especially in this Conference, where multinationals are spreading their propaganda about their supposed capability to solve the world food crisis.

Food workers of developing countries have long and bitter experience of this capability. There are great numbers of agribusiness workers whose low salaries, substandard housing, poor health and squalid working conditions are such that hunger, malnutrition and undernourishment for them and for their families are commonplace. If so many multinational firms do not even allow their own workers to feed themselves properly, then how can we imagine for a moment that they can bring a decent diet to everyone?

IUF bulletins and other sources furnish numerous examples of this "capability." Workers on the tea estates in Sri Lanka are among the worst paid in the world—perhaps because such a high percentage of them are women. Although these workers are directly responsible for earning about three quarters of Sri Lanka's foreign exchange, "The estate worker is in debt to and dependent on the [company] provision store . . . He has to put up with substandard goods and short measures. Malnutrition is written all over his face and during lay-off periods, he lives on the brink of starvation." The infant mortality rate for tea workers is the highest in Sri Lanka. These workers are "housed" in rows of what amount to little more than cages, and they have no land for subsistence farming, while "the Superintendent has a very large house with ample land. Sometimes a swimming pool and a mini golf course. He has opportunities to have a dairy, a poultry run, as well as a flower and vegetable garden. He is provided with servants to work in these . . ." Tea workers are "daily paid labor, *always temporary*. There is no security of employment." This comes from a Ceylonese religious society and applies to all employers. The IUF adds for one of them: "If a new kind of enlightened employer has entered on to the world scene to lead mankind to a new era of abundance, Brooke-Bond Liebig is not one of them. Its tea estate employees . . . live in delapidated housing, with poor water supply and sanitary facilities and suffer the ravages of disease and malnutrition."

South Africa is another country where workers live close to the brink in the midst of plenty. The South African government fixes a poverty datum line recommended wage on which black workers and their families are theoretically expected to exist. It makes no provision for such non-essentials as medicine or education. According to the *Guardian*, a study of wages paid by 100 MNCs in South Africa was carried out by a South African employers' group. "The results of the study were so bad that it was decided by mutual consent that they should not be published." The IUF singles out UK food firms Rowntree Mackintosh and Tate & Lyle as among those employers paying wages below even the poverty datum line. Nestles' non-white plant workers are also reportedly paid below this official subsistence level.

Prior to independence, the British-owned company Sena Sugar Estates operating in Mozambique was paying its 5,000 African cane cutters about £10.40 monthly, according to IUF.

This is the minimum according to Portuguese colonial law but take-home pay is actually less, since £3.48 is deducted for food and clothing. Some Sena employees claim they are paid only £1.70 a month. The firm has also been charged with using forced labour recruited by the colonial government to work for European settlers.

At least *this* situation has been corrected—thanks to FRELIMO.

Agribusinesses' only current worry seems to be that governments may become intractable to their interests. Yet far too many governments have already succumbed to their influence. It is not these governments that control decisions to open or close plants and other operations. As the IUF again points out, "The three key elements that determine food production [capital, technology and control of markets] escape governments' powers of decision. This power is concentrated in the hands of the principal multinational agribusiness companies."

In spite of all the evidence demonstrating that half the world's people are conveniently forgotten by the food companies, these MNCs are precisely the entities to whom a man like Orville Freeman looks as a "model for the political leadership of the world"! He claims that shortages are not the problem and that

. . . efficient management could maximize available supplies. Moreover, with resources scattered around the world, the necessary level of production cannot be achieved within the boundaries of competing nation-states, each jealously husbanding its own sovereignty. Somehow, the nation-states must share critical resources on a global basis.

We have seen how the companies conceive of this "sharing." Mr. Freeman goes on to explain that

. . . one institution, frequently maligned but spectacularly successful, has managed to think, plan and act in global terms . . . These multinational corporations reach out to do business all over the world, regardless of national boundaries. They search everywhere for the best people, raw materials and resources, and then, using the most advanced technology, management and marketing techniques, they work to produce and distribute at the lowest cost and at the best profit—in other words, at maximum efficiency.

For reasons I hope have been made clear, this efficiency does not and cannot extend to the people who constitute "the other half."

The goal for those who do not share Mr. Freeman's enthusiasm is clear: do everything possible to weaken the companies' control of food production and distribution and to strengthen independent, egalitarian nation-states as the only present possible global defense against them. Otherwise, continued malnutrition and starvation will be the only prospect for those hundreds of millions who will never become "consumers": the invisible poor.

8. Food Aid? . . . Or Weapon?

Suppose Dr. Gallup approaches you for your opinion on food aid. You're in favor of it, aren't you? You don't want to go on record as an opponent of charity, generosity and the filling of empty rice bowls. Only a modern Scrooge could say, "Bah, Humbug," where helping people to get enough to eat is concerned. Well, we are not going to argue that food aid has never filled an empty stomach or saved a dying child—but we will contend, in the case of the United States at least, that it has done so only inadvertently. Our concern here is with America, because its food-aid program has the longest history and because this country also has the largest amount of food to use as it pleases. But as the EEC's capacity to produce extra food grows, its aid policies should be given hawklike scrutiny. States use the means they have at their disposal to promote their own economic advantage and their foreign-policy objectives. No one should therefore be shocked by what we will have to say about the way the US has used and is using its food: from a power politics standpoint, all these uses are entirely normal—there are some disinterested individuals; there are no disinterested states. If this chapter is at all convincing, no reader will ever again think of food "aid" without mental quotation marks, nor will he or she consider it as altogether a good thing.

In 1812, the US Congress approved a budget of $50,000 for emergency food aid to victims of an earthquake in Venezuela. Was America's very first act of food aid an act of charity? Not at all. RAND Corporation economist Charles Wolf says it was even then an economic instrument in the service of a political goal—in this case support for a revolt (which failed) against Spain. Ever since then, the US has consistently tied its contributions to the needy to the enhancement of its political leverage over other governments and to the expansion of its own commercial markets.

Herbert Hoover was the first modern politician to look upon food as a frequently more effective means of getting one's own way than gunboat diplomacy or military intervention, and as a means of supporting US farmers in the bargain. He first came on the scene at the beginning of the First World War. Millions of European farmers were bearing arms and producing no grain, while America was even then raising surpluses. America was neutral in the war, and would have been delighted to sell to all comers—but Britain objected to anything that would make Germany's war effort easier and blocked US food shipments. Devising a means to get around this was Hoover's first stroke of genius: he created the philanthropic Commission for Relief in Belgium. The fact that Belgium was the most self-sufficient of all the European nations in food at the time did not make it a less attractive recipient for charity, because the enormous quantities of wheat that arrived at Antwerp could afterwards be shunted east or west, towards France or towards Germany. A German author speculates that "it is possible that the Germans would have stopped the war at the end of autumn 1916 if they had not had access to American wheat which reached them through Belgium." When America entered the war, all its food went to the Allies and it is problematic whether US doughboys or US wheat contributed more to the ultimate victory.

As soon as the Armistice was signed, Hoover was all for starting aid to the vanquished, who still had gold reserves, while America still had eighteen million tons of surplus wheat. He wanted to make a good deal to avoid plummeting prices in the US; he also wanted to fight the "collectivist infection"—a pre-cold-War term for the "Red menace"—which he feared would spread throughout Europe. All these goals were attained: Hoover sold US wheat and summarily forced settlements of several European disputes simply by threatening to cut off food aid to the party of whose politics he disapproved. He was instrumental in the overthrow of Bela Kun's government in Hungary—and immediately afterwards resumed food aid to that country. He "suggested" that the Poles accept his choice of Paderewski for their Premier, in which case they might expect increased food shipments. In Vienna, at a time when a communist-inspired takeover seemed imminent, he staved it off by the simple expedient of posting notices announcing that "any disturbances of public order will render food shipments impossible and bring Vienna face to face with absolute famine." All this is recounted, not without a certain pride, in the volume of his memoirs he titles *Years of Adventure.*

Hoover took time off from famine relief to become President of the United States and to oversee the beginnings of the great depression, but when the Second World War broke out in Europe, he was back behind the same old desk and founded food-relief agencies for Poland, Finland, Belgium, Luxemburg, Holland, Norway and Greece—later grouped under the name of "The International Committee on Food for the Small Democracies." But here, a large democracy got in his way. Winston Churchill, with the whole British government behind him, instituted a blockade. They justified their position in March 1941:

> The blockade . . . is directed against the whole war machine of the enemy . . . it must extend over the whole range of countries overrun by the enemy. The Germans are attempting to organize these territories to form an integral part of their war machine. [The blockade] is intended to deprive [the enemy] of imported goods, to drive him into using in uneconomic ways foods which he possesses or produces, to aggravate his transport difficulties and to render as costly and burdensome as possible distribution of supplies within the areas which he controls and utilizes for his military operations and war potential. Every import of foodstuffs into an occupied territory conflicts directly with one or another of these objectives . . . The British government [regard] it as false humanitarianism to agree to the admission of foodstuffs to the areas concerned, knowing as they do that the result of this action would be to prolong the war and to add in the long run to the sum of human misery.

Considering the aid and comfort Hoover's shipments had brought to the Germans in the First World War, this position seems entirely justified. There was no reason the British should have allowed the United States to carry out a thinly masked commercial operation via the German-occupied countries, at a time when Britain alone was continuing the war and the US was still neutral. The British stood firm, the governments-in-exile of the "small democracies" repudiated Hoover's Committee and he had to wait four years, until the end of the war.

When peace came, Hoover and his staff visited thirty-eight countries, and there is no doubt that the relief efforts he coordinated contributed greatly to relieving the distress of many millions of ordinary people suffering from the immediate aftermaths of a war that had dislocated agriculture like everything else. But as Hoover himself says, "While our major interest was relief of famine, all on our staff were concerned about the forces moving in the world and their impact upon our country—and especially with the spread of Communism." He was alarmed that whereas before the war there was only one Communist country, in 1946 there were "twenty-three nations or parts of nations dominated by Communism . . . and eleven countries which emerged from the war with Communists in their ministries and with organized Communist political parties." Hoover's single-mindedness and the exceptional opportunities for data collecting enjoyed everywhere by his large staff during several decades of famine relief resulted in a unique collection of millions of modern historical documents housed at Stanford University in the Hoover Institution on War, Revolution and Peace. This is without doubt the best place in the world to study communism in the Soviet Union, China and many other countries, as well as what Hoover calls "aggressive nationalist movements." We cannot go into a long digression on this interesting by-product of food aid; nevertheless it is interesting to know that

. . . the United States government has made extensive use of Hoover facilities. Because the collections in political and economic affairs frequently provide materials not available elsewhere in the country, federal departments have entrusted the Institution with special research projects . . . The collections are used by such agencies as the Department of State, the Central Intelligence Agency, the Department of Justice, the Federal Bureau of Investigation and the military services.

After the Second World War, the US channelled enormous grain surpluses to Europe, but by 1954 reconstruction was nearly complete and the Marshall Plan had had the desired effect: Europe was once again a valid trading partner for America. It was clear that the dumping ground for excess agricultural products would have to be enlarged. Hoover's method had been that of sales of surplus food for hard currency or gold, with the cash receipts then partly used to provide for the destitute. But most of the world's currencies in 1954 were anything but hard. It was then that the brilliant idea of sales of American surplus food for *local,* non-convertible currencies was conceived: the proceeds would be put into a US account in country *x*'s central bank and used for such purposes in that country as the Americans might choose. This was the genesis of Public Law 480 (now also called the Food for Peace Law) passed by the US Congress in 1954 with these stated purposes: *An Act to increase the consumption of United States agricultural commodities in foreign countries,* to improve the foreign relations of the United States and for other purposes." The Congress further specifically declared that one goal was "to develop and expand export markets" for American products.

The major sections, or Titles, of PL 480 were as follows: Title I provided for sale of farm surplus to "friendly nations" with food deficits, to be paid for in their own money. These sales were to provide the "counterpart funds" deposited for use by the US or by the country itself with US approval and permission. Title II concerned urgent famine relief and donations, again to "friendly" countries. Title II donations have, throughout the twenty years of food aid, represented only one fifth of US food sent abroad, yet most people automatically assume that food "aid" means gifts. Title III concerned barter of strategic raw materials in exchange for food. For many years the US used this means of constituting stockpiles of minerals, especially those necessary to its atomic-energy program. America's needs are no longer so great in this area and when it is still used, Title III chiefly concerns goods needed by US agencies operating abroad. In recent years its use has been restricted to military procurement in Vietnam.

Title IV was added to PL 480 in 1959. It concerned long-term food-supply contracts between the US and the recipient; under its terms the food had to be paid for in dollars or in convertible currency (which amounts to the same thing) over a period of up to twenty years and with interest. In 1966 PL 480 was amended to provide for progressively switching *all* Title I (local-currency) sales to hard-cash sales: this switch was completed by 1971, although exceptions continued to be made for South Vietnam. "Title I" is the term still used, but now it means *hard-currency sales, the only kind available.* Title IV has ceased to exist. The changeover to dollar payments was necessary and logical, first because the US balance of payments showed a deficit owing to the Vietnam war; second because PL 480 had indeed resulted in developing commercial export markets and disposal of surplus was no longer a concern since the food was being *bought.* During the first Food for Peace decade, "it was almost as though the needy nations were doing us a favor by letting us give away or sell under concessional arrangements our unwanted farm surpluses," as Senator McGovern put it. Indeed, during this period, fully a quarter of all US agricultural exports transited through the PL 480 channel. Still, the program was quietly and gradually fulfilling one of its major aims—that of building up future commercial markets. By fiscal year 1974 (the last for which the Annual Report of PL 480 is available at this writing) the proportion of food aid to total agricultural exports had dwindled to only 3 per cent.

Make no mistake: the question of commercial agricultural exports is of crucial importance to the well-being—even the survival—of the United States. In March 1973, the business magazine *Forbes* asked rhetorically, "Can Agriculture Save the Dollar?" It recognized that "The U.S. has lost, probably forever, its edge over Western Europe and Japan in manufacturing efficiency and technology. At the same time it is burning imported oil at an ever-mounting rate." The previous year had been a commercial disaster—a trade deficit of $6.8 billion was inscribed on the national ledger and 1973 was not looking much better. *Forbes* gloomily forecasted that "under not overly pessimistic projections" and if this state of affairs continued, "by 1980 . . . this would imply a potential trade deficit of $20 billion and international bankruptcy for the U.S." Graphs of the US balance of payments show that the export-import balance for *manufactured goods* has been in the red since 1971—well before the oil-price hike.

The brighter side of the coin is that *agricultural exports* have for many years been consistently in the black. In 1972 they were not able totally to offset the unfavorable trade balance, even though their total value had been over $9.4 billion. But in 1973, farm produce exports came triumphantly to the rescue by nearly doubling to more than *$17.6 billion*—and gave the US a commercial surplus of $10 billion. Simple subtraction shows that without the spectacular showing of US agriculture, the commercial deficit would have been even worse in 1973 than in 1972—about $7 and a half billion. By 1974 the $21 billion level was reached and the USDA now feels the sky's the limit.

So the vital role of Food for Peace in its professed aim of developing commercial markets is definitely not to be sneered at. We will look at its other implications (including the military ones) after examining in detail its role in paving the way for American commercial exports of food products abroad. [Unless otherwise noted, all the following quotes and figures come from one or another of the. official Annual Reports on PL 480 transmitted by the President to the Congress between 1966 and 1974. Emphasis is mine.

By 1966 it was already evident that

... balance of payments benefits have resulted from PL 480 operations. The great expansion in commercial sales of US farm products has resulted in an average annual balance of payments saving of $1.5 billion since the program began. This increase in commercial sales is attributable in significant part to increased familiarity with our products through the concessional sales *and donations programs ... the economic development built into* food aid programs measurably improves US export sales opportunities.

Charity indeed begins at home. Any 10 per cent increase of per capita income in a country receiving food aid is estimated to result in 21 per cent more sales of US farm products. "In this way a number of countries have moved from 'aid' to 'trade.' Japan, Italy and Spain are classic examples." Japan is not only classic, it is positively breathtaking—one of the best investments Food for Peace ever made. From the beginning of the program in 1954, Japan got not quite $400 million worth of food aid, but by 1974 had *bought* over $17 *billion* worth of food. Its purchases of food imports alone are now worth over $3 billion a year to the US.

How, practically, does one develop commercial markets? Whenever possible, one works through the children participating in charitable feeding programs: "Japanese school children who learned to like American milk and bread in US-sponsored school lunch programs have since helped to make Japan our best dollar purchaser for farm products," said Senator McGovern in 1964. He feels those happy days are not over:

The great food markets of the future are the very areas where vast numbers of people are learning through Food for Peace to eat American produce. The people we assist today will become our customers tomorrow ... An enormous market for American produce of all kinds will come into being if India can achieve even half the productivity of Canada [a very good US customer].

The 1966 Report echoes McGovern: "This food aid has improved the diets of more than forty million of the world's school children ... *and built bigger cash markets* for American farm products ...

'Over the past twelve years these rising commercial sales have brought tangible returns to the American farmer and business-man.'''

But one doesn't just sit around waiting for these children to grow up, for the effects of food donations to take hold in market terms, or for people to have more cash to spend on food in the UDCs. There are other concerted strategies for encouraging consumption of US food, and these are largely carried out through the skilful use of "counterpart funds," the cash receipts generated by the sale of food-aid shipments. Although there have been no contracts for aid in local currency signed since 1971, there is still enough money coming in from previous loans to keep these programs active.

Promotional activities are part of the strategy. Food for Peace cooperates on a full-time or part-time basis with nearly seventy private US agricultural producer or exporting groups ranging from the California Prune Growers to the Poultry and Egg Institute—but the most important among them are the producers of food and feedgrains. All these groups cooperate with Food for Peace in sponsoring trade fairs, educational efforts and promotions. By 1973, the cumulative budget—about half of it paid for by counterpart funds—for promotion was $320 million. The Reports describe how "private trade organizations, in cooperation with the Foreign Agricultural Service, maintain 39 permanently staffed offices in 24 key countries and carry out promotional programs in more than 75 foreign markets." Point-of-sale promotions paid for by PL 480 are pictured in the Reports: there are Arabs in flowing robes and keffiehs gathered round an exhibit of US-manufactured food and Japanese in a Tokyo department store gaping at a mountain of Libby's canned fruits. Some of these promotions have brought in as much as $3 million in on-the-spot sales. A computerized system has been set up through which foreign inquiries about US food products can be instantly matched with US suppliers. But the big winners of PL 480 have been the major exporters of feedgrains.

As early as 1966, feedgrains were the biggest single dollar-earner for the US abroad and "the US Feedgrains Council assisted this development through continued education programs to inform trade and farm groups in all principle markets about proper [!] livestock feeding and uses of American corn, grain sorghums, oats, barley and alfalfa in livestock feeds." "The

Soybean Council of America and the American Soybean Association helped stimulate export gains resulting in a multi-million dollar market for soybeans and soybean products. The market in Spain more than doubled with the aid of continued meal and oil promotions." By 1970, PL 480 had helped soybean exporters to top all previous records:

> Substantially increased volume shipments of beans and meal to countries striving to expand their own livestock feeding industries accounted for the bulk of the $359 million gain over the previous year. These results clearly illustrate both the effectiveness of lower 1969-70 prices and the tremendous potential world demand for US soybeans and products at competitive prices.

Three years later, so many countries were hooked on US soybeans that, as we saw in Chapter 6 on "Planned Scarcity," they had no alternative but to go on buying when prices sextupled—there was no longer any need for "competitive prices." Because feedgrains earn big money and because soybean processing is a US monopoly, PL 480 has encouraged feeding high-quality protein to animals rather than to people abroad through its promotional programs. "In Iran, these projects [poultry and beef production] will expand Iran's commercial import market for US feedgrains, soybean meal and other supplemental feeds as well as non-agricultural supplies and equipment." Four joint ventures between US agribusinesses and Korean interests have been directly financed from proceeds of Food for Peace.

> The four Korean private trade agreements, all of which were in various stages of implementation in 1969, are examples of the use of this program authority to open up and develop markets for US agricultural commodities and at the same time assist in the private enterprise sector of economic development of the importing country. Under the agreement with Purina-Korea, Korea Livestock Development Corporation, Nambang and Berger Corp. and Korea-Cargill Co., US firms with extensive experience in livestock and livestock feedgrain production and marketing have invested in and are providing technical services to their Korean partners. The Korean firms will use the funds generated from sales of PL 480 commodities . . . to finance construction and operation of modern livestock feed mixing and livestock and poultry production and processing facilities. As these facilities become fully operational they will substantially expand the market for feedgrain and other feed ingredients.

And give Ralston Purina and Cargill new outlets and plant capacity virtually without charge! By 1972, these joint ventures were working out just as planned. The 1972 Report, although it no longer speaks of the US agribusiness participants by name, refers to the projects and declares that

. . . these firms were instrumental in accelerating the introduction of US technology and were a major factor in the rapid expansion of . . . the increase in Korea's imports of US corn, soybean meal, breeding stock and other supplies and equipment. For example, annual Korean corn imports increased from about 3,000 tons just prior to the conclusion of the first PL 480 private trade agreement in 1967 to over 450,000 tons in fiscal 1972.

The Food for Peace Reports are infrequently accommodating enough to announce in black and white exactly which US firms are being directly helped by the program, but there is no doubt whatever that aid and comfort to agribusiness is one of the major goals of PL 480. In the first place, and contrary to what might be supposed, the selling of the commodities themselves is handled by the private traders, not by the US government in contract with the government of the recipient country. Although the US government "finances the sale and export of commodities under Title I, actual sales are made by private US suppliers to foreign importers, government agencies or private trade entities." In other words, PL 480 directly finances the commissions that Cargill, Continental *et alia* make by handling Food for Peace. All the figures concerning the value of "food" sent abroad also include the shipping rates—markedly increasing these days—and the produce must be carried by American vessels whenever available.

It is safe to assume that the traders are kept better abreast of PL 480 intentions than the American farmers from whom they buy. The farmers are the last to know when the price for a given commodity may go up. The Korean example shows one way that agribusiness can get its feasibility studies done for free and assure itself of future markets with little or no cash outlay.

That, of course, is not all. PL 480 is in addition specifically authorized to make loans to US companies who want to set up abroad. The counterpart funds are used to defray all their local costs such as land and labor for factory building.

There is provision also that local currency sales proceeds be made available to (1) US firms or their branches for . . . business development and trade expansion in the foreign country or (2) either US firms or firms of that country for establishing facilities to increase markets for US agricultural products.

In 1966, the private enterprise loans were already flourishing: "A total of 397 loans have been approved for private business firms in 25 countries with a dollar equivalent of $341.3 million. These loans were made for such varied activities as the production of . . . foodstuffs in Israel and . . . animal feeds in the Sudan and Peru." Another of the few recipients of a loan mentioned by name has established a 25,000-acre ranch for "beef cattle breeding in Morocco. Controlling interest in the project is owned by King Ranch Texas." Food for Peace has also financed the construction of luxury Sheraton and Hilton Hotels in Bombay, through companies locally known as "East India Hotels" and "Metropolitan Hotels"; but still American and still luxury. Since 1971, owing to the decline of local currency funds, and direct payments for food to the US Treasury in hard currency, the local-currency loan program has been phased out. Still, the grand total in 1974 was 419 loans in 31 countries for $413 million—not bad when one considers the hard-cash savings of the MNCs.

Since the termination of soft-currency loans, a new twist has been added. Provision is now made for private corporations to sell PL 480 food commodities and the proceeds from these dollar sales can then be considered as loans and used to finance the companies' own projects. These new "private trade entity loans" are even more directly related to agricultural expansion than were the local-currency loans. They must, by law, "result in the expansion of sales for dollars of US agricultural commodities" or must aid future market development.

PL 480 has also been one of the major promoters of the Green Revolution. In 1966, when the "surplus" concept was dropped in favor of gradual conversion to dollar sales, the law added a certain number of provisions known as "self-help measures" to which recipient country governments were obliged to commit themselves when they contracted for PL 480 aid. These measures vary slightly from country to country, but they include in all cases "creating a favorable environment for private enterprise and investment" and "development of the agricultural chemical, farm machinery and equipment, transportation and other necessary industries," the use of "available technical know-how" as well as programs to "control population growth." The leverage that the US gains through the imposition of "self-help measures" in the contracts allows it to push HYVs and mechanization. For example, proceeds of food sales "are also being used to help finance a broad project for mechanizing agriculture in the Ivory Coast." In Indonesia, the "government will make every effort . . . to encourage farmers to use optimum quantities of fertilizers, pesticides and HYVs of seed" through a guaranteed price for rice. (Recall what Ingrid Palmer says this imposition has done to the diets of the Javanese, who have attained a "new world record of protein deficiency.") "Ghana has liberalized import licenses for agricultural equipment and machinery." In India, a state corporation had held some control over the distribution of agricultural inputs, but in "1970–71, several private firms were given permission to compete." In Brazil, fertilizer consumption went up a third in three years and in 1970 "the market for agricultural tractors reached 14,000 units, an increase of 3,500 over 1969. The sale of agricultural chemicals is also increasing rapidly." Etcetera, etcetera.

Every country with a food-aid contract must submit a twice-yearly report describing how well it is progressing in the implementation of the imposed "self-help measures." The 1967 PL 480 Report notes with pride that in India fertilizer consumption has tripled in two years and that "India has sought to . . . increase the attractiveness of private investment in fertilizer, particularly from overseas. Earlier restrictions on investment, pricing and distribution, which had been deterrents, have been eased." In all aided countries, the Reports say, "strong emphasis has been placed on improving conditions for foreign private agribusiness investment." Each time a government has displayed a deplorable tendency to favor state-organized agriculture, PL 480 has put it back on the right track. As early as 1964, Senator McGovern described how "an interesting by-product of our food shipments to Poland and Yugoslavia is that both countries have discarded the Communist technique of trying to raise farm products through government collectives." He credits food aid with strengthening their independent stance towards the Soviet Union. Food for Peace much later notes that "an encouraging trend in Ghana is the government emphasis on private enterprise in agriculture. Ghana has phased out some of its state farms and is encouraging private farming, both large and small."

Food for Peace counterpart funds also finance research in the recipient countries. Most of these research contracts are held by scientific institutions in Israel, Poland, Yugoslavia, India, Tunisia and Pakistan. This research can hardly be qualified as disinterested, since no bones are made in the Reports about its direct applicability to problems in the United States. There are of course "awards of grants . . . for commodity research aimed at expanded markets for US farm crops"—this is in keeping with the basic aim of the Law, as are the purely market research grants. One example is the discovery of a soybean variety particularly suited to the Oriental taste for *miso,* a traditional food resembling cheese. These beans are now grown in the US and "shipped to Japan, where 6 million bushels of beans are used annually for *miso* manufacture." Many other study programs relate to development of plant varieties resistant to diseases prevalent in America. A research breakthrough on cotton made in Egypt has been useful in the Southern United States; other programs have resulted in "supplemental documentation of value to US companies in securing registration of new pesticides for use in the US and other countries." The high priority placed on family planning in UDCs by the US is proved by an especially repugnant example of research financed by PL 480. In Yugoslavia, "major studies" were carried out on the "relative safety of oral contraceptives" and of abortion techniques. The goal of the latter was to discover whether there were fewer complications with the curettage or with the suction method. One assumes that the "unsafe" oral contraceptives used on Yugoslav women guinea pigs were thrown out before being tried on US women. Many other scientific programs are carried out through the spending of counterpart funds: they include translation of scientific works into English, teacher exchange programs, bilingual education and the like.

Perhaps the most startling use of counterpart funds is "common defense," a euphemism for military expenditure in the country receiving food aid. Senator Proxmire was furious when he learned of this, but he should have known better. It has been a feature of PL 480 since the beginning. By 1974, over $2.2 billion in local currencies had been devoted to military and to police uses ("internal security" is specifically provided for). However, a 1973 amendment to the Foreign Assistance Act prohibits future use of these funds for military spending unless specifically authorized by Congress. "Common defense" spending of counterpart funds provides a handy guide to US political priorities. In 1966, Korea was the front-runner, but even then Vietnam was a close second, followed by "China" (i.e., Taiwan), Turkey and Pakistan, with lesser sums spent in Greece, Iran, Indonesia, Japan, the Philippines and Spain. Barter agreements (Title III, now defunct) in 1967 provided for "the needs of military installations in Belgium, Germany, Italy, Turkey, the United Kingdom, Japan, Thailand, Vietnam and the Philippines." By 1970, Vietnam was at the top of the common defense list, soon joined by Cambodia. The twenty-year cumulative totals (1954–74) show that Vietnam and Korea between them accounted for more than three quarters of all the military uses of PL 480.

It is next to impossible, and an academic distinction anyway, to separate the economic and the political aspects of Food for Peace. What is important to understand is that the local-currency counterpart funds accumulated by the US in almost all the aided countries *far surpass the budget at the disposal of the country's own Ministry of Agriculture.* India has been the largest recipient of both Title I and Title II aid. She has also been the "beneficiary" of half the total loans to the private sector. It is thus not surprising that India's agricultural policy has been largely determined by US foundations, universities, corporations and by the US government.* An Indian scholar has, furthermore, presented a detailed and convincing argument that in his country PL 480 shipments have been directly responsible for higher food prices: "It is most unfortunate that this undermining of price stability should have occurred under the benign auspices of the Food for Peace program . . . The inflation generated by PL 480 . . . [has caused] incomes to be shifted from the pockets of the poor to feed the affluence of the few." Professor Shenoy sees such inflation as directly responsible for any number of violent urban and rural disturbances and concludes, "To persist in PL 480 deficit financing in such an explosive background would be to feed these forces of social and political instabilities." He also argues, as many others have done, that food aid has discouraged local production aimed at self-sufficiency.

Title II donations also illustrate major US foreign-policy aims. Only "friendly countries" may receive food aid at all, and in 1966, specific provision was made to exclude from this category any nation permitting trade (or even transit of trade) with North Vietnam or Cuba. This same year also saw an amendment providing for "termination of [food] programs in countries

*As of the end of fiscal year 1974, PL 480 counterpart funds for use in India amounted to nearly $6 billion.

where damage or destruction by mob action of US property" has occurred, and where the country concerned has not taken firm enough steps to prevent same—or to pay the damages.

Title II aid is dispensed in three ways: through voluntary agencies like CARE or Catholic or Lutheran Relief; through government-to-government donations, and through the FAO World Food Program. Over 60 per cent is channelled through private charitable organizations; about 20 per cent goes directly to foreign governments (which are free either to *sell* or to distribute the food locally) and about 16 percent goes through the UN/FAO. (Exact figures depend on the year.) Funds spent by the UN World Food Program appear to have the fewest political strings attached; the voluntary agencies have shown themselves much more likely to follow the political lead of the US government; choices of aid-worthy foreign governments obviously reflect US political priorities. At no time do the Food for Peace reports simply come out and say, "This year so-and-so got the most, followed by *x*, *y* and *z*." Statistics for Title II largely concern "number of recipients"—but with no indication whatever of duration. How often were 19 million people in India or 588,000 in Malawi fed? Once? For six weeks? All year? More useful information is to be found in the total cost of each country's program. Between 1972-3, the *overall* donations budget was cut by 28 per cent, so most recipients suffered cuts in free food aid. There were a few countries, however, which received more aid that year, some in the Sahel among them—but they started from very low levels, and none got more than $2½ million—while Morocco and Tunisia got twice and four times that much respectively. India's donation food budget was cut by half in 1973, Bangladesh's free food declined by about $10 million worth, while Pakistan's and Korea's stayed the same, Vietnam's increased, that of Laos doubled and that of the Philippines was three and a half times as great. America has been much criticized for cutting off food aid to Chile during the Popular Unity period (while Chile's commercial imports of food from the US went up) but in the light of across-the-board cuts, this action really concerns many countries besides Chile. The whole donations program gets very short shrift: in 1973, all donations amounted to $290 million, down from $406 million the previous year.

All-time winners in the food-gift sweepstakes over the 1954–74 history of PL 480 are the following top ten, in descending order:

India, Korea, Brazil, Morocco, Yugoslavia, South Vietnam, Egypt, Tunisia, Pakistan and the Philippines. In fiscal 1974, US political preferences were again reflected in food aid since the top recipients of PL 480 (Titles I and II) were Vietnam, Cambodia, India, Pakistan, Israel, Morocco, Bangladesh and the Philippines. The first two absorbed nearly half of all loans and gifts. Vietnam alone got over five times as much as all Latin America put together; Cambodia $40 million more than the whole of Africa. The other countries that follow them on this list, along with virtually every other country in the world, *all actually paid out at least three times as much for US commercial agricultural exports in 1974 as they received from PL 480.* New Title I programs were started in Egypt, Syria and Chile.

Naturally, dollar credit sales also reflect political concerns. Cambodia, for example, got very little free food, but its contracted purchases were viewed by the US, according to the 1973 report, "not merely in terms of economic stability, but in terms of the survival of the government." Perhaps the best proof of all that food aid is only incidentally humanitarian and related to real hunger comes from the sequels of the Indochina War. Millions of tons of Food for Peace were poured into Cambodia, Laos and especially Vietnam; the US created refugees through bombing and then set up food programs for them; it introduced any number of "self-help measures" and made exceptions for repayment terms—yet as soon as these countries became independent, the US cut off all aid and is even reported to have diverted in mid-ocean sorely needed food and fertilizer shipments. America left Indochina with farmland full of mines and thousands of hectares devastated by defoliation from which it will take years to recover. These countries will have—and they admit it—a serious food problem until the next harvests come in. Presumably the people are more or less the same Vietnamese, Cambodians and Laotians as the previous year; but the US has lost all interest in them. As Dan Morgan of the *Washington Post* remarks, the credits for food aid "often go to countries in which the United States has a political or military interest, officials concede."

Officials sometimes concede a great deal. Earl Butz was widely quoted as saying, "Food is a weapon. It is now one of the principle tools in our negotiating kit." He was backed by no less a personage than ex-President Ford, who made headlines in September 1974 by announcing from the rostrum of the United

Nations that the OPEC countries had better watch their step, or the US would have to use food as a weapon, as he claimed they were using oil. For the United States, this would be nothing new. The French daily *Le Monde* commented that such statements do very little to gild the image of a "generous America" and that the warning itself rang hollow as far as the oil producers were concerned. This paper pointed out that in 1973 the Arab countries got only a few crumbs of the Food for Peace loaf. Tunisia and Morocco did have contributions in the millions, but all the other Arab states received only a few thousand dollars worth when they received anything at all. But Egypt, cut off for five years, is now to become a major food aid recipient as a reward for being more reasonable.

The use of food as a weapon has frequently been advocated by some of America's more prominent intellectuals. The director of graduate studies in international relations at Yale University, Professor David Rowe, suggested just such a use when furnishing "expert advice" to a Congressional Committee in 1966. His target was China. He suggested that the US buy all surplus Canadian and Australian wheat so that there would be mass starvation in China. "Mind you," he said, "I am not talking about this as a weapon against the Chinese people. It will be. But that is only incidental. The weapon will be a weapon against the government because the internal stability of that country cannot be sustained by an unfriendly government in the face of general starvation."

The idea of withholding food from the political enemy is as old as warfare and the scorched-earth policy. But the twentieth century has contributed a refinement. This is the policy known as *triage*. It comes from the French word meaning to pick or sort out, and was first used in its new sense by French doctors during the First World War when there were not enough of them to save all the wounded. They practiced *triage*, operating only on those who had a good chance for survival. This theory, born of battlefield necessity, is now being considered as applicable to whole countries where people are starving: you pick out the ones that are too far gone and shunt them to one side, reserving all your food aid for those you think may still have a chance. This proposal is now being seriously discussed by leading thinkers and respectable academics. Dr. Garrett Hardin of the University of California is speaking all over the US on what he prefers to call "lifeboat ethics"—some have to be thrown overboard or we all sink. He has been joined in his crusade by Dr. William Paddock, who was recently interviewed by *Forbes:* "Paddock's conclusion simply put: We will have to let people starve to death in societies that fail to cut their birth rates . . . Paddock sees the cruelty that is inherent in his logic, but he adds, 'There are no nice solutions.'" Dr. Jay Forrester, a computer-model specialist from MIT, has also taken up the banner, or the cudgel. He speaks of a policy of "directing aid to those countries with the greatest chance of survival, while abandoning others to famine." Moral support, so to speak, comes from the theologian Dr. Joseph Fletcher, author of *Situation Ethics.* He suggests that "any action, however 'criminal,' can be right depending on the situation." He says he "hates the idea, but cannot resist the lifeboat logic."

Such serious academics and moral leaders also have partisans in positions of power. A Mr. Denny Ellerman, who represents the National Security Council in interdepartmental US Government meetings on food aid, is quoted in an article by Dan Morgan as having said, possibly in an unguarded moment, "To give food aid to countries just because people are starving is a pretty weak reason." Mr. Ellerman, reached by telephone, confirmed the remark, but said it was a "personal opinion." Personal or not, the opinion is becoming dangerously widespread.*

The CIA looks at the food weapon from a slightly different angle. In August 1974 it published a secret report (everyone prepared for the World Food Conference in his own way) which concluded that grain shortages were likely to increase in the near future, and that these circumstances "could give the United States a measure of power it had never had before; possibly an economic and political dominance greater than that of the immediate post-World War II years." In bad harvest years, "Washington would acquire virtual life and death power over the fate of the multitudes of the needy" . . . "Not only the poor, less-developed countries, but also the major powers would be at least partially dependent on food imports from the United States." Heady stuff! This is a far cry from Senator Hubert Humphrey's frequently quoted and rather naive remark about food in 1957:

I have heard . . . that people may become dependent on us for food. I know this is not supposed to be good news. To me that was good news,

---

*But it is not a new opinion either: "Some people are going to have to starve," said the US Secretary of Agriculture to a Congressional committee. "We're in the position of a family that owns a litter of puppies: we've got to decide which ones to drown." The Secretary of Agriculture was Clinton P. Anderson; the year, 1946.

because before people can do anything they have got to eat. And if you are looking for a way to get people to lean on you and to be dependent on you, in terms of their cooperation with you, it seems to me that food dependence would be terrific.

According to a friend of mine who confronted Humphrey with this remark at the World Food Conference, he is now ashamed of it. "That was a long time ago," he replied, and hurried off. This did not prevent him from saying at the Munich Soybean Conference that "Food is a new form of power . . . Food is an extra dimension of our diplomacy." To a greater or lesser degree, US politicians are in favor of brandishing the food weapon, although most will probably have the good sense not to espouse *triage* publicly.

Everything in the history of Food for Peace indicates that America is fully prepared to use agripower as it sees fit. "'We have the food, and the hell with the rest of the world,' snaps one high-level State Department official," according to *Business Week*.

This same publication lets the man who knows best describe the political clout US food can wield:

Butz gives two examples of how, as he says, "food talks." Referring to Kissinger's Mideast peacemaking efforts, Butz says: "The Russians could have blocked that agreement between Egypt and Israel when Henry was shuttling back and forth." The reason they did not, the Secretary contends, is that they needed millions of tons of US grains, and "they knew it was no time to be fooling around." Asked if there was such a link between the Mideast peace agreement and the Soviet grain deal, a high State Department official conversant with both negotiations concurs in one word: "Undoubtedly."

The Agriculture Secretary also credits much of the warm-up in US-Egyptian relations to food. When he visited Egypt a year ago, he says symbolically, "I had a little wheat in my pocket"—in fact, 200,000 tons worth $37 million. According to Butz, President Anwar Sadat told him that if he could improve Egypt's infrastructure, it would increase political stability and turn the country's mind away from war with Israel. On the spot, Butz signed an agreement that allowed Sadat to sell the wheat in Egypt and use the proceeds for such things as road construction. "That's agripower, and the tool is food," Butz says with satisfaction.

Food aid is a means for developing markets, for helping agribusiness, for gaining a stranglehold on the policy decisions of needy governments and for promoting US foreign policy and military goals. It is also intimately tied to the overall US agricultural policy. At one time it served as a channel for getting rid of surplus, but when this era ended, it forced countries whose hands were already tied by contract to switch to straight hard-currency commercial purchases. Aid represents a lower and lower proportion of total exports, as "export market development" under PL 480 has met with remarkable success. When food stocks go down, so does aid. The USDA admits this:

> Partially at least, in response to scarcer supplies and the related higher commodity prices, the US during 1973 suspended procurement of commodities for even the Title II (donation) program for several weeks. Several individual country programs were terminated and others sharply reduced. The smaller quantities of food available for long term dollar credit sales were rationed among requesting countries . . . important for security reasons.

In other words, in exchange for giving up their power of decision and a large degree of political and economic autonomy, food-aid-recipient nations cannot even be sure that the food will continue to arrive, at what time, or in what quantities.

As I said at the beginning of this chapter, I make no claim that food aid has never brought temporary relief to hungry people. But considering the political and economic strings attached, considering also the power it gives to the MNCs and the military—wouldn't it be better if the poor produced their own food, and if international, no-strings aid did the job in the meantime?

9. Et Tu. UN?

There is only one institution in the world that even approaches the concept of global government: the United Nations. It is the umbrella for a host of specialized bureaucracies: the Scientific and Cultural Organization (UNESCO), the World Health Organization (WHO), the Industrial Development Organization (UNIDO), the Development Program (UNDP), the Food and Agriculture Organization (FAO) and a great many others. Its close collaboration with the International Bank for Reconstruction and Development (the formal name for the World Bank) makes the UN system the greatest single outside influence—for better or for worse—in the UDCs today.

The word "development" is to be found either in the title or in the official ideology of all the various organizations that make up the UN family. Through the World Bank Group and its own member agencies, the UN controls outlay, geographical destination and purpose of enormous sums of development money, and it is the UN and the World Bank teams of experts who design the development packages that will be delivered to the poor countries. UN publications carry the mention that over 85 per cent of its human and financial resources are devoted to social and economic development.

In late 1973, President Robert McNamara of the World Bank announced to the annual meeting of his Board of Governors in Nairobi that agriculture, too long neglected, would henceforward become a major focus of the Bank. He has reiterated his concern in subsequent declarations. The World Food Conference, sponsored by the UN in Rome where FAO is headquartered, turned the spotlight on food as the most pressing of all the many international crises for which a solution would have to be found. It is therefore of particular interest that we attempt to understand how these organizations look upon development and how their vast resources weigh upon the balance in the Third World.

FAO has been going for thirty years now. Currently it has "more than 1,600 projects going in 127 countries and territories involving 2,100 field specialists. Another 1,200 technicians backstop the projects at FAO headquarters. Nearly 3,000 other workers in more menial jobs are also on the staff." Somewhere, somehow, over 6,000 people must be doing some good.* Seven of them, for the more senior positions, work in a little known FAO bureau called the Industry Cooperative Program (ICP).

This program was established in 1966. Let us return for just a moment to Mr. Ray Goldberg's meeting of top agribusiness brass and US government officials in May 1966. Another of the recommendations of this meeting was that "the [US] government should encourage cooperation with FAO of the UN in its effort to interest specific companies in the private sector to engage in business in the developing countries." This has apparently been done: about 25 per cent of ICP's hundred-odd members are US firms including several who were present at the Harvard meeting (Ralston Purina, Corn Products—CPC, Archer Daniels, General Mills). Nearly a third of ICP membership is made up of Common Market country agribusinesses. Four out of five of the largest UK industrial companies belong: BP, Shell, ICI and Unilever. Japan and Switzerland count seven members each and the rest come from other countries including two from Poland and one from Hungary. To belong to ICP, all companies pay an annual fee of $5,000 into a trust fund administered by FAO to support the program's activities.

ICP's stated objective is to "demonstrate that far-sighted and responsible business contributes to social and economic development by means of fostering profitable private enterprise." It is worth quoting the benefits ICP promises *in toto:*

---

*FAO's new Director General, Edouard Saouma of Lebanon, took office on 1 January 1976. Since then he has chopped staff, junked 94 publications and cancelled 155 international meetings. With the savings of nearly $20 million, he has set up an emergency fund (but also spent $26,000 to redecorate the DG's office, irreverently referred to by staff as "the throne room"). It is far too early to assess Mr. Saouma's mandate which has five years to go, but it is already evident that he will stress FAO technical cooperation in the field in UDCs over analytical work/information gathering centered in Rome. He has also called for "greater emphasis on stimulating a larger flow of investment from all sources into food and agricultural projects in the developing countries"; an orientation which could well give added prestige and influence to the Industry Cooperative Program and the Bankers Program, examined in this chapter.

For Government: A UN system program for relating industry's managerial skills, marketing know-how, technology and financial resources to agro-industrial development goals; a forum for objective dialogue between government officials and industry executives; a channel to establish new agro-industries with foreign partners.

For the UN system, especially FAO, ICP is a source of expertise in planning and implementing projects concerned with production, processing and marketing of agricultural, fisheries and forestry products; new technology; information inputs for long range development planning, and

For industry [ICP is] a unique organization for participating in the development process through the UN system with governments at the highest level; a channel for new applications of expertise and technology; [and allows] access to information and intelligence of long-term market and resource development.

We shall now attempt to decode this message.

ICP has several working groups which include dairy, fisheries and forestries industry development; farm mechanization, meat development (this usually means feedlot technology); use of plastics in agriculture; pesticides, and protein food development. These working groups sometimes act in an advisory capacity to FAO as a whole. In 1974 much of the groups' energies were devoted to preparing for the World Food Conference.

Since its inception, one of ICP's chief activities has been to sponsor missions to UDCs, including Pakistan, Ethiopia, Dahomey, Cameroon, Sri Lanka, Colombia, Venezuela, Brazil and Liberia. The mission teams are made up of industry representatives who spend a week or two in the concerned country, meeting with government officials and members of the local financial community, and visiting sites which are, or could be, involved in agricultural production. The team, upon its return, prepares a white paper on its findings and provides a summary of business possibilities and priorities, specific possibilities for agro-industrial investment, and "general factors influencing investment," i.e., government policy towards foreign capital.

One major mission of recent years was the April 1973 one exploring Brazilian Amazonia. If Amazonia were a country, it would be the ninth largest in the world, and it is also, as the mission report put it, "the world's test case for humid tropics area development." Mission members, including executives of the UK sugar firm Tate & Lyle, Liebig and an IBEC subsidiary, examined the agro-industrial possibilities of livestock raising (*the* top priority, government officials told them); of such crops as sugar cane, oil palms and tropical fruits, as well as the potential of forestry and fisheries industries. Needless to say, these areas were inspected with an eye to their present and future export capabilities, which is entirely in keeping with Brazilian government policy. The report tells us that the mission "frequently asked officials and entrepreneurs at all levels, 'Why invest in the Amazon?'" Among the several answers invariably figured, "Because it is profitable." The mission was not wholly convinced of the present economic value of the tropical forest and felt that the virtually uncharted, virgin state of the territory might "confuse if not deter some investors." However, the long-range opportunities for profitable enterprise more than offset such disadvantages: the report points out that

... the world's fifth largest nation has committed itself to a huge, costly, long-term effort to develop the largest underdeveloped area in the world. This means the geo-political advantages of the region will, we trust, be translated into operating and marketing realities, possibly faster than in any other major developing area.

The members saw their initial visit as a starting point for permanent cooperation between ICP companies and the government and promised that once the report had been circulated among them there would be "an active follow-up campaign."

In early 1974, another, more specialized mission set out to explore the possibilities of meat development in Ethiopia. It found that sanitary conditions, both of animals and of processing facilities, left something to be desired, but if this situation could be corrected, prospects for increasing beef exports should improve. The mission pointed to the success of feedlot operations like ELIDCO (30 per cent American, 30 per cent West German) already underway as "an ideal model which could be followed." The mission's essential concern appeared, however, to be with feeding DC animals: the possibilities for pet-food "raw materials" and manufacture are also good (executives of the UK Pet Foods Mars Co. and of Spillers dog foods were mission members) although up to now "the scattered nature of the product has hindered the Pet Food Industry" (i.e., cattle are raised over a wide area) and there is "still a requirement for further knowledge on what improvements can be made with collecting arrangements." At the time of this ICP mission, at least 100,000 Ethiopians were about to die of starvation or had just finished doing so.

The year 1974 witnessed a curtailment of missions as ICP

devoted all its attention to "two major international developments: the world food situation and the growing debate on the
role of the multinational corporation . . . [which] brought sharper
focus to ICP's work in 1974 . . .International agro-industry was
involved in both issues through ICP [ICP *Annual Report*]."

In 1973, the UN suddenly became aware of the existence of the
Multinational Corporation and appointed a Group of Eminent
Persons to study the question. Eminents included Senator Javits,
Sicco Mansholt, presidents of corporations, a former Governor of
the Bank of India, a Russian specialist in American studies, etc.
As reported in *Business Week*, the "issue [was] whether a set of
institutions and devices can be worked out that will guide the
multinational corporations' exercise of power, and introduce
some form of accountability to the international community."
The outcome of the Eminents' report was a very watered-down
confrontation of this issue. The Economic and Social Council of
the UN (ECOSOC) decided, on the advice of the Eminents, to
establish an "advisory body to assist it in dealing with the issue of
transnational corporations" which could hold hearings and
"exchanges of views," "develop a comprehensive information
system on the activities of the transnational corporations and
[disseminate] such information to governments." This advisory
body could also undertake "work which may assist the ECOSOC
in evolving a set of recommendations which, taken together,
would represent the basis for a code of conduct dealing with
transnational corporations." This is the most daring part of the
resolution and it would be hard to hedge one's language more
thoroughly.

Meanwhile, back at ICP, the corporations are *already* inside the
UN system. For the first time in history, industry representatives
participated in an official UN Conference (World Food), not as
observers (the status given to *all* other non-governmental organizations) but as delegates (status given to official international
organizations and to governments). ICP was very proud of this
achievement, although it notes that "industry had never before
been given an official role in a major UN Conference, and
growing international criticism of the multinational corporations made the situation even more sensitive." Sensitive or not,
"ICP was accorded official status in all World Food Conference
Committees"—a privilege no one else had except governments—
"and industry participants were able to make interventions on a

number of resolutions." In its annual report, ICP misprints (?) the number of these agro-industrial leaders with delegate status as thirty-nine. Actually there were sixty-nine, plus three from the fertilizer industry which is not represented in ICP but in FAO proper. We may note with a certain curiosity that the names of these industry delegates appearing in the provisional delegates list published at the beginning of the conference had mysteriously disappeared from the definitive list published a few days later. They were nevertheless the *largest delegation at the conference* (beating even the USA) where "several resolutions were specifically supported by industry."

Agribusiness arrived neither cold nor empty-handed in Rome. Its participation in the World Food Conference had been carefully prepared at a meeting two months previously in Toronto, where not only ICP members but a total of 180 agro-industry leaders met to hear papers on major questions and to formulate specific proposals which were circulated before the conference to "all member governments of FAO, and . . . to all FAO Country Representatives in developing nations for discussion with government officials" as well as to media people, university seminars and non-governmental organizations. ICP fairly gloats that "as a result, Industry's views were known to a number of key delegations well before the Conference."

Proposals formulated at the Toronto meeting for "immediate action" include "organizing industry advisory assistance to government agricultural planning and project identification efforts" and the group also hopes to "establish appropriate government fiscal and price policies, including especially those providing incentives for the small-scale producer and those encouraging foreign investment" (one might think this would be a task for governments themselves). On the whole, proposals for immediate and longer-term action on the part of agribusiness stress the new trend away from land ownership or outright concessions and towards the control of *activities*, not property. Thus one finds that many of the proposals concern management and technical expertise for bringing plants up to full production capacity, research, and the "effective use of farm mechanization," coordination of national stockholding policies, expansion of trade and the "integrated use of inputs in agricultural production," meaning a Green Revolution type of approach.

One of the most interesting-sounding papers presented at

Toronto was titled "Utilizing international agribusiness resources in developing countries where conventional methods of improvement are *not permitted* or impractical" [my emphasis] presented by the President of Ralston Purina, who ought to know. In response to a request for this paper, the RP President, Mr. Cornelsen, replied, "the data we could send you which I feel you might find intriguing and helpful is privileged information due to it being part of a long on-going dialogue with FAO members" followed by a phrase of refusal [letter to the author]. All the other authors of papers presented in Toronto contacted very courteously sent the material requested, often with long letters of further explanation.

Orville Freeman's suggestions presented at this meeting are particularly innovative and show that agribusiness is adaptable to current facts of economic life. He proposes a system of "triangularity," involving UDCs' land and labor, agribusiness technology and management expertise, and OPEC-country money. This, he feels, would be a profitable solution for everyone, for it is in this connection that he tells us that "a well-run agribusiness project can bring in up to 30 per cent a year on investment." US and other companies may from now on, in certain instances, renounce equity interest entirely and content themselves with management fees and royalties (as well as with sales of inputs); while Arab capital could hardly be better invested! According to Mr. Freeman, it is too early to tell if his suggestion will be taken up, but, as an example of the uses of petro-capital, Iran is not only a host country for foreign agribusiness—it is also itself "investing in agribusiness in the Sudan, Morocco, Australia and New Zealand" according to *Business Week*. The triangularity approach places emphasis on "satellite farms to help channel industry's resources to the smaller farmer and provide adequate market outlets for his products."

ICP also held a follow-up meeting to the World Food Conference to assess the outlook for the future. Here it was explained that the FAO Bankers Program "has been growing steadily and has increased the flow of financing to agricultural projects including several that could be models for the type of approach proposed by Mr. Freeman." Private banks and agro-industry are both thus happily integrated into the structures of the UN: "If ICP can identify a project, the Bankers Program can finance it," said a spokesman for the latter. ICP country missions are geared to just such project identification.

There is no doubt that the UN system as a whole is increasingly calling on private industry and private banking for solving development problems. FAO is, however, so far as I know, unique in its integration of both multinational industry and commercial banks into its official structures. Certainly ICP itself is in a touchy position, and does not want to be seen as "neo-colonialist" or as fostering the interests of the transnational corporations with whom it works. ICP bends over backwards to avoid this, declaring, "We bring in a multinational company only when the project is beyond a country's technical capacity . . . Clearly, our duty is to member nations of the UN system, to FAO and to the other UN organizations." And ICP never tires of stressing that it works for the development of countries, not for the profits of corporations.

Because I hoped to learn more about how the Industry Cooperative Program actually works than is possible through documents, I spent a few days in Rome at FAO talking to both officials and critics of ICP and the Bankers Program. This is what I came home with.

There are some positive aspects to ICP. Its pesticides working group perhaps provides the best example. Pesticide-producing firms represented in ICP account for 90 per cent of the industry's total output. These companies are now cooperating with FAO to the extent of giving classified information on a confidential basis so that FAO will have a clearer idea of the supply–demand situation and can inform member governments of what to expect. This might have happened without ICP, but the fact remains that the Program has been the agent responsible for this useful cooperation. Some of these companies are beginning to envisage joint programs to eliminate "trips and ticks" (tripanosomiasis/ tse-tse flies) among African livestock. The other working groups do not seem to have anywhere near this level of activity. The pesticides group's record is due to dynamic leadership and this comes from industry representatives themselves, not from ICP.

The Executive Secretary of the Program, Dr. A. G. Friedrich, maintains that it is the quality of the people that makes the quality of his Program. ICP refuses to accept a company representative at lower than a vice-president level and never accepts the local (Italian) manager for membership. Friedrich feels that ICP directs member companies' attention to projects that would not be undertaken otherwise because they would be considered too risky. Obviously good investment opportunities do not need ICP

which deals only in "marginal" projects. Modern MNCs understand the necessities of government planning and are willing to
cooperate with government aims, he says. ICP acts as a brokerage
service, allowing these government planners to meet top executives who would not otherwise be considering investment in this
or that country. No mission is undertaken without a specific
government request. The major objective, according to Dr.
Friedrich, is to create more agro-industrial capacity in the UDCs,
"to turn a report into a factory chimney." Industry is now much
less interested in equity participation (too likely to be nationalized) and much more so in supplying technology and expertise.
ICP would probably refuse to accept for membership a corporation with an unsavory reputation in the UDCs like United Brands
or ITT (though ITT is already present through its St. Regis Paper
subsidiary). At the close of our interview, Dr. Friedrich rather
lyrically reminded me that even corporation presidents wanted to
have a sense of contributing to the needy, that their interest in the
Third World was "not merely a question of business," and that
they, too, had to "face their own children."

I have not undertaken to poll a cross-section of ICP members'
children; nonetheless I am not entirely convinced of the benefi-
cence of this program.

Some of the people working in it are the first to admit its
limitations. The most serious of these appears to me to be that
*ICP has absolutely no structure for monitoring the results of the
contacts it facilitates, nor does it want one.* Counting entirely on
the "quality of the people involved," it does not learn in any
systematic way what, if any, contracts may have come about
through its good offices. In a conversation with one of the
Program's officers, I pulled what I thought was an example out of
a hat: What, I asked, did he feel were the relative negotiating
strengths of, say, Unilever and Dahomey (now Benin)? (Unilever's sales in 1973 amounted to about $10 billion; Dahomey's
GNP is about $300 million. Unilever spends almost three times
that in a single year on advertising alone.) It turned out that this
was an actual case—one of the few that ICP knew about. The
official replied that if a government felt diffident about a contract
it was free to consult the legal services at FAO. (I asked several
other people in FAO outside of ICP about these services. None
had ever heard of them, although they may indeed exist.) But ICP
itself never participates in actual negotiations; it imposes no

conditions on members with regard to their contacts or contracts in UDCs; nor does it expect adherence to any particular code of behavior once they are set up there. This lack of monitoring equipment, or imposed feedback from member companies, prevents ICP from pinpointing any successes it may have had—it also "absolves" it from further responsibility. Once the contact has been established it is up to the local government to fend for itself.

When asked if it wouldn't be to ICP's own advantage to know more about the results of its own work—if only to defend its projects against considerable criticism within FAO itself—officers reply that they wish it could be done but that this appears to them impossible because member companies do not want to "admit" that they need the services of a broker to identify investment opportunities and that even some governments would be reticent on this point. The next obvious question, which, because of my careful upbringing, I did not ask, is "If you can't even trust a multinational to report back to you on a service rendered, how can you possibly trust it to put the interest of a UDC above its own?" Certainly the governments involved have no reason not to admit to using ICP's services, if such they are— they officially asked for the missions in the first place.

The only way to get around the monitoring, follow-up problem would be to have a more integrated approach to industry participation, rather than an individual company approach. ICP recognizes that all its efforts to date can only have resulted in one-shot affairs—a packaging plant here, a vegetable-processing factory there. They would like to get groups of members organized to do integrated work in certain countries, but this hasn't happened yet. The only project of this nature currently under discussion—at least that I was told about—is for dairy development in Pakistan, where a group of ICP member companies would take care of every aspect—from pasture improvement, to breeding stock, to feedlot processing and right on through to the baby's bottle. ICP feels that governments would be better off dealing with a consortium of companies and then it, ICP, would also know what was going on. The latter is doubtless true, but I can hardly say I agree with the first proposition. With an "integrated approach," whole industrial sectors could pass from the control of the national government into the hands of MNCs. The technology package would come complete from start to finish and tied with red ribbons. If a single MNC is a tough customer, a consortium would be worse.

There is evidence that some companies are not getting exactly what they bargained for when they joined. I asked, in essence, "What's in it for the members, besides possible contract opportunities?" Mostly they want information on commercial prospects in the UDCs. They tend to use feasibility studies prepared by various UN agencies just the way they use information disseminated by ICP. But requests for specific information are not always honored—for example one from Del Monte. "If we had provided them with what they wanted, it would have taken twenty people three weeks to do it." So what do you expect for $5,000? Other companies find an 'opportunity to push their products with governments through ICP-sponsored regional seminars: such seminars concerning pesticides have been held in Costa Rica, Brazil, Thailand and Kenya.

ICP has no policy on food crops versus cash crops—a great many of its members could, by the very nature of their business, be interested *only* in cash crops, in livestock feeding or in food for export. Here again, the Program says, "We do not intervene, but follow the policy of the government concerned." On the whole, there is a good deal of starry-eyed confidence in ICP not only that government policy is always "good" and will prevail, but also that "the attitude of industry is changing." ICP believes it can promote such "change," while not actually insisting upon any particular standards. The Program points to the Booker-McConnell sugar project (Mumias) in Kenya as a model. So do I. But it cannot cite any other similar ventures—or at least did not do so when I visited. The Chairman of Booker McConnell, Sir George Bishop, has now become President of ICP as well. Perhaps he will attempt to encourage the "fade-out" business approach in the UDCs with his fellow-members.

Whatever Sir George's Presidency of ICP may bring, so long as firms like Unilever, Nestles, Ralston Purina, General Foods *et al.* continue to appear on its roster, there seems to me little hope that it can contribute in a meaningful way to the well-being of small farmers—although it may help in a marginal way the balance sheets of its 100-odd members and some of its working groups may enhance FAO efforts in certain areas.

Is the Industry Cooperative Program really necessary? It was the brainchild of former FAO Director-General B. R. Sen of

India, who wanted closer links between the developed countries and the UDCs and who thought that industry could provide those links. The first Executive Secretary of ICP was a retired millionaire Swedish industrialist who worked for $1 a year. But another department already exists in FAO that ought to be able to provide necessary services to UDCs in search of access to industry. This is the Agricultural Services Division (ASD) that employs specialists in industry and technology covering all the areas of farm production (fruits and vegetables, fibers, dairy products, fats and oils, etc.). The job of these people is to visit, at government request, particular areas in order to formulate projects; to recommend specific management and technological services that will be necessary to carry them out; and to follow up on how these are procured and utilized. ASD is also concerned with technology training programs in FAO member nations. In essence, it is a feasibility-study service aimed at promoting the development of indigenous agro-industries in the UDCs in which no private corporation is directly involved at the outset. The ASD technical staff never recommends a particular company or brand of food-processing machinery, for example, but furnishes specifications to the UN agency that is helping fund the project (FAO, UNDP, etc.). It is then up to their purchasing departments to ask for bids from companies able to supply the equipment. I was given the example of palm-oil processing in Nigeria: there are only two companies in the world that can supply the necessary machinery. If one of them were to serve as a UN consultant on this project, that company would be barred automatically from bidding on the actual contract. Obviously, there is follow-through on government-industry agreements by the UN agency doing the tendering. An ASD person I talked to said that in the 1970s money was no problem—the difficulty was identifying worthwhile projects. (This same viewpoint was later confirmed by the Investment Center.) The same person told me it was his personal opinion that MNCs can have "a tremendous [favorable] impact, even if some of them are bastards." A lot, he thinks, depends on the company. He said Del Monte had had several commercial failures abroad, and this was in itself enough to prove it was a "terrible company." It pays foreign nationals half what is paid to Americans in similar positions; while for a company like CPC (ex-Corn Products) "a manager is a manager" no matter what color he is.

It's none of my business to gauge how much love may or may

not be lost between ICP and ASD—the latter told me it had "very good relations with ICP" and that often it tried to identify projects "that would appeal to members of ICP." On the other hand, it was pointed out that ICP policy was set by its membership, who also furnish its budget; whereas the ASD budget comes from FAO member governments, its policy is set by FAO, and if there were to be a merger "it could only be through the absorption of ICP" which will "never have control over its member companies because of the way it's structured."

ICP admits as much, but says that "ASD never meets the President of a corporation" [Dr. Friedrich]. ICP places its faith in the top brass, and says ASD is not able to get the factory actually built, which ICP, or at least its members, can do. ICP also feels it provides a unique forum for corporation Presidents to meet *each other*. It definitely does not want to merge with ASD because it "would lose its freedom." For ICP, MNCs are a fact of life and it is better for everyone concerned that they be inside the UN rather than outside. The Executive Secretary points out that President Echeverria of Mexico made a vehement speech against MNCs at the World Food Conference—yet now his government has asked for an ICP mission which is currently being prepared.

Unfortunately, the overall tendency I detected in *both* these bureaus at FAO is that they are extremely *production*-oriented and seem very little concerned with *consumption*. (This of course was also the general drift of the World Food Conference and this attitude seems still to orient the general policy of FAO.) In other words, not much attention is paid to *who* will eat the food that may be produced with the help of the MNCs—rich consumers? small farmers? animals? Europeans and North Americans? their pets? The important thing is that food production be increased. Both ICP and ASD support, for instance, satellite farming, and an official of ASD said, "The small farmer doesn't know how to grow for the big corporation. The fewer growers you have the better"—as if growing for corporations were an end in itself; as if the fact that the corporation might "produce" more was more important than the number of people actually benefiting from a project. ICP has as one objective the growth of food-processing industries in the UDCs themselves. Certainly one can have no quarrel with that—but here again there are no criteria as to who is to produce for the factory that is the core of the satellite system, nor who will benefit from what it produces—ICP has absolutely no control over this aspect either, for reasons already made clear.

Through the FAO, for example, Del Monte has moved into Greece—and "Del Monte had been looking for an alternative source of peaches to California for years." People in California may lose their jobs and Del Monte will doubtless run true to its usual form in Greece. ASD told me that "in Kenya, Del Monte now controls the plantations and exports of all pineapple, about 15,000 tons. Very little money comes back into Kenya." There is absolutely nothing—certainly not in the structures of ICP—to prevent the same thing happening in Greece and elsewhere, with Del Monte or with others.

* * *

There is another area in the UN system in which the private sector plays a major role and that is in the FAO Investment Center. This is quite a complicated set-up and a chart will help sort out the complex relationships. The specific role of the World Bank,

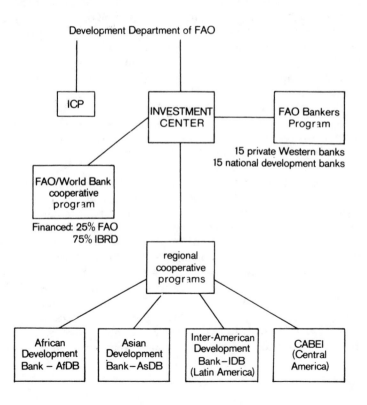

which is part of the tableau, will be discussed in more detail in the next chapter.

The FAO Investment Center is the catch-all bureau responsible for the agency's efforts to promote outside investment in agriculture, forestry, fisheries and agro-industries in UDCs. It is not a particularly weighty bureaucracy and manages to do a great deal of work with a permanent staff of ninety experts who provide the multi-disciplinary teams of agronomists, economists and financial analysts who identify projects and determine how they can be practically carried out. It works, from left to right, on the chart, in cooperative programs with the World Bank (including its subsidiaries, the International Development Association and the International Finance Corporation); and with various regional development banks. The Investment Center can call on FAO's technical staff and on private consultants for help when need be. Ideas for projects come from a number of sources: World Bank surveys, FAO or UNDP country studies, requests from governments or financial institutions in member countries, or missions carried out by the Investment Center itself. Most of the projects identified and implemented through these various institutions are long-term and multilaterally financed. They may or may not call on MNCs for technological assistance—in any event, such cases and companies are not identified by name in any of the available documents.

What we will look at here is the box on the right of the chart labelled FAO Bankers Program, because that is where private money is directly involved. There are now fifteen major Western banks enrolled in the program: they include Barclay's, National Westminster, United Dominions Trust for the UK; American Express, Bank of America, Bankers Trust, First National City and Wells Fargo for the USA; plus commercial banks from Italy, France, the Netherlands, Norway and Austria. They have been joined by several national development banks from Third World countries including Pakistan, Morocco, Gambia, Brazil, Yugoslavia (not really Third World!), Venezuela and Sierra Leone.

I was lucky enough to meet an offbeat banker on the inside who provided me with the chart and who explained that while the Bankers Program used to be called the "Private Banks Program" it now stresses the presence of national development banks for public-relations reasons. The latter make more requests for loans than they make loans themselves—so the real financial backbone of the program is unquestionably the network of private Western banks who actually supply the money for projects. The projects themselves have to be short- or medium-term—no pay-back period can exceed ten years—and the loans carry commercial interest rates. During 1972-4, this program committed over $400 million. A fifth of this went to Brazil for five projects and Egypt was also slated for five investments at a total cost of $65 million. The largest customer by far, however, is socialist Yugoslavia with $145 million in outstanding loans, mostly for livestock development on both state and private farms. Foreign banks will own 50 per cent of the equity. Altogether there are loans outstanding in sixteen UDCs, mostly for processing industries of one kind or another—fish, timber, vegetables/fruits, oil, dairy products, wine and paper. There is no way of learning—at least I did not discover it—which MNCs may be called in after the financing arrangements are completed—the Bankers Program documents occasionally say which bank is interested in which project, but not which company it may hook up with afterwards for the industrial side of the project. I did learn, however, that once a project has been "identified," financing arrangements completed and the package approved, the Bankers Program then goes to ICP which may single out four or five companies who are alerted to the opportunity. Any firm showing interest is then put in direct touch with the local government and/or the local development bank for negotiations. That Del Monte is to run the Greek fruit-processing project for which the Bankers Program found $5 million is clear only because this could be cross-checked with the International Finance Corporation's annual report in which Del Monte is named. What *is* certain is that many of the projects are geared to export production. A commercial fisheries project for Pakistan "involving the purchase of modern trawlers and related equipment, port and cold storage facilities" (with the cooperation of the private Norwegian group Norinvest) sounds like a re-run of the Kerala-Norwegian fisheries fiasco.

Other projects sound more beneficial to local interests—at least the way they are presented by the Bankers Program. For example, in the poor Nordeste area of Brazil, the *babaçu* oil palm grows wild, but its nuts could be processed for edible oil and starch and its bark for fiber. The Bankers Program is putting $50 million into an integrated system for using *babaçu* which will employ several thousand poor families for collecting the nuts. A processing plant will be the nucleus and there will be a transportation network. A Dutch company will hold 40 per cent of the equity in exchange for management and supply of technology and the Bankers Program claims that 40,000 small farmers' families will benefit from the project. Surely they can't be any worse off than before.

The senior officer I talked to in the Bankers Program assured me that none of his projects could involve moving peasants off their land—that this would have no chance of getting by the FAO approval board—and that MNCs were increasingly willing to "work through the local system." "Nothing decrees," he said, "that growing has to be done by tractors and multinationals can get perfectly acceptable produce with local farmers using local methods." When I remarked that most of the projects seemed to run to the satellite farm-for-export model rather than to food crops for the local people, he said that was quite true. But he justified this position by explaining that "certain land, for example in the Nile Delta, should be used for high-value crops for export, not for wheat for local consumption." Wheat, he said, was a "low-value crop." In Egypt, a Banker's Program project for tomato growing, including a processing plant for tomato paste, "provides a stable and secure market allowing the small farmer to change over to contract farming and to raising a crop that will be worth twice as much to him." The choice of technology intervenes not so much in the factory itself as in the method of growing. If the farmer gets the proper inputs and enough guidance, he can produce up to specifications and be well paid for it.

This officer was nice; he was also busy, so there seemed little reason to argue this point. He would, in any case, have fallen back on the standard FAO reply, which is "we only do what the government wants." But I do want to argue the point here. The first question is whether national priority should be something approaching self-sufficiency in major foodstuffs or not. A press dispatch tells us that in 1975 "booming Egyptian imports of US food probably reached a record $500 million and could hit $1 billion by 1978, the Agriculture Department has reported." Egypt also receives hefty supplementary food aid. In the seven years between 1964–71, its own wheat production went up only 4 per cent, not nearly enough to cover population growth. As I have been writing, in the space of three weeks, wheat prices have risen 17 per cent on the US futures markets and the quotations for corn and soybeans are going up as well. Egypt no more controls the world price of wheat than it does the world price for tomatoes— which can decline just as wheat can go up. If cheaper sources of supply for tomatoes are found by the big firms (and Heinz, to name only one, is growing them from Turkey to Venezuela) nothing proves that Egyptian tomato exports will continue to be competitive or that to keep them competitive farmers will not be paid less than today. Tomorrow there can be a glut of tomatoes on the international market. And up to now, the price of tomatoes has not been indexed to the price of wheat. This is the argument on the national level: If you want to be self-sufficient in the most necessary foods, you grow what *you* need in the Nile Delta, and you don't measure what it "costs" in terms of hypothetical exported tomatoes.

I am sorry to report that since my conversation with the Bankers Program officer in June 1975 the above analysis has unfortunately proved accurate. The FAO *Monthly Bulletin of Agricultural Economics and Statistics* (September 1976), in its Commodity Note on "Tomato Products: Market Trends and Outlook" explains that due to expansion of tomato growing in 1973-74, in response to higher world market prices, there occurred a sharp reversal—

. . . which led to a heavy build-up of stocks in 1975 in major producing and exporting countries. . . Although the market situation is likely to be more favorable by the end of 1976, this improvement will be mainly the result of sharp downward adjustments in processing in many countries. These reductions would follow those of 1975 which led to considerable hardship for tomato growers . . .

There are currently excess stocks of canned tomatoes, paste and juice and "market prospects . . . in 1976 are unfavorable." By mid-1976, prices paid for tomato paste had dropped to *less than half* the 1974 price. So much for my banker's "stable and secure market," supposedly so beneficial to small farmers.

As for the peasant who grows these tomatoes to specifications laid down by the food firm, he becomes a sort of "piece-worker" on the agricultural assembly line, getting his inputs, being told when to plant, when to fertilize and when to harvest. I don't know what the contracts for these Egyptian farmers look like, but I have a copy of one used by Campbells in New Jersey, in which the price paid the farmer for "Number 2" tomatoes is 40 per cent less than that paid for "Number 1"—and if the tomatoes have yellowish tops or are undersized, they are Number 2s. The company pays nothing at all for culls—that is, vegetables with more serious damage than yellow tops—but makes use of them, all the same. Any tomatoes that ripen before or after the specified delivery period are not accepted. So the small farmer is left with the problems of weather and of disease. If his crop is "sub-standard," the company has all the negotiating power, because tomatoes have the additional deplorable habit of rotting quickly—for the farmer, on the other hand, it's now or never. At least with wheat he could hang on to his crop surplus and bargain for a better price.

In the system encouraged by the FAO Bankers Program in many countries, the peasant will get his inputs from the company (or the state corporation—it doesn't matter much) which is also his only outlet. The "guaranteed fixed price" only applies to perfect specimens—so the peasant is caught between the two ends of the production-marketing chain.

A nation loses its freedom of decision when it gears its production to exports whose prices it does not control in exchange for imports of the vital foods whose prices it does not control either. A farmer loses his freedom of decision when he becomes part of a satellite or contract system that controls both inputs and marketing. But this is exactly the global design that powerful international bodies like FAO and the World Bank are pushing—and to fall back on the old saw that "this is what the government wants" is to beg the question. Is this "what the government would want" *if* the world's major lending facilities were presenting it with a viable alternative of greater benefit to the small farmer and to the self-sufficiency of the national economy as a whole? Projects are identified, financing is concocted and implementation is planned by Western interests that have only one development model to propose. Countries with other ideas do not get financing.

There is another good reason for not hitching one's wagon to private capital from the affluent nations. These banks have a stake in making sure countries are run in ways best adapted to protecting their overall interests. Before Allende came to power in Chile, five US banks (including First National City, active in the FAO Bankers Program) had supplied about $220 million yearly in short-term credit, or more than three quarters of Chile's short-term needs. One third of this money went to buy food. In 1972, in the midst of Chile's foreign exchange crisis, outstanding loans from all US banks came to just $35 million. The political conclusions one may draw from these facts are obvious.

Perhaps the most distressing trend in official thinking, and by "official" I mean those who have the money or the prestige to impose their own conceptions of development throughout the less advanced countries, is what I have called their production orientation. The trouble is that food production has become almost incidental to consumption. There is no particular relationship between the amount of food produced in the world—and hunger itself. The question, "Who will eat?" is almost never asked. Farming for export to rich countries is encouraged because half of the world's people *are not in the market system* even if they "belong" to market economies. Food production is relative to the food *industry* but it is not relative to hunger nor to the *poverty that causes this hunger.* The idea that the poor should be producing first for *themselves* and not for "the market" has not yet officially surfaced in most quarters.

There is no reason to believe that ICP and Investment Center FAO people are not sincere. There is no reason to believe either that many agro-industry leaders and private bankers would not be gratified, even proud, to see food reaching the mouths of the hungry through their offices. Many people in ICP's membership are scientists who have reached the top of their companies' pyramids through valuable research. They honestly want good technology to be put at the service of the poor and they think channels such as ICP are the most efficient means of doing so. The rub is that agribusiness and private banks cannot be *expected* to invest in anything that is not profitable—this is simply not the nature of the beast. This is where the question of the individual sincerity of industry leaders is answered: they themselves—even if they are corporation presidents with the best will in the world— are not free agents. They *must,* under the logic of their system, market produce in countries that can best pay for it; they *must* get the best possible return on investment, which means either cheap labor or less labor and more amortizable machinery; they *must* control all the facets of food production and distribution for maximum profitability from field to supermarket shelf.

And willy-nilly the UN—the UN which through ICP sends industry representatives instead of independent agronomists and economists on country missions for project identification; the UN that through the Bankers Program finances only the bankable projects—is helping them do it.

10. IBRD, or, Is the Bank Really a Developer?

Despite a decade of unprecedented increase in the GNP of developing countries, . . . nearly 800 million individuals . . . survive on incomes estimated at 30¢ a day in conditions of malnutrition, illiteracy and squalor . . . The average citizen of a developed country enjoys wealth beyond the wildest dreams of the one billion people in countries with per capita incomes under $200; his calorie intake is 40% greater . . . the mortality rate of his children is 90% lower, his life-expectancy 50% more . . .We must. . . give as much attention to promoting the inherent potential and productivity of the poor as is generally given to protecting the power of the privileged . . . Land reform is not exclusively about land. It is about the uses and abuses of power and the social structure through which it is exercised.

This is neither an idealistic churchman nor a Third World revolutionary talking: this is Robert McNamara, President of the World Bank Group, the most powerful single lending institution on earth, all of whose money is now pumped into the Third World. In its first quarter-century of operations, less than $4 billion out of a total of $25 billion went to agricultural projects, but now the Bank has decided to enter the field, so to speak, of UDC farming in a big way. It is therefore important that we understand what the Bank is, how it works and has worked in the past, and what it plans for the future.

Readers seeking a concise history of the Bank will find a good one in *The Trojan Horse* (Ramparts Press, San Francisco 1974). Here is merely an outline of its structures and operations, before we look at its policies for rural development.

International Bank for Reconstruction and Development (IBRD) proper. Made up of governments (now 127) which must previously join the Bank's sister institution, the International Monetary

205

Fund. Each country is assigned a subscription on the basis of its economic strength, but need pay in only 10 per cent of its subscription, and only 1 per cent in gold or convertible currency. The other 9 per cent, in local currency, can be loaned only with the consent of the member, and the remaining 90 per cent is "on call." Voting rights are proportional to subscriptions; the US controls 23 per cent of the votes and the US, Canada, UK, France, Germany and Japan together control a majority, although the Bank claims that its decisions are reached through "consensus." Well over half the Bank's lending resources come from *private capital* markets. Its loans are almost always long-term (ten to thirty years) currently at about 8½ per cent interest. As of the end of fiscal 1976, it had made 1301 loans on which it had never had a default. One of the reasons for this excellent repayment record is the existence of the affiliated International Development Association. In 1976, IBRD's net profit plowed back into loan funds) was $220 million. The Bank's priority sectors for cumulative loans totalling $20 billion as of 1973 were transportation ($6 billion); electric power ($5.7 billion); industry ($3.3 billion); with smaller sums going to agriculture, telecommunications, water supply, education, tourism, population control and urbanization in that order.

It is evident that the Bank's main thrust has been infrastructure loans leaning heavily on roads and electric power supply. One of the contentions of this chapter is that the Bank acts as paver of the way for private-industry investment in the UDCs.* Industry cannot operate without a certain level of infrastructure—meaning literally the underpinning of its activities—but such projects are rarely profitable in themselves. It is no wonder the Bank is so favorably regarded in private capital sectors. Not only are its loans remarkably sound financially (indeed they must be and are guaranteed by governments) but it also acts as a bridge for those same markets' subsequent investments in poor countries when industrial or other ventures—owing to the Bank's prior activities—become profitable.

Until recently, IBRD's contribution to agriculture has been minor, again concentrating on large infrastructure projects like dams. Many of these irrigation projects in UDCs have been

---

*IBRD's Articles of Agreement set as one of the institution's principal objectives "the promotion and encouragement of private investment for productive purposes." [Article I (ii)]

grandiose; they have not necessarily been valuable. As President McNamara himself notes,

There are far too many cases in which it has taken ten year or more after the dam was completed for the water actually to reach the farmers. Major irrigation schemes often pre-empt necessary resources for on-farm improvement. The drama of harnessing a major river may be more exciting than the prosaic task of getting a steady trickle of water to a parched hectare, but to millions of small holders that is what is going to make the difference between success and failure.

It is a pity that the World Bank did not foresee that this would inevitably be the case. In 1968, it awarded "probably the largest-ever single civil engineering contract . . . to a consortium of Italian and French firms, subsequently joined by German and Swiss partners." According to the Bank's periodical *Report* this billion dollar baby, the Tarbela Dam on the Indus River in Pakistan, has brought nothing but headaches. The saga of mishaps—jammed sluices, implosions and explosions, collapsed tunnels, 500,000 cubic yards of earth inadvertently swept away— is recounted in the paper's lead article. This series of disasters occurred immediately after a first attempt to fill the fifty-mile-long Tarbela reservoir. Extensive damage has had to be repaired at an additional cost of $60 million, while Pakistan has borne further heavy local-currency costs. Now the reservoir is filling up again. "Emergency plans have again been prepared. This time it is devoutly hoped they will not be needed." Seven years after con-struction began, not a drop of water had reached a single farmer. The dam's only effect on local people so far came during the initial filling of the reservoir, before all the calamities. The Bank's writer peevishly remarks that at this time "filling began on schedule, and initially went according to plan, except that for a short period, the rise of the reservoir had to be slowed to allow some of the 80,000 people who had been slow to move out of the reservoir area, to get away from the rising waters." The Bank does not seem concerned, officially or journalistically, by the fate of these 80,000 people its project has forced to leave their homes.

René Dumont reports on another Bank foray into the "pro-vision" of water to the rural poor.

In Sri Lanka, as in many other countries, the World Bank finances the harnessing of the biggest river on the island, the Mahaveli. This project is very expensive, especially in terms of foreign exchange, and it will be a long time before it brings any benefit to the country (although it will rapidly benefit the foreign construction firms building it). Yet in the Kandy district alone, I saw possibilities for at least a thousand small earth dams which would be immediately productive, with next to no outlay in foreign exchange and with much use of local labour. But the Bank, to date, has refused to finance such small irrigation works.

The Bank now says it has had a change of heart.

McNamara's leadership of the Bank since 1968 has been dynamic in the extreme. During his first five years, he doubled the Bank's loans compared to the previous five-year period—in real, not just monetary terms—raising them from $5.8 billion (1964-8) to $13.4 billion. From the *beginning* of the Bank's existence after the War until 1968, it had loaned $10½ billion—so McNamara even topped this cumulative loan total. Now he intends to do even better.

For the period of 1974-8, his pledge is to loan $22 billion to nearly 1,000 projects, an annual cumulative expansion rate of 8 per cent, representing a 40 per cent increase over the previous period and 175 per cent above the 1964-8 period. McNamara promises that 7 billion of this will go to agriculture and that an "increasing share" of this will go directly to "assisting the small farmer to become more productive." "In the next five years, we expect that about 70 per cent of our agricultural loans will contain a component for the smallholder."

International Development Association (IDA) Established in 1960, IDA is tailored to the needs of those countries whose external debt has become so crushing that they can no longer afford even the long-term, relatively moderate-cost IBRD loans. Such countries bear intolerable debt burdens, "often devoting 20 per cent or more of [national] earnings to the service of their debts." IDA has the same structure and voting procedures as the Bank. It has 116 subscribing members and its funds are periodically "replenished" by governments. The fourth replenishment went through with considerable difficulty in 1974 after McNamara had threatened his Board that "there is now a danger of the complete termination of IDA's activities next July 1 [1974]." In 1976, he reported to the same audience that progress on the fifth replenishment had been "painfully slow" and that IDA would again be in jeopardy as of June 30, 1977.

IDA also receives direct transfers of funds from IBRD. Its loans bear no interest, merely a service charge of ¾ per cent; they provide for a ten-year grace period and allow for repayment in up to forty years. In many cases, IDA loans contribute to debt service and are in fact the *only* way to insure that previous IBRD loans can be repaid. IDA gives with the right hand, while the Bank takes back with the left. Certain countries hold no Bank-proper loans at all, only IDA concessionary credits: Afghanistan, Jordan, and several Sahelian countries among them. India is by far the prime recipient of IDA credit: over $4 billion in 79 separate grants, or more than three-quarters of its total Bank group loans; Pakistan is second with over $700 million in credits, followed by Bangladesh and Indonesia both with over half a billion. Thirty per cent of IDA's credits go to agriculture—the largest proportional share—with transportation the next largest sector.

International Finance Corporation (IFC) The third and last member of the World Bank Group has as its exclusive purpose loaning to private enterprise. Its structure is the same as that of the Bank and IDA; 100 countries to date are members; the US controls 32.8 per cent of the votes, and with Britain and France controls a majority. The cumulative gross total of the Corporation's investments between 1956–75 was "$1,262 million in 249 enterprises in fifty-seven UDCs, in which other sources had concurrently invested approximately $5.131 million." "Of the cumulative total of the Corporation's investments . . . about 62 per cent has been committed in the last five years." Most of IFC's past investments have been in manufacturing; other enterprises in mining, tourism, utilities and agriculture have also received loans. IFC does not take on projects by itself, never holds equity capital of more than 25 per cent and "only rarely is IFC willing to be the largest single shareholder in an enterprise." Outside of country-member subscriptions, to which the same 10 per cent rule applies as in the Bank, the Corporation raises all its money in private capital markets; it is also authorized to receive loans from IBRD. Its most recent loans have been contracted at 9½ per cent, usually repayable in dollars. Among its stated objectives is "giving advice and counsel to less developed countries on measures that will create a climate conducive to the growth of private investment." IFC looks for private commercial banks as partners in its projects. Presidents and managing directors of some of the US's and Europe's most well-heeled investment banks sit on its International Advisory Board. A bank participating in an IFC project need not do any of the administrative work concerning loans, which IFC continues to supervise, and the private bank "often has an opportunity to obtain collateral business for itself in connection with the transaction," according to a speech called "How IFC Works with Banks" by its then President, William S. Gaud. Gaud also explained to his audience of commercial bankers that "no taxes are withheld by the host country in respect to the loan portions of our investments," and this tax break is "not affected by reason of foreign participations." Of its total investments, IFC has placed 44 per cent in Latin America, 24 per cent in Asia, 17 per cent in Europe, 10 per cent in Africa and 5 per cent in the Middle East. Countries that have received more than $50 millions in loans from IFC are Brazil, Turkey, Yugoslavia, the Philippines, Mexico, Indonesia and India in decreasing order.

Although IFC's total commitment to agribusiness is small ("food and food processing" ranks twelfth out of seventeen investment categories), it is significant that in 1974 it made three loans to private agribusiness. The largest was to the RFM corporation of the Philippines for meat and vegetable processing in which "two [unspecified] US companies are providing technical assistance" and which should produce 4,500 tons a year of processed food.

Smaller, but more interesting, is the loan to the "House of Bud" in Senegal. IFC's fellow shareholders in this project include "Bud Antle, Inc., a large US agribusiness company" (through its European subsidiary) and a "prominent Dutch agricultural engineering firm." The company's purpose is the "growing and *exporting* of vegetables . . . as favorable market conditions exist in Europe for off-season vegetables . . . the hope was that these [vegetables] could supply the European winter markets."

According to UN figures, Senegal's population is expanding at a rate of 2.2 per cent a year, but food demand is growing only at 1.2 per cent, one of the lowest figures in the world. As I have attempted to make clear, food-demand figures reflect purchasing power more than anything else, and do not mean, when low, that the population is already well fed. In the food-saturated countries, a 1.2 percent growth rate would also be extremely low—for example the upward trend for food demand in the US is 1.6 per cent a year, whereas the US population is stable. World Bank figures further tell us that Senegal is one of the few countries in the world actually to have a *negative* growth rate for the whole period of 1965-73 (-2.8%). As to the "European market," in 1974 the EEC countries "spent 225 million francs ($53 million) to 'withdraw,' from the the market, in other words to destroy, fruits and vegetables which could have caused prices to drop" [*Le Monde*]. I leave it to readers to determine whether Senegal should be more concerned with the IFC, the House of Bud and its European exports, or with the Senegalese.

The third 1974 IFC loan to agribusiness concerns a sugar plantation in Nigeria. One of its partners in this venture is the Mehta family group of India, which apparently cannot find enough profitable investments in its own country.

In at least one case, the effects of Bank/IFC lending policy to agribusiness have become tragically clear. In the late 1960s, IFC invested $9 million for sugar production in Ethiopia, in cooperation with HVA, a Dutch agribusiness firm (and Industry Cooperative Program member) heavily into sugar, palm oil, tea and similar cash crops in more than a dozen UDCs. By 1970, HVA controlled over a fifth of all the cultivated land in the Awash Valley. Smaller areas are occupied by British (a cotton company of the Mitchell Cotts Group), Israeli and Italian agribusinesses.

In 1973, Ethiopia experienced widespread famine, particularly affecting semi-nomadic tribes dependent upon animals for their livelihood. This famine is estimated to have killed about one third of the Afar tribespeople alone. Although the famine did not become public knowledge until several months after it had occurred, it has now been established that the Ethiopian government was warned that certain of its policies, particularly as concerned concessions to foreign growers, would inevitably bring about severe hunger. When this prediction came to pass, the official reasons advanced for the disaster were "drought" and "overgrazing."

Any phenomenon that wipes out, at a conservative estimate, 100,000 people deserves to be examined in more detail. People who raise animals count on just two interdependent resources: water and grass. Since at least the sixteenth century, the Afars of the Awash Valley had grazed their cattle through the eight-month dry season on the rich lowland plains inundated by the Awash during the rainy season. But these excellent pastures were also the areas most coveted by agribusiness growers and it was these lands that were awarded as concessions. Tribal custom that had designated vast pasturelands as communal property for hundreds of years was erased with a stroke of a Minister's pen; HVA and others were entitled to occupy thousands of acres; the Afars were obliged to seek new pastures and there was nothing left for them but rain-fed land, distant from the river.

The colonization of the Awash Valley created a new situation for the original inhabitants who were suddenly exposed to the vagaries of the weather. In addition, the relative overpopulation of these less fertile areas brought about overgrazing and famine for the animals, followed by a decrease in the size of herds and consequent malnutrition for the people.

It is not that there were more Afars or more animals than before—there was no population explosion and no drastic change in rainfall—merely the fact that local policy and foreign corporations, one of them aided by IFC, suddenly and brutally obliged a whole society to "make do" with land wholly unsuited to their ecological and traditional needs. These are the conditions that set the stage for famine. Those Afars who remain and who have tried to water their animals at the Awash after HVA installed its sugar mill claim that the river has been poisoned by residues and that more of their animals have died.

Local production of sugar has not even improved Ethiopia's balance of payments (equipment is all imported, capital and profits repatriation contract clauses are "liberal"); the price of sugar for Ethiopians has increased 30 per cent in ten years, while salaries have remained the same; the whole sugar operation is capital- rather than labor-intensive and the outflow of money is said to amount to seven or eight times the total salaries paid to Ethiopian workers.

Neither HVA nor the International Finance Corporation mentions any of these aspects in their annual reports. HVA notes increases in plant capacity (its land concessions have also, necessarily, increased) and that on part of its land "the cultivation of French beans and green peppers has been somewhat extended... the products were exported to the Netherlands." In its "search for diversification," HVA is also carrying out experiments in *raising cattle itself:* "The first objective of these tests was to determine whether this operation offers a sufficiently attractive margin. In view of the high prices for beef, the prospects seem quite favorable [HVA annual report, 1973]." And considering that local competition has been conveniently eliminated ... The ICP meat-development mission to Ethiopia visited the HVA center in

1974 and noted, "A feedlot is planned to cover 50,000 head per year . . . anticipated mainly maize silage," meaning that the animals will be corn-fed.

Although its efforts certainly do not always contribute to outright famine, there does not seem to be a single IFC venture in agribusiness concerned with helping to feed the local people. A 1966 loan-and-equity operation in Morocco involved cooperation with "Lukus, S.A., an established manufacturer of food products . . . to help increase exports of tomato and paprika products principally to Europe and North America."

IFC's 1975 contribution to Western agribusiness is the Hellenic Food Industries S.A. (that's Greek for Del Monte), for which IFC contributed a quarter of the capital. It is "located at Larisa, Thessaly, in an area where irrigation has been developed with World Bank assistance"—a good example of way-paving. "Local farmers will be helped to meet high-quality standards with improved seeds, nursery stock and other forms of technical assistance. The Company will produce mainly for export to Western Europe . . ." And like our friends raising tomatoes in Egypt, these farmers will be growing perishables. Good luck to them.

IFC's private investment, although it can influence commercial banks far beyond its own financial capacity to intervene, is still peanuts compared to the funds available for development to the World Bank Group as a whole. IBRD intends to loan $7 billion to agriculture in 1974-8, as compared to $3.1 billion for 1969-73 and only $872 million for 1964-8. In his 1976 address, President McNamara announced that this goal would be not only met but exceeded.

The rural development program now gets more funds than any other. What has caused this shift in priorities? McNamara, speaking to his Board of Governors in 1973 and 1974, gives several reasons. One of them is moral. For his audience, he defines the concept of "absolute poverty" as

. . . a condition of life so limited as to prevent the realization of the potential of the genes with which one is born; a condition of life so degrading as to insult human dignity—yet a condition of life so common as to be the lot of some 40 per cent—800 million individuals of the people of the developing countries. And are not we who tolerate . . . such poverty failing to fulfill the fundamental obligations accepted by civilized men since the beginning of time?

McNamara is afraid his remarks may be interpreted as those of a "zealot"; he defends himself: "You have hired me . . . to report to you the facts. These are the facts." The greatest proportion of the absolute poor live in the countryside, and this will continue to be the case until at least the year 2000. McNamara identifies these poor on the whole as "small farmers" (not until 1975 does the Bank give serious thought to the landless) and he says that "the truth is that despite all the growth of GNP [in UDCs] the increase in productivity of these small family farms in the past decade has been so small as to be virtually imperceptible." Furthermore, "The decade of rapid growth has been accompanied by greater maldistribution of income in many developing countries and the problem is most severe in the countryside." So the Bank's task will be to reach these small farmers and to attempt to bring them the benefits of growth directly.

McNamera also gives the Governors a list of nine different projects approved or in preparation for Sudan, Upper Volta, Kenya, Mali, India, Tanzania, Nigeria and Northeastern Brazil which should benefit 839,000 small farming families and 1,950,000 individuals (depending on how he tallies them) as well as an unspecified number of people in Mexico who will profit from the "most complex program with which the Bank has ever been associated" involving a total investment of $1.2 billion over a four-year period. A subsequent Bank paper makes far more grandiose claims for the number of people who will benefit from rural projects, stating that "the agricultural and rural development program of the Bank would reach a total rural population of 100 million, of whom 60 million would be in the poverty target group" if loans attain $7 billion for 1975–9 as they are now expected to do.

McNamara sees no alternative to the Bank's almost single-handed efforts to benefit the rural poor directly. The countries these people live in are caught in a double bind, a kind of noose that the rich countries draw ever more tightly around them. Their terms of trade, for one thing, are wholly unequal. Because the rich countries refuse to allow them to expand the markets for their exports, they do not have vital foreign exchange for imports, and thus their underdevelopment "tends to become self-perpetuating." Bank studies indicate that "if the affluent nations were gradually to reduce their present protectionist trade restrictions against agricultural imports from the developing world, the poorest of the poor nations could, by 1985, increase their annual export earnings by at least $4 billion," while the nations known as "middle-income developing countries" could increase theirs by a highly respectable $29 billion. The rich countries show few signs of doing anything of the kind, although there was one breakthrough in 1975.

This is the Lomé Agreement signed between forty-six European and African, Caribbean and Pacific (ACP) countries. Under the terms of the agreement, which came out of eighteen months of negotiations, the ACP countries can ship their industrial products duty free into Europe, and the same goes for their Agricultural produce if it does not compete with food already produced in Europe—which means about 85 per cent of what ACP countries grow. Even the remaining 15 per cent of their crops will meet with lower tariffs in the EEC than farm produce from, say, the US. The poorer signatory countries also have the right to use tariff protection for their own infant industries against European manufactured goods, if they so choose. The Lomé Agreement shows a good deal of foresight on the part of the EEC governments signing it—they have realized that increased trade is in everyone's interest—although Lomé may have the negative effect of encouraging poor countries to keep on producing cash rather than food crops. It also remains to be seen whether or not such trade agreements will have any effect at all on the lives of the rural poor—although they will certainly benefit the élites . . .

Another reason why the World Bank finds itself virtually alone in its concern for Third World small farmers is that the affluent nations are becoming more and more miserly as the years go by; less and less interested in helping UDCs. The seventeen richest nations in the world all belong to the Development Assistance Committee of the Organization for Economic Cooperation and Development (OECD). The United Nations has set a development assistance goal for these countries at 0.7 per cent of each one's GNP—a very modest figure. In 1976, only three of the seventeen rich countries, Sweden, the Netherlands and Norway, met this goal. The richest of the lot, the US, has almost the most dismal record of the bunch—only Japan, Switzerland, Italy and Austria give less proportionally. Moreover, American aid contributions from 1960 to 1974 have steadily *declined* (from 0.53 to 0.26 per cent of GNP) while most of the other OECD member countries are at least trying to improve their showing or keep it stationary. US performance is expected to decline still further until it reaches the all-time low of 0.21% in 1980. The latest Bank figures (1976) indicate that Denmark, France, Canada and Belgium are inching toward the UN target; while aid from the world's other two richest countries, Germany and Japan, is expected to dwindle even further.

When the political will exists, the United States is capable of far greater efforts. By way of comparison, in 1949, at the beginning of the Marshall Plan, US Official Development Assistance amounted to 2.49 per cent of GNP. Total development aid in 1975 for *all* the member countries of OECD represented 0.36 per cent of their collective GNP, or half the UN goal—and far less than what the wealthy countries could actually afford. In constant prices, and in spite of the current recession, their total GNP, according to the Bank, will "grow from $2 trillion in 1970 to approximately $3.5 trillion in 1980; an increase in output virtually beyond one's capacity to comprehend," says McNamara. The argument of problems in one's own society taking precedence over foreign development aid simply doesn't stand up to scrutiny. To reach the modest target of 0.70 per cent of GNP, all the rich countries would need to do would be to contribute "less than 2 per cent of this *additional* income by which they themselves will grow richer during the period" (up to 1980). The remaining 98 per cent of their incremental income would provide them with more than sufficient funds to meet their domestic priorities.

It is almost impossible to make the implications of such colossal selfishness come alive when one is dealing with figures in the trillions. What the numbers mean, in terms of you, me and our neighbors, is that between 1970 and 1980 every man, woman and child in the seventeen richest nations will have enjoyed a per capita increase of $900. For one billion people in the impoverished world, the increase, if we are to believe the World Bank, will have been exactly $3.

Usually, at this point in the argument, critics of development assistance say, "Let George do it," George in the present case being the Arabs. OPEC countries are supposed to be rolling in money now. The truth is that in terms of GNP, their "vast wealth," so begrudged to them by the richest countries in the world, amounts to a piddling 2.5 percent of the GNP of the OECD countries, and will not amount to more than 5 per cent of OECD GNP in 1980. Calculated in *per capita* terms, in 1973 per capita share of GNP in OPEC countries was only 20 per cent that of the OECD nations' average; by 1980, OPEC citizens will still be way behind, with only 35 per cent of GNP per capita compared to what OECD citizens will then enjoy.

As for Arab development and efforts, "[the OPEC countries] are making contributions which are larger in proportion to GNP than those of the OECD nations" and they "have already taken a number of initiatives which may lead to an increase in the flow of their development aid," according to McNamara. In 1975, he said present Arab contributions to development aid represent 3 per cent of their total GNP—more than the US gave during the heyday of the Marshall Plan and more than eight times what OECD countries are currently giving. Many of these nations are also making bilateral agreements with poor countries for delivery of oil on deferred payment terms; several are establishing their own development funds which the World Bank is helping organize and staff to accelerate their impact. Not only is OPEC's bilateral assistance far more generously accorded than that of the US, Europe or Japan—these countries are also making extra funds available to the Bank for loans. McNamara says, "The proposed Bank Group program is large. It will require net borrowing [in 1975–9] of over $13 billion. Much of that amount can, I believe, be borrowed from OPEC countries. They have been most cooperative with the Bank, and in recent months we have received commitments from them totalling $2 billion." The Bank adds that "since 1974, OPEC members have made available about $5 billion per year in loans to other developing countries . . ."

OPEC countries are growing justifiably tired of being told that they are responsible for the so-called crisis in the West, and that they are doing nothing to alleviate the misery of the Third World. The fact that they are themselves developing countries is rarely remembered.* A poll taken in February 1975 in the US showed that "an overwhelming majority of Americans are bitterly hostile to OPEC," and one would be surprised if a similar poll in Europe produced a different result. "Mr. Kissinger has succeeded in convincing his constituency that OPEC countries are selfish, greedy and irresponsible." The prevailing attitude is illustrated by this cartoon. (see next page.)

*Say "OPEC" and everyone immediately thinks "Arab." The complete list of OPEC countries is: Algeria, Ecuador, Gabon, Indonesia, Iran, Iraq, Kuwait, Libya, Nigeria, Qatar, Saudi Arabia, United Arab Emirates, Venezuela.

International Herald Tribune, September 15, 1975

'Upstairs-Downstairs in the Third World.'

OPEC public relations must be terrible, because the unvarnished truth—if they could only get it across—is that they are now giving in foreign aid, concessional oil sales, and outright gifts *at least the equivalent of the increased cost of oil to the poor countries.* Kuwait and the United Arab Emirates are giving away an incredible 8 per cent of GNP, but Saudi Arabia, Venezuela and Iran are also strong donors. Algeria is one of the poorest of the oil nations—and still giving the UN goal of 0.70 per cent of GNP.

OPEC is now responsible for at least one sixth of all foreign aid by all countries and this does not count its loans to institutions like the World Bank.

Another popular superstition (that is, when OPEC aid is even recognized) is that all their money goes to Arab countries. Not so: India, Bangladesh and Pakistan (Moslem, but not "Arab") are major recipients, although a greater proportion of aid is indeed going to Egypt, Jordan and Syria—and why not? Venezuela is concentrating on Latin America. It has also just made the largest loan the World Bank has ever received. In late 1976, the OPEC Special Fund announced another $200 million in loans, entirely interest-free, to 45 UDCs "described by the UN as those most in need" (28 in Africa, 12 in Asia, 5 in Latin America).

When Westerners accuse OPEC of practically murdering people in the Third World by increasing the price of its oil imports, they conveniently forget the fact that these prices are determined by the cost of crude oil, naturally, but also by the Western oil companies that control shipping, refining and marketing. Nor do they mention the phenomenal price hikes for food and fertilizer we have already discussed. One thing OPEC countries could do with their money, besides give it away, would be to hire a top-flight PR firm to help them outshout Kissinger and Co.

Because in reality, for Official Development Assistance, trade terms conceded to the poor countries and proportional contributions to multilateral loans, the score is OPEC-3, OECD-nothing.

* * *

Besides suffering vastly discriminatory trade terms and wholly inadequate Western development assistance, the neediest nations are also confronting a heavier and heavier debt burden. Outstanding debt of the poor countries (what they owe to bilateral or multilateral, public or private suppliers of credit) has reached an astronomical $135 billion—on which they ought to be paying interest of more than *$11 billion* a year. The amount they owe *in interest alone* is growing faster every year than their incoming hard-currency revenues (again because of unfavorable trade terms their collective trade deficit was about $37 billion in 1975— rounding out the vicious circle). For all of these reasons the Bank is increasing both IBRD loans and IDA concessionary assistance to unprecedented levels. Whatever the Bank may do, however,

GNP in the so-called "most severely affected nations," those with per capita incomes of less than $200 a year, is probably going to *decline* by 4 per cent a year during 1974–8.

To summarize, the gap between rich and poor nations will continue to grow until at least the year 2000, largely owing to the selfishness of the rich. McNamara laments that "nothing we can do is likely to prevent this. But what we can do is begin to move now to insure that absolute poverty—utter degradation—is ended." Since most of the absolute poor live in rural areas, the Bank's efforts must be directed towards these people, particularly the small farmers whose production and consequent incomes have stagnated when they have not declined. After this enormous build-up, it is something of a let-down when the Bank announces that only 20 per cent of the Bank's resources for the five-year period will go into agriculture (subsequent documents say 26 per cent*) and that there will be only a "component" for the small farmer. But heaven knows this ought to be better than nothing and warrants an examination of just how the Bank plans to go about it. Does it propose radically new strategies for rural development justified by its apocalyptic analysis of an intolerable situation, or does it suggest more of the same old unsuccessful remedies? (Any emphasis given to McNamara's remarks or Bank documents is added.)

McNamara's declarations and Bank documents are full of *implicit* criticism of the Green Revolution. The whole thrust of the Green Revolution has been to modernize the methods of the already better-off farmers to the detriment of the poor, who, unable to afford the costly inputs it requires, are being progressively pushed off their land. McNamara seems to realize this: "There is only a limited transfer of benefits from the modern to the traditional [farming] sector. Disparities in income will simply widen unless action is taken which will directly benefit the poorest." The zero growth productivity of small-scale agriculture must be improved. Elsewhere, speaking of the Bank's most-complex-ever program in Mexico, he explains that it is necessary because "although the nation has achieved over the last three decades the highest sustained growth in agricultural production in Latin America, *rural poverty appears to have worsened* in many regions throughout the country . . ." These three decades

*In 1976 "Agriculture and rural development lending accounted for about 25% of all Bank and IDA commitments." (IBRD Annual Report 1976).

correspond exactly to the application of the Green Revolution in Mexico, which has created large, productive commercial farms of the agribusiness type side by side with "worsening rural poverty" for those left out. Or, again, we learn from McNamara that India had to add an extra $500 million in hard currency to its budget in 1974 in order to import fertilizer and "India is the world's largest importer of this essential ingredient of increased agricultural production." A few paragraphs later we learn that what the "energy crisis" has added to India's outlays could have been avoided altogether! "In many countries, for example India . . . [it will be possible] to generate power using alternative sources. Petroleum-based plants can be replaced with hydro-power, geo-thermal power or with coal, lignite or nuclear-fuel plants." He does not add that the fertilizer base could also be changed—or could have been, before Westerners moved in. India's Green Revolution agricultural system has largely been based on oil. Now the Bank discovers that India could have been energy indepen-dent (although this might have been less profitable for various US firms). An even more recent Bank document tells us that "poverty is found in the highly productive irrigated areas of Asia" (where the Green Revolution holds sway) and "that the number of landless or near-landless workers is growing, especially in Asian countries" (for which we have given examples of land concentra-tion in the hands of the largest farmers and of eviction suits).

McNamara and the Bank are equally hard—and much more explicit so—on the glaring inequalities within the poor coun-tries themselves. The President of the Bank speaks of the concen-tration of land in the hands of a privileged minority; he notes that "the politically privileged among the landed élite are rarely enthusiastic over the steps necessary to advance rural develop-ment"; he knows full well that "income distribution patterns are severely skewed within developing countries"; he castigates the many purely rhetorical land reforms that have been passed in UDCs and which have "produced little redistribution of land, little improvement in the security of the tenant": He even goes so far as to suggest that the answer for the small farmer lies in "various types of communes" and says "experience shows that there is a greater chance of success if institutions provide for popular participation, local leadership and decentralization of authority."

Recognizing (at least implicitly) the pernicious effects of the

Green Revolution and the obvious obstacles to a better life for an estimated 100 million poor rural families posed by present land tenure and power structures, what does McNamara propose in order to put his Bank's stated policy of "reaching the absolute poor" into effect? Alas, more of the same.

First, he confesses to ignorance: "Neither we at the Bank, *nor anyone else*, have very clear answers on how to bring the improved technology and other inputs to over 100 million small farmers." This statement, in the first place, is not true. The Chinese, to give only one example, have brought improvement with very "clear answers" to far more than 100 million rural families. In the second place, it shows that in McNamara's thinking, the solution to the problem consists wholly in bringing "improved technology and other inputs" to still passive recipients. What is more, the only cure for underdeveloped agriculture seems to be increased intervention by developed countries: "There is ample evidence that *modern agricultural technology* is divisible and that small-scale operations need be no barrier to raising agricultural yields." It is of course the rich countries that will continue for the foreseeable future to control and produce this "modern agricultural technology." Another recent Bank document explains that

. . . in recent years, considerable progress has been made in getting the beneficiaries of agricultural investment down to the small farmer through use of commercial banks, cooperatives, input suppliers, etc. *The scope for profitable agricultural investment has also been notably expanded by the technological advances of the "green revolution"* . . . as a result the Bank has been able to increase its lending for agriculture substantially . . . [January 1974].

On the whole, Bank policy would seem to provide for a sort of technological mini Green Revolution—directed this time at the poorer sector. Meanwhile, "employment of the landless and near landless on rural public works can provide them with income to purchase food while creating productive facilities for agriculture," but there are no other plans in evidence for these millions of people.

The question of land reform presents McNamara with far more annoying contradictions, given that his realization of the magnitude of the problem is far more explicit, and his condemnation of local rural élites much stronger than that he expresses for the Green Revolution. Even so, his Bank's agricultural program for the next five years "will put primary emphasis *not on the redistribution of income and wealth*—as necessary as that may be in many of our member countries—but rather on increasing the productivity of the poor, thereby providing for a more equitable sharing of the benefits of growth." Elsewhere, McNamara has specifically admitted that possession of land in poor countries *is* wealth—but this is not to be "redistributed." How far it is possible to "increase the productivity of the poor" when the poor have almost no access to land is a question that is not faced. In fact, land reform and redistribution may not even be necessary after all, for according to a Bank *Policy Paper* (February 1975), "Small-holders can increase their incomes considerably *without land reform* (1) in densely populated areas where the tenancy ratio is low, the distribution of land is not excessively skewed and the private marketing system effectively reaches the small as well as the big farmers" (one wonders where in the Third World such idyllic conditions might prevail) and "(2) by participating in settlement schemes in areas where there are large tracts of land which can be exploited productively" (that is, by leaving their present homes).

Still, there is no doubt that IBRD has had a change of heart. For twenty-five years, it pushed development based on the trickle-down theory—from the top dogs to the underdogs—and these twenty-five years have proved that this conception has resulted in a monstrously expensive failure. The Bank is furthermore conscience-stricken that during so many years of heavy investment in roads and electricity, it gave only a tiny fraction, less than 5 per cent, to rural development; and thus to the places where most of the world's poor people live. The sheer weight of reality and of steadily deteriorating conditions in the Third World have forced the Bank's analysts—its far-flung teams of economists, financiers and sociologists—to arrive at conclusions that were news 120 years ago when an obscure scholar named Karl Marx announced them, but which are hardly original today. In the Bank's various papers, *Land Reform, Agricultural Credit* and *Rural Development*—and in McNamara's speeches—one can almost hear these anguished analysts crying out, "Great Scott, there *is* a class struggle!" "By George, poor people *are* exploited by rich ones!" In all these documents, the Bank is constantly sidling up to the only available verdict: that total social upheaval is necessary if such exploitation and poverty—the real causes of hunger—are to be eliminated; then slinking away from it again.

QUESTION: What does the world's most formidable capitalist lending institution do when confronted with the inevitability of a quasi-Marxist analysis of present reality?

ANSWER: It abandons the hoary trickle-down credo of development in favor of what it calls "new-style projects" with a "comprehensive approach." In no case does it call for social and political structural change, much less revolution. How could it do so when its major stockholders and lenders would not be exactly overjoyed at such a prospect? And it tries to find a middle ground, because it "measures the risks of reform against the risks of revolution." This middle ground is constituted by a super-hyper-broad-scale technocratic approach with a scope far beyond that of the Bank's previous projects, even when they were as grandiose and as costly as the Tarbela Dam. I am indebted to the "offbeat banker" mentioned in the previous chapter for explaining the nature of this approach. He deserves a wider audience—his only published paper on the Bank's current strategy has appeared in Swedish. So with a bow to "Henri Labouret," as he calls himself, who was kind enough to supply me with his original draft in a language intelligible to me, as well as with further explanations, here is the story as seen from inside the Bank, and from its recent papers read in this light.

The Bank is making many new recommendations. Perhaps the most unexpected are those that favor some kind of limited land reform and better organization of small farmers so that they will have more access to credit and to the market and greater protection from the pressures of privileged landowners. Unfortunately, these recommendations are being made more or less in a vacuum, because the Bank refuses to consider the political context.

The Bank's managers remain convinced that somewhere, somehow, there exists a methodology without ideology, a purely technocratic view of development—and that it can and must be discovered. So the Bank's rhetoric becomes a mere justification for its own program—it has no particular bearing on the real political inclinations of real governments even though it frequently mentions the "political factor" in the abstract. Nevertheless, the new program for rural development is under way, even though the Bank recognizes that this must be necessarily a trial and error process for a while. As McNamara says, "We will have to take some risks . . . and if some of the experiments fail, we will have to learn from them and start anew." The few projects of the "new style" already in action differ widely and it is difficult to trace a uniform profile: for instance, they may concern 3,000 farmers in one case and 30,000 in another. Furthermore, the Bank does not know exactly what it means by "small farmer." Labouret says he thinks the return on investment/profitability criteria of most projects would generally exclude farmers with less than 1 or 2 hectares. Still, the projects all have certain things in common. First, they are implemented within a certain area, and to this geographical territory is applied the approach variously called "sectoral," "integrated" or "functional." Beyond giving small farmers the necessary physical inputs to help make them more productive, the novelty of the Bank's "new style" is that investments are also made in social services which are not immediately profitable, such as schools, health care, roads, credit, extension services and the like.

This strategy amounts to creating *ex nihilo* an island of development in an ocean of poverty. The Bank hopes that its efforts will be "replicated" once the island has been proved a success. The creation of these development enclaves, according to Labouret, gives rise to one of the greatest gaps between Bank theory and Bank practice. In the old days, a "good" project, from the Bank's standpoint, was one that could furnish an immediate return on investment of 12-15 per cent. The criteria of project evaluation applied to classical Bank projects were approximately the same as those applied to any large commercial or industrial enterprise.

An integrated rural development scheme is of an entirely different breed. Here one is not merely buying cement and steel and hiring foreign firms to build a dam; but rather putting money into keeping educational, health, credit and other services going. Improvements in productivity are slow to come, but one must not discourage the small farmer, so subsidies may even become necessary (although this is theoretically outlawed by the Bank). Smart commercial money—which supplies most of the Bank's funds—is not going to become involved in nebulous schemes with no immediate return, so the Bank must use interest-free IDA credits for much of the financing, particularly the social costs. IBRD has not yet sorted out to its own satisfaction how it is to account for so many intangible investments.

But the major problem, because it is a problem for the concerned country and not just for the Bank, is the way in which the project fits into the nation as a whole. In principle, a project is decided upon by a member government which then seeks out financing from the IBRD or from one of the regional development banks. This is not at all the way things happen in practice.

A Bank project actually defined by a government is a very rare bird. In the first place, although they may have a general idea of what they want, governments of UDCs usually do not possess the techniques for defining a project according to Bank standards, nor do they know how to manipulate the various components to Bank satisfaction. Secondly, they are too busy trying to define and organize their own national budgets. So what really happens is that the Bank itself establishes schedules of possible loans—one per country and one per type of project—and *then sends out its own experts to find bankable projects.* About 40-50 per cent of these projects are "discovered" by the FAO-World Bank Co-operative Program's experts. The net result is the paradoxical situation in which it is the Bank's directors that solicit the government to accept a project that has been identified—in fact created—by the Bank itself. The government then asks the Bank to be kind enough to study the financing. It is still the Bank's teams that have defined the location, content, organization and priorities of the project—and of course, finally, its financing. Governments generally agree to these arrangements. They have no reason to refuse financial help that comes to them with next to no exertion on their part.

Just as the Bank's experts are masters of decisions as to how, when and where a project will be set up in the first place; so they remain masters of its implementation. Local governments often lack the trained personnel to man large, complicated schemes, and they have been only marginally involved in the planning. Because the projects *are* complex both economically and socially, the Bank, in fact, literally takes over the functions of public administration in the area of the country chosen for the rural development scheme. This is what Labouret justly labels "a technocrat's dream." The technocrat has a whole area to play with, he has created a zone fenced off from the country at large; an enclave in which he may be able to accomplish "rural progress" *which is absolutely beyond the reach of, and not necessarily related to, the country as a whole.*

As US Secretary of Defense, McNamara tried the enclave system in Vietnam. As President of the World Bank, he is giving it another go. One wonders if the second attempt will be any more successful than the first. Twenty-five years was too long for the poor to wait before the Bank discovered that nothing much was trickling down. But IBRD is so enthusiastic about its "new style," capable, in its view, of steering such an enviable course between total collapse in the Third World and revolution, that we may have to wait even longer for it to discover that the "integrated approach" won't work either. One cannot recommend highly enough the Bank's documents as *descriptions* of present social inequality and injustice in the UDCs. One would like to see the same lucidity applied to the predictable results of the Bank's own current policies. In the late seventies, IBRD is not just tinkering with 80,000 Pakistani peasants who had better run for their lives before the Tarbela reservoir fills up. It is talking about the 100 million people in the Third World it is going to "reach"—and this is to be only the beginning. Nor is it just pottering about with irrigation and roads—it is going to determine and develop whole social systems whose management will be largely in its own hands. How these technocratic "development" enclaves can bring anything but greater disequilibrium to the societies concerned is difficult to see. The enclaves, whatever their relative importance, will have very little in common with the global problems of development on a national scale. If a government balks at land reform, there is little reason to believe it can be instituted in an enclave in any meaningful way. In spite of the Bank's numerous "policy guidelines" concerning land reform, it has been proved over and over that *in nations most assisted by the Bank,* the government prefers to develop large-scale cash-crop agriculture, taking care of the small peasantry, when pressed, through a well-oiled repressive machine. This would not appear to be accidental.

Time and again, the Bank laments its impotence to do anything about this situation. How sad it is, but true, that "many countries have legislated for land reforms but relatively few have achieved them—and these only with a change in the government." But the Bank does not encourage national movements that might bring about such changes in government. How sad it is, but true, that "effective popular participation of rural people may be a critical condition of successful land reform." But again, the Bank does not aid peasant organizations directed against the large landholders. How true, but sad, that "few [of the Bank's projects] have supported land reform as such," although the "Bank group has taken an active interest in land reform on a number of occasions." Doubtless one of these occasions on which the Bank was able to manifest its active interest was in Chile,

which was cut off without a cent by the Bank as soon as it
instituted genuine land reform. It is, however, gratifying to know
that two agricultural projects for Chile, approved in 1970 and
placed in limbo during Popular Unity, are now being effectively
funded under the Junta. And finally, how true but sad that "the
Bank has to recognize that its leverage is limited as it seeks to
redefine its position with regard to land reform . . . the potential
for using Bank influence to press or even force the issue of
structural reform on member countries is severely circum-
scribed." McNamara accepts that the "need to reorient development policies in order to provide a more equitable distribution of
the benefits of economic growth is beginning to be widely
discussed." But he announces with sinking heart that unless
"national governments redirect their policies toward better distribution, there is very little that international agencies such as
the World Bank can do to accomplish this objective."

Is the World Bank really so helpless to orient national policies?
If it were firmly committed to reform of land-tenure structures
and to the redistribution of national incomes to the bottom half of
the population, could it not have enormous influence on its
member governments and aid recipients? McNamara says the
question is one of *political will* on the part of governments who
must "measure the risks of reform against the risks of revolution," but that the Bank cannot supply such political determination.

Here we really must depart from a polite, scholarly, examina-
tion-of-the-Bank's-own-documents approach. Sorry, Mr. President, but this is rubbish. The World Bank *could* make *all* its loans
conditional upon structural change in the recipient countries. It
has consistently imposed economic policy conditions, including
major currency devaluations, on loan recipient countries, just as
its sister institution, the International Monetary Fund, has done.
The worst-off among these countries, who get most of their
credits through concessionary aid from IDA, could be *mightily*
influenced if the World Bank raised a single finger. Once again,
the Bank gives outsiders enough rope with which to hang it, in
spite of its cautious language:

Indirectly, the influence of IDA, as of the World Bank, can be an
important restraint on the adoption of unsound policies by member
countries. IDA's borrowers, in particular, would be unlikely to obtain
finance on terms as satisfactory as IDA's from any other source; they are

therefore *unlikely to disregard the kind of advice* they may be given by Bank/IDA missions whose periodic surveys of their economies include assessments of the soundness of their economic policies.

If that is not the Power of Positive Blackmail, I do not know a better example. IDA credits in 1973 represented 46 per cent of all Bank loans (although by 1976, the proportion had dropped to one-third).

If McNamara wants land reform, McNamara can have land reform. He can, most especially, have it in India, Pakistan, Bangladesh, Indonesia and the Sahel countries of Africa which would rapidly disappear as they presently exist without Bank loans and particularly IDA concessionary grants. Moreover, the Bank constantly applies "evaluation procedures," meaning inspection missions to aid-recipients, to "assess their development progress and problems" . . . "As a result of these missions, the Bank often recommends to the host country certain policy changes which it believes would further the country's economic development."*

And yet, the Bank insists that it is a purely economic institution. Its professed criteria have nothing whatsoever to do with politics; in fact

. . . under its articles, the Bank cannot be guided in its decisions by political considerations; they must be based on economic criteria alone. The Bank is further required not to interfere in the domestic politics of member countries. *These prohibitions, however, do not mean that it must not take into account political situations or developments in member countries that may have an impact on their economic situation. . . . thus Bank decisions may be influenced by or have an influence on the domestic affairs of a country.*

One example of IBRD's "neutrality" and of its capacity to intervene is provided by Bangladesh which had refused all but IDA grants and bilateral aid until October 1974. But the floods were too much for this poorest of poor countries, and it has now accepted an aid consortium made up by the Bank from among its several wealthiest members. The *Guardian* describes some of the implications for Bangladesh. Up to now the country had refused to devalue its currency, but at present, "All the signs in Dacca

---

*The Bank could also refuse to finance any crops-for-export projects until it was entirely satisfied that the entire population of the loan-recipient country was assured of a decent diet.

point to the devaluation as part of a 'package deal' between the IMF and Bangladesh." Now that the country will be getting its aid through the IBRD consortium,

> . . . devaluation is only the most dramatic measure in the program, which to be successful must be accompanied by fiscal and other changes which will restore monetary stability. An integral part of the program is the creation of a "favorable investment climate" which would encourage market forces and provide initiatives for private capital, both foreign and domestic . . . In spite of the clinically neutral language . . . [this] stabilization program is not simply a technical exercise in monetary management. It amounts to imposing lower real incomes mainly on the urban and other working classes, and so calls for unpopular measures . . .

among which may be higher prices in government food shops upon which "nearly the whole urban population is dependent for up to half of their daily needs for food grains . . ." This may not be political intervention, but in that case my vocabulary is too weak to supply me with another term.

The Bank, naturally, reserves the right to define "political" as it sees fit. Just as for Humpty Dumpty in *Alice in Wonderland*, words mean what the Bank wants them to mean, as do stated policies. Is it an accident that the Bank withdrew, as early as 1951, all support from the Iran of Dr. Mossadegh when he attempted to nationalize his country's oil industry, thus acting against the interests of the Bank's two principle stockholders, the US and Great Britain?* Is it an accident that the Bank never loaned a cent to Indonesia—presently one of its most indebted clients—until after the pro-Western generals stepped in, massacred hundreds of thousands they labelled as communists and overthrew Sukarno? Was the Bank's more recent policy toward Chile another accident? Bank "support" for reform must be measured against its actions with regard to countries that seriously try to give the poor, especially the peasantry, a better deal.

In fairness, and because I do not want to discount *anything* that may be beneficial to small Third World farmers, I want to report that according to a *Washington Post* article headlined "World Bank Aids African Socialism," Tanzania, Ethiopia and Somalia are now getting loans for socialist rural development, while Algeria is being aided for industrialization. A new note of "undisguised bias among many of [the Bank's] top officials

---

*This is a complex question, but I think my one-sentence resumé is fair. See Mason and Asher (bibliography) pp. 595-610.

towards the more daring attempts in Africa at rural and industrial development" has been detected, and according to one of the Bank's permanent staffers in Africa, "Somalia is one of Mc-Namara's favorite countries." Tanzania has received a $310 million loan for resettling milions of peasants in planned villages and according to the same official, "an awful lot of the things the Bank hopes to be doing in the future are now being done in Tanzania." Perhaps, where the government is behind it on a *national* scale, the "enclave" method will have a chance of success.

As to Chile, the Bank has a ready answer. Chile had expropriated American copper interests—which had already repatriated many times over, in profits, the capital invested there.

As far as expropriation is concerned, this is the right of any country; the Bank is neutral in this matter. It is, however, concerned that the expropriator shows good faith by taking serious steps to reach agreement on the payment of fair compensation, and *it may refuse to lend to members* who fail to make reasonable efforts to settle expropriation claims or similar disputes.

Now that the Junta has paid off US copper producers, the Bank has a perfectly good excuse to resume loans.

Le Monde reported that a secret meeting between IBRD and the Asian Development Bank was scheduled for June 1975 in Manila to determine how Western aid could best be channelled to Saigon through a consortium like the one created by the Bank for Bangladesh. The meeting was to discuss especially the "special fund for the development of the Mekong Valley" of which Saigon's share would be "by far the greatest." Such meetings were also held in October 1973 and October 1974 "under the auspices of the World Bank . . . in secret, whereas they commit member governments both financially and politically . . . who do not inform their own Parliaments." By now, the Vietnamese themselves have altered the Bank's plans for the Mekong Valley. But the case proves that when the Bank does not want its so-called "political neutrality" questioned, it acts in secret.

We finally come, as we did for the agribusiness leaders, to the question of the personal sincerity of McNamara. As a good Presbyterian Elder, he doubtless hopes at least on Sunday mornings that the absolute poor may benefit from the policies of his Bank. He came to its presidency after being one of the chief architects of the wanton destruction of Indochina and may have seen the error of his ways, though that is a slim defense. But before he ever joined the Bank, he gave his reasons for favoring "development" in a book called *The Essence of Security*. Here are the real reasons we must help the poor:

. . . We are beginning better to understand that stability of relationships among rich nations is affected by the stability of the institutions of poor nations. And, in the long run, stability in the poor nations is a function of development. That is obvious enough in the case of those impoverished nations whose peoples are seething with growing frustrations, nations racked with famine and disease and the cruel pressures of expanding populations on diminishing resources. But while we have begun to recognize the obvious correlation between social, economic and political stagnation and volcanic internal violence, we have yet to do enough about it. But I believe that we will begin to do more, and soon. We will do more because we will have to do more.
. . . The wealthy and secure nations of the world will realize that they cannot possibly remain either wealthy or secure if they continue to close their eyes to the pestilence of poverty that covers the whole southern half of the globe. They will open their eyes and act, if only to preserve their own immunity from the infection.
. . .[They will give more to development] not because the rich nations will suddenly become more philanthropic, but because they will gradually become more realistic. They will reach a point of realism at which it becomes clear that a dollar's worth more of military hardware will buy less security for themselves than a dollar's worth more of developmental assistance . . . Collective security and collective development are but two faces of the same coin.

So McNamara is caught between the Devil and the deep blue sea. He knows we must help the poor if only to save ourselves from their "infection." But a World Bank dominated by the interests and politics of the rich—with the US, UK, Germany, France and Japan at the top of the heap—cannot help them more than marginally however many enclaves it creates; however much it may try to extend the Green Revolution. The poor, in fact, can only profit from the kinds of truly radical structural changes whose necessity McNamara recognizes, but whose political implications would involve power shake-ups his Bank cannot possibly foster or accept. But should you undergo a real conversion, come join us, Mr. McNamara. It won't be as well paid, but there's room for you on the other side.

Conclusion to Part Three

Let us imagine anywhere on the planet a country which has mile-high walls instead of conventional boundaries. After a period of, say, a thousand years, the walls crumble, and for the first time curious outsiders can see what sort of a society has evolved within. They will find, of course, a more or less large group on top that holds power—political and economic—over a more or less large group underneath which submits to this power. But the thousand-year history of this fantasy country will show that there has always been a limit beyond which the powerful group could not go without provoking revolt on the part of the underlings; without automatically insuring its own overthrow. So if the powerful have been reasonably benevolent, if disparities in living standards between them and those over whom they hold sway have not been too glaring, we may find that the same class has perpetuated its control for the whole of the thousand years. If, on the other hand, each powerful group has repressed those beneath them beyond the limits of human endurance, even the most refined police methods the society has been able to devise will not have prevented several upsets from taking place. A sort of physical equilibrium establishes itself between the interests of the dominating and the dominated—the former cannot tread too heavily on the latter without causing serious imbalance in the system and eventually their own downfall and replacement.

Now let us imagine the same country without any walls, and on the contrary with totally permeable frontiers. The dominant class in the country is still repressing those beneath, but sensing their growing restiveness, it looks for allies. It finds them in the dominant groups of other countries with which it can communicate and who share, on the whole, its principal goals. If our country's dominant class can do so without really sacrificing its own privileges—which are control over part of the country's wealth and over the productive labor of its own poor—it will seek out the most powerful allies it can find. Usually the latter will be only too glad to oblige. Both groups will get something out of the deal. But the previous natural balance between repression and revolt within the country will have been destroyed in the process. Now the dominant class can count not only on its own methods of oppression, but also upon the enormous force of its partner that can be permanently brought to bear on the dominated. In order to react to this combination of forces, the underdog class will have to be ten times stronger, twenty times more determined. It may, in fact, be pushed beyond the "limits of human endurance"— because there is nothing else it can do. The alliance between the two (or more) dominating classes may be more or less visible— ranging from "merely" economic assistance arrangements or "technical cooperation," to overt military presence. The ideology of the allied partner may be democratic, fascist, socialist or what have you. That is not the point. What matters are the *physical* laws of politics by which outside intervention allows the domi- nant class to bear down with all its weight—and all the weight of its ally—upon its own poor.

This law applies to the United States and to the international agencies in which it plays so large a part, just as it would apply to France in Africa, to the Soviet Union in Eastern Europe or to any other power. But the sphere of influence of the US still covers, in spite of recent and spectacular setbacks, the greater part of the planet, inhabited by two billion people. Most of them are poor. If we take the above theory seriously, we should not be surprised to see the élites of these nations competing for American invest- ments and for World Bank loans. They know, instinctively if not consciously, that without such help they might wake up to- morrow on the other side of the power fence.

Intelligent spokesmen for Western interests, like McNamara, have understood that it is not in the rich world's long-term interests to keep the poor too downtrodden—but they are too fettered by their short-term interests to initiate meaningful change. Their "development" efforts are therefore attempts, politically speaking, to square the circle. Since little is to be expected from our half of the world, we must hope for heroism in the other, and that the wretched of the earth may soon decide that they will not starve quietly.

PART FOUR

What to Do?

11. What Can "They" Do?

By "they," I mean those ill-defined groups in positions of power who are supposed to be able to alter the status quo, as in, "Why don't they do something about [pollution, inflation, etc.]." The answer, of course, is that it is usually not in their interests to change anything that would simultaneously reduce their power, prestige or profits. An economics professor friend of mine, commenting on an early draft of this book, asked me why I was so strident about governments and corporations taking advantage of hunger. Who, he asked, would expect otherwise? While I don't think anything worth reading can be written without a certain degree of passion, I have since tried to deal with "them" as matter-of-factly as I could. But the only answer one really wants to offer when asked what they—in positions of power in the West—can do to eradicate world hunger is to say *nothing. Let them alone. Stop it.* Stay out of other peoples' affairs. Stop sending out your experts whose training suits them only for proposing Western-oriented "solutions." Stop forcing your unadapted and usually unadaptable technology on radically different societies. Stop shaping their environments to suit your needs. Stop educating people to think that yours is the only road to "progress." Stop sending the kind of aid which will aid *you*, in the form of myriad commercial advantages, a hundred times more than it will ever help the poor. Stop running the multilateral agencies and the UN. Stop giving aid and comfort, political and material support to repressive local élites that have no intention of changing the lot of their people, and give the people a chance. Put a leash on your corporations, your foundations, your universities, your bureaucrats and your banks. So much for utopia.

Life is not like that, neither are MNCs, neither are states. Their methods may change; their basic goals will not. We are not going to see another American intervention like Vietnam—not because it was brutal, immoral and uncivilized, but because it didn't work. There will also be fewer Chilean-type interventions. Chile was still too visible. The alternative methods of domination chosen will make the task of power-watchers more difficult; they will not mean that power is no longer being exercised. The people that may get in the way will not be napalmed, but they may still die, frequently of hunger. Agripower, like other kinds of power, will be used, and the goal of food dependency for the Third World—and even for the rest of the developed world—has become a permanent feature of United States foreign policy. As we have seen, the economics of soybeans can be better for keeping any number of countries in line than the best-trained police forces. Such realities should always be kept in the forefront of the mind every time one hears of a new "solution" for world hunger proposed by Western institutions; and especially by the United States, which holds most of the agricultural trump cards. The latest key word seems to be "interdependence" which means that the US will supply food as long as UDCs continue to supply raw materials, cash crops and labor on terms basically unfavorable to them.

It is in this context, I think, that we should look at two types of solutions "they" are currently proposing. One is technological and concerns alternative sources of food and/or proteins; the other is the constellation of new institutions that have grown out of the 1974 World Food Conference and which are grouped around a brand-new UN agency. In each case, the question, "Who is in control?" is the crucial one.

ALTERNATIVE FOOD SOURCES

For several food crops now being raised, up to 80 per cent of the total weight is wasted. Leaves, stalks, hulls and roots are thrown away. They could become biological fertilizers, animal feed or even food for humans if proper technology were applied, and several large firms and research institutions are now setting their sights on such uses, spurred on by very real charges that animals are eating too much precious grain. It is not entirely concern for the starving that has prompted such activity: meat consumption is becoming too expensive even for many rich consumers. Animals are now being experimentally fed everything from newspapers to their own processed manure—and thriving. One 1350-lb bull at a US research center who has spent eleven years on a diet of wood pulp and urea got loose on the lawn but "appeared mystified by the grass." Animals may turn out to be nature's most inventive garbage-disposal units with no loss in weight gains and may solve some of our pollution problems in the bargain. Certain scientists predict that in the future, cattle raisers will also be poultry growers, realizing what may be the ultimate in recycling technology by feeding chickenshit to steers.

Another animal feed that has great possibilities, including some for humans, is already being industrially produced. This is SCP, short for single-cell protein—micro-organisms like yeasts that can reproduce themselves at prodigious speeds when provided with a gassy or liquid hydrocarbon food base. The production of SCP is about sixty times as efficient, in terms of energy, as the production of beef protein. British Petroleum has one 20,000-ton SCP production unit operating in France and is joining the Italian firm ANIC for a 100,000-ton plant in Sardinia. The Japanese are also reportedly active in the field. SCP can be fed to animals with absolute safety and with no change in meat quality—quality sometimes appears actually to be enhanced. BP scientists say that although other substrates than hydrocarbons might not produce such great quantities, there is no technical reason why "waste" products like cheese-whey, left-over liquid from paper processing and wastes from breweries, distilleries and canneries should not be used for making SCP. The most encouraging item I have seen in the scientific literature on the subject is this one:

> By sacrificing a little in the way of efficiency, high protein foods and feeds may be produced on a village level. If a labor intensive system of medium preparation and cell harvesting is used together with cheap plastic fermenters, an acceptable food can be produced; the basic concept being that an organism or combination of organisms is used which has the ability to use many different substrates in a similar manner. In this way the microbiology and engineering required for such projects are cut to a minimum.

The concept of total crop utilization can be applied to the leaves, stalks and roots of any plant so as to extract syrups or sugars, alcohols or feedstuffs presently going to waste. The technology and expertise to do this already exist. But when one sees Harold Geneen, the President of ITT who showed such concern for Chile, pushing for a government crash program in SCP and the "total crop" concept which "could grant contracts to private industry and other entities with capabilities in food technology"—it gives one pause.

A dozen liberal US Congresspeople headed by Representative John Seiberling are sponsoring legislation to provide extra money for advanced agricultural research stressing recycling and alternative sources of food. Seiberling points out that public money for R&D in agriculture is lagging way behind inflation while the military eat up half the total of all public money spent on research. (US Defense gets $10.6 *billion*; agriculture, $468 million.) Furthermore, if the US continues to rely on its current energy-devouring food-production system, its own fossil-fuel reserves will be exhausted within twenty-five years. The extra clout such research could predictably give to US agripower may not have fallen on entirely deaf ears: *Business Week* reports that the National Academy of Sciences fully expects a Ford-administration promoted "Manhattan Project in food that would rival the effort that produced the atomic bomb." They claim this may show up in the Administrations's budget next year [1976].*

If the US government is not yet visibly convinced of the necessity for research in the food-production technology of the 1980s, this is certainly not the case for industry. Besides developing SCP and protein-extraction techniques, it is busy learning how to make animal digestion more efficient, how to make plants fix more nitrogen, how to prepare soils to eliminate weeds and pests from, so to speak, the ground up; and how to make recalcitrant turkey hens lay an egg a day. Really far-out chemical techniques can slow or hasten growth and can force plants to stop wasting energy by "useless" reactions with oxygen. When plants like soybeans are experimentally flooded with carbon dioxide nutrition at DuPont's research station, they fix more nitrogen, quadruple yields, and their growth can be regulated. "Monsanto Co. has already begun selling Polaris, a sugar cane ripener or regulator. DuPont would like to come up with a similar product for soybeans."

If this technology were developed and then shared in such a way that it could make a real difference to hungry people, such research could be a boon to the human race. But we know a little more now about who has benefited from previous research. We might also mention that in countries like Brazil and India USAID

*It didn't.

is encouraging the downgrading of legumes like peas and beans—which *already* contain protein—in favor of soybeans for which US industry holds all the patents. A certain degree of skepticism thus seems warranted as to what "they" can do in the domain of food research. New crop technology will very likely remain a paying proposition, reserved for the well-endowed, and become a part of the food weapon arsenal.

THE NEW BUREAUCRACY

In its final resolution, the November 1974 World Food Conference called for follow-up machinery in the form of yet another full-fledged UN agency whose authority would extend to "all aspects of world food problems in order to adopt an integrated approach towards their solution" and which would be charged with coordinating "all relevant United Nations bodies and agencies giving special attention to the problems of the least developed countries and those most seriously affected." This new body, which has not had time to become an elephantine bureaucracy—it presently occupies just eight offices at FAO in Rome—is called the World Food Council. It is headed by Dr. John Hannah, an American who was President of Michigan State University during the period MSU was notorious for its contracts with the CIA concerning Vietnam. He also served as Administrator of USAID and as Board Chairman of the Overseas Private Investment Corporation whose activities include insuring US agribusiness abroad. The chart on p. 242 shows how his organization looks on paper.

Connoisseurs of organigrams will immediately warm to the rich variety of built-in disputes that are bound to arise from such re-shufflings of organizational priorities, and indeed the press reports that at FAO "the air is already crackling with jurisdictional squabbles" over who reports to whom and who can spend what money. The WFC retorts that FAO is rife with bureaucratic ills, and that it, for one, will by-pass paper pushing in favor of telephone, telex and cable to disentangle multiple jurisdiction over the world food situation and to really get things done.

Two of the subdivisions under WFC authority merit special scrutiny. The first is the International Fund for Agricultural Development which might have over a billion dollars a year at its disposal. Several countries, Britain, The Netherlands, Saudi

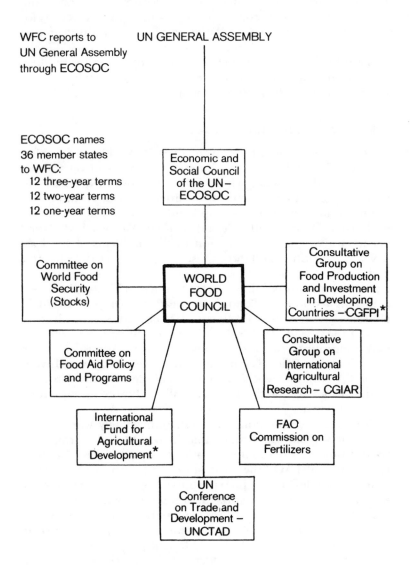

WFC reports to
UN General Assembly
through ECOSOC

UN GENERAL ASSEMBLY

ECOSOC names
36 member states
to WFC:
   12 three-year terms
   12 two-year terms
   12 one-year terms

Economic and
Social Council
of the UN –
ECOSOC

Committee on
World Food
Security
(Stocks)

WORLD
FOOD
COUNCIL

Consultative
Group on
Food Production
and Investment
in Developing
Countries – CGFPI*

Committee on
Food Aid Policy
and Programs

Consultative
Group on
International
Agricultural
Research – CGIAR

International
Fund for
Agricultural
Development*

FAO
Commission on
Fertilizers

UN
Conference
on Trade and
Development –
UNCTAD

*Expected to get underway in 1977

Arabia and Iran among them, have already made concrete pledges
to the Fund. Dr. Kissinger announced that the US would endorse
an overall $1 billion annual level, but has not made a specific
commitment to the Fund,* which should start operating in 1977
if all goes well. With heavy OPEC participation, the Fund could
have a real impact on the Third World, and would, in any case, be
the first big gun in the development armory whose trigger could
not always be pulled by the major Western governments. The
second important committee is the Consultative Group on Food
Production and Investment in Developing Countries. The role of
CGFPI will be to "increase, coordinate and improve the efficiency of financing and technical assistance to agricultural
production in developing countries" from bilateral and multilateral investors. This committee is also headed by an American,
also a former high USAID official, who served as chief of the
American delegation to the World Food Conference, Edwin M.
Martin. The CGFPI has its headquarters not at FAO, but at the
World Bank in Washington. It is already working not only with
the Bank, but with the Industry Cooperative Program and the
Bankers Program at FAO. Between Hannah and Martin, the
United States has pretty well sewn up its traditional share of the
power in this most recent UN agency.

The heavily American slant of the World Food Council has not
been lost on the Third World member nations of the new
organization which held its first meeting late in June 1975.
Delegates from the three poor continents arrived already somewhat ill-disposed towards the WFC, partly because of Hannah's
CIA—AID—OPIC reputation, partly because working documents were often unavailable in languages other than English.
The meeting that ensued can only be described as a shambles. The
agenda was supposed to concern the establishment of the International Fund, commitments of emergency aid for the worst-off
countries, concrete measures for establishing a rational system of
world food and fertilizer stocks, as well as longer-term measures
geared to increasing food production.

What actually took place was rather a far cry from this agenda.
Delegates from the West made speeches reiterating positions
taken at the World Food Conference, but no new pledges for aid

*The US has now promised $200 million to IFAD; OPEC contributions will
amount to $400 million. At the end of 1976, total pledges came to $930 million.

or for changed stock-holding policies. Britain was the exception: it pledged an extra 100,000 tons of fertilizer for 1976. In addition to the absence of working documents in all UN languages, overworked interpreters were sent to cover a rich-country sub-group meeting, but were not provided for one held by the UDCs. "This is not an isolated case, but part of an effort to prevent the developing countries from presenting their views," charged the Mexican delegate on behalf of the Latin American group. In the course of a seventeen-hour marathon debate on the nature of internal structures in the new agency, the interpreters gave up the struggle altogether and went out on strike. In the midst of the resulting chaos, the Egyptian Chairman threatened to leave the chair. Finally, Latin American and African delegates demanded a suspension of the meeting and, accompanied by some apprecia-tive desk-banging, their Senegalese spokesman called for Han-nah's resignation. Delegates from nations most dependent on US aid (India, Pakistan, Bangladesh and Egypt) kept negotiations open as best they could, while Western spokesmen took the line that the WFC meeting was supposed to provide only guidelines and was never intended to be a pledging meeting. Five days of procedural wrangling and intercontinental in-fighting resulted only in a declaration reiterating what the World Food Conference had clearly stated seven months previously—that the world is still in the grip of hunger. The poor nations got no more than they had already gotten in Rome.*

So long as the WFC's power of decision and power to finance remains largely in US hands it is doubtful that the UDC members can expect much more than compromise declarations, and even these will be painfully arrived at. We in the West should not

---

*Between the Conference in November 1974 and this meeting in June 1975, the US pledged an extra four million tons of food aid. An FAO official says privately, "Quite frankly, the US was sloppy at the Conference. If it had pledged the extra four million tons then, its delegation could have left after a positive rather than a negative step." As to the second annual meeting of the WFC (June 1976), it was far more sedate but no more productive. One observer remarks that this forum merely restated goals already called for elsewhere and that "no new initiatives emerged from the second session, no progress was made on the major issues." This reinforces the impression that the rich countries do not, in fact, want "the WFC to interfere with negotiations of political significance" and that "the Western industrialized countries, forcefully headed by the US delegation, are able to dictate the conditions for international cooperation in food policy matters. They can unilaterally define the rules of the game. . . " The WFC is consequently "in no sense a 'Food Security Council.' "

expect that "they" will take concrete steps to eradicate world hunger through another UN body bound to traditional Western conceptions and interests. If, however, the balance of power in this new body were to shift (we won't go into what this would imply for global politics), here are some of the useful things "they" might try.

Immediate Food Aid FAO estimates that the grain import needs of what are called the Most Seriously Affected nations for the 1975-6 (July to June) year will be a minimum of fourteen million and a maximum of twenty million tons, depending on the quality of the harvests. These calculations, however, do not include "several other developing countries not on the current MSA list, such as Egypt, which will have large import needs." Not even half of this minimum amount has been pledged and the MSAs may have to do what they did last season—make up most of their shortfall through commercial grain imports. (Estimates of import needs between June '76 and June '77 amount to 18 million tons). This makes the hunger cycle a particularly vicious one. The poorest countries must spend money to buy grain, so they have that much less to invest in agricultural development. An aid crash program is clearly necessary: not to encourage dependency but to free resources for the kinds of investment that can alone insure food production for the future and thus make aid unnecessary. The same reasoning, and the same urgency, applies to fertilizer and pesticide aid.

A World Food Security System Such a plan, which exists only at the preliminary discussion level, would include both an emergency food reserve (ten million tons above and beyond committed aid) and buffer stocks of major food grains aimed at preventing wild oscillations of prices on the world market. At present about fifty nations have signed a declaration of principle for establishing national foodstocks that would be internationally coordinated. Effective world food security would have to involve bringing the now dangerously low stock levels back up to par, financing them internationally, placing them under international supervision and setting an agreed floor and ceiling price for their release. The United States has expressly opposed any such system, preferring the free market for the setting of foodgrain prices.

An Early Warning System Through information volunteered by governments (and when they prove recalcitrant, through satellite photographs), predictions of world food needs could be made more accurately and with enough advance notice to prepare for emergencies. Unfortunately, under present circumstances such a system would best serve the interests of the grain traders, not those of the hungry, as is already the case for satellite data.

Investment in Agricultural Development This is the only possible long-term strategy, but the richest countries, and again the US, are dragging their feet over the International Fund for Agricultural Development because OPEC would foreseeably wield a good deal of power in it and recipient countries (those that need the development) would have their own say in the uses of the fund.* Rich nations want a political or commercial return on their investments, and this particular Fund is not likely to provide these.

In a general way, the food issue is providing another theater of confrontation for the US and OPEC as chief players, with bit parts being taken by the EEC and members of the "Group of Seventy-Seven" (the UDC group that now counts over a hundred countries as members). Not all of the US Establishment is in favor of Henry Kissinger's tough stance against OPEC: Geoffrey Barraclough reports on a speech by George Ball (once a State Department man; now a senior partner in an investment bank) who told his high-powered audience that "the entire financial structure of the non-Communist world" was threatened with collapse. The main reason was the "strategy of confrontation" pursued by Kissinger and his determination to "confront the oil-producing nations rather than seek their cooperation." Ball and many of his colleagues see that both sides have a stake in "keeping the floundering capitalist ship afloat," says Barraclough.

In the area that concerns us, this means that many financial interests have endorsed proposals such as Orville Freeman's for "triangularity" in agribusiness: if Arabs supply the capital, the West will still be able to supply technology and management and make money on it. US Secretaries of State will probably not be allowed to indulge in confrontation strategy very much longer, in so far as it conflicts with the felt needs of the US financial

---

*As previously noted, the US has now pledged $200 million to IFAD.

community. Whether the OPEC nations will still play ball now that the US has gone so far is another question. They seem to be far more allied with genuine Third World interests than they were two or three years ago. Perhaps Kissinger served a useful purpose, albeit against his will.

* * *

What can "they" do in UDCs? Many of the recommendations one could make for the UDCs are the mirror image of advice to the DCs—and for the moment just as utopian. They too should stop it. Stop devoting so much land to cash crops, stop paying royalties for expensive and often detrimental farming technology, stop educating their best people in Western universities, stop the massive borrowing that carries fantastic interest payments, stop welcoming MNCs onto their national soil—in a word, put an end to dependency.

Some UDCs are beginning to exhibit backbone and guts undreamed of even five years ago, partly thanks to the OPEC example; also because of the increasing misery of their own people. Confrontation with the affluent nations in the UN and its agencies or international cooperation through trade agreements like Lomé are not enough. The affluent governments have amply demonstrated, not least at the World Food Conference itself, their refusal to grant fair trade terms to producers of agricultural raw materials. In spite of all the pitfalls and obstacles, these nations should attempt to form commodity cartels on the OPEC model. They will have a tooth-and-nail battle on their hands, but as long as the British tea companies, to return to only one example, can manipulate Sri Lanka because they also control India and African countries (and, of course, vice-versa) no nation can be sure of a fair and stable price for its exports. At the very least, they have nothing to lose from a strategy of unity. Consumers in the wealthy countries might pay a little more for tea and coffee, but it is up to them, after all, to fight the marketing monopolies at home that skim off most of the margins anyway.

Moreover, many UDCs are reinforcing their dependency on the advanced nations year by year because they are investing in costly new productive capacity while simultaneously under-utilizing the capacity they already have. One expert estimates that they have, on the whole, about the same industrial potential as the now-advanced countries had at the end of the nineteenth century, but that much of it is going to waste. The UDCs are now contributing far more to the DCs (in payments of all kinds, repatriated profits of firms, etc.) than the latter are bringing to them through investment or aid. They must slow down the outflow of scarce capital and one way to do it is to make maximum use of the natural and industrial resources they have on hand.

Any basic change in the present world hunger crisis must come about through internal policies and planning in the UDCs. This book has tried to show the responsibility of the rich for the fate of the poor, but it will have failed if readers have not gained an equal sense of the absolute necessity for structural change inside the worst-off countries themselves. As long as the majority of the population has an inadequate food supply because it is maintained in abject poverty—not by the climate or other mysterious natural forces but by the concerted actions of the dominant class and its allies—these people will go hungry and so will their children.

LAND REFORM

Giving poor people in the essentially rural UDCs a livelihood and enough food, means primarily giving them access to land. Wherever this has happened, in socialist or in market-economy countries, serious food crises have disappeared, although problems resulting from centuries of colonialism have not entirely vanished. Nations like China, Vietnam and Cuba are the first to admit their own shortcomings—but the admirable difference is that they use such self-criticism to move forward—and best of all, they do it without us.

Decades of cold-war rhetoric have caused the words "land reform" to flash a red flag in many Western minds. The first prejudice we must get rid of is the one that equates agrarian reform with "communism" or with "revolution." If the political will to create an egalitarian society existed, it could be done under any number of social systems. The bitter truth is, however, that landowning classes consistently refuse even limited concessions and thus eventually tend to bring revolution on themselves. Nobody—except the odd stray sadist and the lunatic fringe—wants revolution for its own sake. It is obviously bloody, but it is also inefficient because so many of the best worker and peasant leaders invariably get themselves killed in the process. Yet how long must deprived people be expected to witness calmly scenes like this one, described by René Dumont:

> At the Dacca Club, in the center of the capital [of Bangladesh] in August 1974 during the worst of the famine, a wedding feast for 3,000 guests cost 94,000 francs [about $20,000 or £10,000]. If starving guerilleros armed with machine guns had come in and mowed them all down, I, for one, would have had trouble blaming them.

History's first land reform actually took place in ancient Greece before communism was born or thought of. Small peasants had been getting into deeper and deeper debt with local merchants and had been obliged to mortgage their land. In the sixth century B.C. the plain of Athens was covered with standing stones bearing notice that x's land was now mortgaged to y. Farmers and their families were reduced to conditions of near slavery, and for the first time a class of landowners who did not themselves farm appeared. Landless farmers were obliged to take refuge in the mountains, where the first "guerrilla movements" sprang up. Peasants allied in political parties with small shopkeepers who had also been dispossessed by wealthy merchants. Finally, pressures for reform became overwhelming. The mortgage stones were razed, debts were abolished, and in 524 B.C. Pisistratus confiscated the big estates and redistributed land to its former owners. In Greece, this refusal to allow great wealth to concentrate in the hands of a few was called democracy.

After hundreds of years of seeing their best efforts enriching other people, it is self-evident that the first and most normal desire of peasants will be to have land of their own. That is why the societies that have made the most progress toward eliminating food problems have not denied this land-hunger but have made it a part of their system. China and Vietnam both leave room for individual plots; but perhaps more important, the large tracts of land farmed collectively belong not to the faraway state but to the commune itself. Major decisions, with full democratic representation, are locally made, and any surplus earned goes into financing improvements for the commune from which everybody benefits. Such an incentive system is undoubtedly the reason people are willing to work so hard. No serious visitor to China or Vietnam, however unfavorable to their politics, has dared go so far as to speak of "repression" or "coercion" as the explanation for the startling gains in food production. The simple truth is that people have organized themselves and they have a strong personal and collective stake in their own productivity.

In some areas where there is plenty of land but where it is very unequally distributed (Latin America, parts of Africa), cutting up of huge estates and redistribution to small farmers could theoretically be sufficient to produce more food, but in unindustrialized societies things do not work that way in practice. Along with distribution of individual plots, some form of regrouping of holdings seems to be by far the more efficient system. This is normal, because land is not the only input that goes into successful farming. (See Appendix for some others.) Some sort of coordination, some cooperative system must be devised for channelling all the other inputs to all the farmers in a given area. Regrouping in Western industrialized nations like the US or France has taken place through common or garden free-enterprise competition—a phenomenon that continues as fewer and fewer farmers each feed more and more people. The people pushed off the land in the process eventually find employment in the cities because previous industrialization has created enough—or nearly enough—jobs for them. The costs in individual suffering are not measured in such systems, but what economists call "economies of scale" are made possible through them. For example, a tractor is used with maximum efficiency only above a certain number of acres; the costs of an irrigation system or of crop-dusting can be amortized only on a large scale, etc.

In countries where not enough off-farm jobs exist—and in the UDCs this is everywhere the case—economies of scale cannot be created in the same way without simultaneously creating unbearable social tensions. This is why the socially planned regrouping of holdings subsequent to (and as a corollary of) land reform is vital. This does not necessarily mean that fully mechanized, as opposed to labor-intensive, systems should be used—only that on large tracts the best elements of both can be combined in the most rational way.

The higher food productivity of the more egalitarian countries has been decisively demonstrated, but when we look at their policies, we find that their efforts have not been confined to questions of production alone. Plenty of countries are *producing* a lot more food now than they were ten years ago, yet their people are worse off now than they were then. Even land reform, when not accompanied by measures effectively giving purchasing power to the worst-off people, is nothing but a sham. Real reform means that through a cooperative system the farmer can get his inputs and necessary credit; but it also means he can be guaranteed access to the market at fair prices. In one Asian village after another, the most important man is the money-lender who functions not only as the monopoly seller of inputs but also as the monopoly buyer of harvests. If state agencies do not eliminate the need for his services the farmers' lifeblood will be sucked just as before. Only through guaranteed purchasing arrangements can a fair income be guaranteed to the farmer—and a fair price to the poor urban consumer. Any reform worthy of the name will have to get rid of such middlemen. Industrialization in the UDCs is essential, but priority should be given to industries that service agriculture. This may mean fertilizer and pesticides, but it also means state expenditure for irrigation works, better transportation and storage for food and better education and training for rural workers. Such industries and public works can and must be labor intensive.

Once again, the UDCs would do well to imitate China and rely on their own strength rather than on the aid of the West. Any real progress in eliminating hunger will mean social change; any massive commitment of Western aid will require a political and economic return. The propositions are mutually exclusive. The only available choices are self-reliance or dependency. If governments of poor nations continue to walk the road of food aid, the MNCs or the World Bank, they do so in the full knowledge that solutions offered for their problems will continue to be technocratic and exploitative and that all the strings will be pulled by outsiders. Doubtless for such governing élites even total loss of dignity and national self-hood is preferable to loss of power and of a comfortable life.

Others have learned that there is honor in austerity, that charity is no substitute for justice and that nothing can equal the people's strength when their leaders have the courage to speak a single word to their would-be masters: No.

12. What Can I Do?

I hope you have not come this far with nothing to sustain you but suppressed rage or grim despair! As I said in the very first paragraph, famine and hunger are not "inevitable, but are caused by identifiable forces within the province of rational, human control." I have tried to identify some of the forces. You are part of humanity; you can be part of the control.

First of all, learn to educate yourself. Learn to see the news behind the news, and who wants it to read as it does. Don't let editorials or cartoons like the ones included here pass without protest. Write to the newspaper, write to the author or the artist, and explain, nicely, why he hasn't understood the problem. Remember that governments, corporations, foundations, and multilateral agencies together control a gigantic public-relations machine, and that many articles that are printed as straight news are in reality their handouts. Journalists are just as rushed and harassed as the rest of us and frequently do not have the time to countercheck and scrutinize what may even go out under their own by-lines. Keep this in mind when you read an article about food "aid" or any other intervention-for-their-own-good on the part of your own country's government. Agribusinesses have the money to put the best possible face on their activities and many innocuous-sounding institutions are nothing but MNC mouthpieces. Find out who finances an institution before you take its word for anything at face-value.

Help to educate other people. Learn to resist the blandishments of business and other interest groups—these people have millions to convince us to think along their lines. Their opponents are a small, if growing, group, and poor. So help spread the word and complete the research. Summarize this book for example, and get your article printed in the magazine or news-sheet of your church, professional or civic group. This book has been written to be "pirated": exploit it and pass it along. Take a chapter or a section that interests you particularly and do it better than I did. "Research" can be a frightening-sounding word, but anyone with an interest in the subject can do it and it does not require three or four college degrees. Any competent librarian can point out to you in about ten minutes the major reference works you will need. Pay special attention to the business periodicals which will give you the most hard facts to the column inch and which are far from dull. You may have noticed that in this book I try, whenever possible, to use what people and institutions *say about themselves* rather than rely on what their critics think. References follow the Appendix, partly to reinforce my arguments for skeptics, mostly to help other people with suggestions for further reading. Clip newspapers (and date your clippings—otherwise they will be unusable!) In the food field, things are changing every day and I often had to resist the temptation—not always successfully—to return to a finished chapter to include a new development I learned about in the press. Government printing offices will send you, usually free, official documents on aid policies, committee hearings and the like. So will the World Bank, and agribusinesses are usually delighted to let you have their literature. What you do with it is your own business. You will discover other sources as you go along and you will invent your own system of pulling things together. Index cards for specific companies are useful. My own system was extremely messy, comprehensible only to me; it consisted largely of piles in folders on the floor according to subject, and I summaraized a lot of reading on cards. All of this must sound elementary, but I include it for novices, which is exactly what I was. The chances are that if you like reading detective novels you will like research. (Aha! The head of the UN Development Program used to be President of the Bank of America. Hmmm. Earl Butz used to be on the Board of Ralston-Purina.) Whatever your system, believe me, the pieces do eventually begin to fall into place. The worst decision you will have to make is to stop reading and start writing. You will never know *all* there is to know about your subject, but you will know more than most people and there is a certain urgency about getting the word out. The main thing is not to be afraid you can't contribute to knowledge we all need. You can read, can't you? (A final note of caution: as you write, note your references in the margin as you go along, or you will *never* find them again).

Here comes one of the most important sentences in this chapter: *study the rich and powerful, not the poor and powerless.* Any good work done on peasants' organizations, small farmer resistance to oppression, or workers in agribusiness can invariably be used against them. One of France's best anthropologists found his work on Indochina being avidly read by the Green Berets. The situation becomes morally and politically even worse when researchers have the confidence of their subjects. The latter then tell them things the outside world should not learn, but eventually does. Don't aid and abet this kind of research. Meanwhile, not nearly enough work is being done on those who hold the power and pull the strings. As their tactics become more subtle and their public pronouncements more guarded, the need for better spade-work becomes crucial. If you live in an advanced country, you undoubtedly have the social and cultural equipment to meet these people on their own terms and to get information out of them. Let the poor study themselves. They already know what is wrong with their lives and if you truly want to help them, the best you can do is to give them a clearer idea of how their oppressors are working now and can be expected to work in the future.

Join something, and if you can't find anything to join, start a group yourself. Your own energy can be multiplied x-fold when you add your strength to other people's. No one has a talent for all aspects of organization work; everyone has something to contribute. Anyone who has ever tried working for social and political change has moments of discouragement—after the meeting to which only twenty people came, for instance. And in those dark post-mortems, we are not human if we do not sometimes ask, "Does it do any good?" The only answer I can contribute is that if you do nothing, you know you have had a zero effect, or even a negative one. You will very rarely have the satisfaction of knowing that you have achieved visible, positive results, and this simply has to be accepted. Those who worked against the Vietnam war occasionally learned that they had prevented *worse* horrors from taking place when military men refrained from certain actions through fear of public opinion (this came out in the *Pentagon Papers*). Anti-war people very rarely had major satisfactions, and when they did, these sometimes proved to be setbacks for the movement—people thought too soon the battle was over. One has to go into any struggle for change with a certain humility, and realize that the kind of action that can and does bring results in the long term is usually minority action. The political "machine" is the least efficient ever invented if purely physical criteria are applied: it takes an enormous amount of energy in input to produce a tiny output. This too has to be accepted.

If you feel a burgeoning talent for local organization, here, quickly, are a few tips. Beg, borrow or steal the best equipment you can get your hands on—and if you are lucky enough to have some, share it with other groups. Unless you just want to give a feeling of togetherness to people who are *already* convinced of your point of view, you have to remember that we are all conditioned by slick media presentations and that few people will trouble to read sloppily typed, tackily mimeoed information, even if it is *true*. Good souls exist in every profession—advertising, journalism and printing among them. Try to take advantage of their professional skills to make the information you want to get across really speak. Try also to gather together people with technical skills. When did you last go to a meeting for a "cause" at which the movie projector and the sound system worked perfectly from start to finish? How can we expect to change the world if we can't even change the reels? None of this means you ought to try to confront the other side on its own terms of computers and four-color brochures, but there is no reason why material cannot be well conceived, well presented and imaginative. It costs no more.

Even if only twenty people came to your meeting, it's a start. Don't let them get away. You can hand out cards and ask people to give you their names and addresses as well as note special skills they may have and whether they would be free for future actions and planning. Each one can also address his own envelope (maybe even stamp it!) so that most of the work is done next time you call a meeting or want to send out information. Never waste a chance to find out who supports you. If you set up a photo-exhibit about hunger, for instance, ask people to sign a book and leave their address. There is a good deal of "how-to" material around on everything from silk-screening posters to teach-ins and street theater which you can use to make your actions more interesting to other people. One mistake action groups make astonishingly often is to neglect to put their own address on every leaflet, poster, etc. A person will have to be exceptionally motivated to seek you out if you don't give him a chance. Never be well-bred when it comes to talking about money. Working for change is usually volunteer, but it is never free. People should contribute (and be told specifically why they are being asked to do so) every time you can get them together.

Try to establish good working relations with local media people and political people—they have a built-in audience which is larger than yours. Radio, television and newspaper people cannot always help you as much as they would personally like to do, but the least you can do is to keep them fed with information. Explore the possibilities in your area for public service announcements, television debates and the like.

Several good groups exist already. (See addresses after Appendix.) If you don't know what to join, you can write to the Freedom from Hunger Campaign/Action for Development at FAO and ask what may already exist in your area. If nothing does, FFHC/AD can supply you with materials to start something yourself. Most church and civic groups concerned about world hunger have their hearts in the right place but often lack an analysis that would allow them to tackle problems with greater efficiency. If this book and other sources have helped you with such an analysis and you want to help others along, such groups would be an excellent place to start.

This part is for women (and for men who do not wish to qualify as male chauvinists). Particularly in these times of high food prices, the women's pages and the women's magazines are full of advice telling us to shop around for the best bargains, how to make inexpensive dishes, how to stretch a chicken into three wholesome meals while still keeping husbands smiling and other nauseous items of this nature. The implication always is that we are not being Good Wives and Mothers if we do not manage well within our food budgets. Why do we take it? How can we tolerate being told, in essence, that we must lengthen our working days and solve the food problem on an individual level by buying new cookbooks with cheap recipes or by walking four extra blocks to buy cheaper butter? *We* are supposed to be the ones to adjust to our dwindling food purchasing power, but these same magazines never encourage us to get together with other women, to boycott agribusiness companies that never pass on their profits to us, or to fight the junk food that can make our children hyperkinetic and give our husbands hardening of the arteries. I do not have the answers to this, but here again, I feel sure the key word is "organize." I would rather devote my vital energies to getting a better deal for *every* wife and mother than to making hearty tuna-fish and noodle casseroles (though like everyone else I have to do that too). Consumer groups exist almost everywhere, and they, too, provided they had a better analysis at hand, could be more effective. In Buffalo, New York, a few women joined forces and prevented General Mills from using their city as a test market for a particularly revolting breakfast cereal made almost entirely of sugar and fat. They got nutritionists to sign a petition, they used local press and television and parent-teacher meetings to spread the word . . . "General Mills became so defensive about charges . . . that it took out full page ads in Buffalo newspapers to refute them. But the company finally gave up and removed Mr. Wonder-full from the supermarkets." Presumably to thrust it upon less active consumers elsewhere. Groups of women could also take the women's pages to task for their individualist attitudes—newspapers can be very sensitive to complaints from their readers. But if possible, establish good relationships with food and women's editors too: it is always preferable to have the media on one's own side, because unfortunately, an event which has not been "covered" to some degree has not really happened.

Our problems in the DCs are very real to us, but they are almost ludicrous when compared to the problems of people who merely hope to survive. One reaction to world hunger in rich countries, and it is a generous one, is the "one less hamburger" school, which believes that if individuals eat less meat, such action will release more grain for the starving in the Third World. I wish I could share this optimism. We should encourage any policy that calls for feeding animals with feed unfit for humans and plenty of these feeds exist. But if grain stocks were to reach the point where surpluses again existed as they did in the 1950s and 1960s, governments with surplus would not react by shipping grain free to people without purchasing power, but merely allow land to lie idle and subsidize farmers not to grow. Reducing meat consumption also reinforces the near-monopoly position of the largest feedlots at the expense of smaller animal raisers who cannot survive economically during a period of crisis. This is happening in the US right now. I do not want to discourage any ethical action on the part of the rich in favor of the poor, but unless the "one less hamburger" is accompanied by a cash donation of the savings to some development group or to some indigenous liberation movement, I cannot see how it will do anything valuable but reduce the cholesterol level of the practitioner. Here again, the individual approach cannot be as strong as a collective one. It would be better advised to join in lobbying governments so that they make it public policy to eliminate wasteful forms of animal feeding—and in the bargain reject their own costly dependency on US soybeans. Show a government that its own self-interest is also the interest of the Third World, and it will be more ready to act than if you try to use purely ethical tactics.

Power is a word that occurs frequently in these pages, but "power" does not mean "invulnerability." The agribusinesses in particular are not invulnerable and like any other large corporations they are extremely sensitive to criticism and to public opinion. It is not good business to be singled out as a "baby-killer." Because of the very nature of agribusiness—its vertical integration—it operates at home and in the Third World and can thus be pressured from both ends. The same wonderful people who bring you high supermarket prices and foods riddled with chemicals also exploit their Third World workers (and fire workers in rich countries). If you want to tackle agribusiness it is preferable (at least in the beginning) to pick a particular target on which to focus: a particular company's actions in a particular place. The role of British tea companies in Sri Lanka has been chosen by some action groups in the UK; and an excellent report on Unilever already exists (see page 178). One tactic that can work well when carefully prepared is to buy stock in a company so as to attend the annual general meeting. Any agribusiness quoted on the stock exchange is fair game and one share will do the trick. This is another type of action that is most successful as a group effort: you can prepare better what you want to say and you won't feel so lonely facing the Chairman of the Board. Among the things you can demand to know is exactly how much workers are paid in the Philippines or Kenya and how much profit is made a year, and repatriated, on individual ventures in the Third World. How much of what the business produces is for export and how much remains in the host country? What does it sell for there (as compared to the workers' wages)? How many people are employed per acre? If it's a low ratio, you can be sure the agribusiness is contributing to unemployment. If they tell you they don't have such data, ask them how, in that case, they can run their company. They have it, and the very least you can do is to embarrass them. This book and other sources will suggest enough pointed questions to get you through several annual meetings—but tell the local press and TV you are going and what you intend to do so that what transpires does not get smothered in the corporation's cloistered halls.

A certain number of "commodity campaigns" have been carried out by action groups in various parts of Europe. These can be used either to help cooperatives in the Third World sell their products directly without agribusiness middlemen, or to publicize injustice to food workers in producing countries. In Switzerland, one group set out to sell Tanzanian coffee, processed in Tanzania and of direct benefit to Tanzanian Ujamaa villagers; they also chose this commodity in order to publicize the unfair trade relationships between First and Third World and the role of Nestles in the control of the coffee trade. Another Swiss group chose bananas to dramatize the terrible working conditions of the plantation labor force. They actually got Swiss consumers to pay 15¢ more a kilo for bananas; the chain-store distributor handed over the difference, and they contributed the funds to a worker's project in Guatemala through a Protestant church group. This project both educated consumers and was of direct usefulness to far-off producers. The World Development Movement in Britain has run commodity campaigns on sugar and textiles; a German church group also chose sugar to point out unfair trade relationships; while the Netherlands Angola Committee organized an education/boycott campaign on Angolan coffee when Angola was still a Portuguese colony. Details on the organization and evaluations of commodity campaigns are also available from FFHC/AD at FAO. All these campaigns were organized by relatively small groups of people. The Swiss banana project was the brainchild of eight housewives at the outset—although their numbers rapidly swelled.

We all have a duty to sweep in front of our own doors, and therefore action in one's own country—both education and pressure on one's own corporations and government—is essential. Many people still want to do something directly for the rural poor in the Third World. Some of the brightest and best will want to put "their bodies on the line" and serve as volunteers, sharing the living conditions of the world's worst-off. This course is full of pitfalls and dangers, not the least of which is that generous but untrained people may unwittingly harm the very people they want to help. The various national associations of the Ex-Volunteers International have done a great deal of critical thinking about the role of the volunteer, and no one should depart for the Third World without first getting in touch with this organization in his country and making himself thoroughly familiar with its publications. (The best I have seen is called *Thinking About Power* and helps the future volunteer reflect on exactly what is meant by "development" and just *which* groups he may be aiding in the society he intends to join for a time. This brochure describes how the American Committee of Returned Volunteers called for the abolition of the Peace Corps in 1969. The Peace Corps, they declared, supports the status quo in the countries to which it sends volunteers "by giving legitimacy to the local power structure which invited it and by reinforcing the belief already held by many of the world's poor that their underdevelopment is their own fault." It furthermore supports "the world-wide vested interests of US business and the US government by capitalizing on the idealism of US youth to present a false image of the US presence in the Third World" and by promoting a kind of "development" which "American interests can control for their own benefit."

Most of us will have obligations that will prevent us from following this course, but we still want to do something. In spite of the economic crisis, American citizens gave a record $25 billion to charity in 1974, of which religious organizations received 43 per cent. It is safe to say that a hefty proportion is going into development projects and it is therefore of crucial importance that these actions, particularly those carried out by the religious groups, receive the most careful attention. If your church group, or other charitable agency with which you are involved, is supporting programs in the Third World, you must help them to ask the basic question: *Aid to whom?* The first criterion should be the regime of the country itself. If it is particularly minoritarian and repressive, and if the group is not *absolutely* sure that the money or the project will directly benefit the oppressed, then it is better to abstain. Nothing much, as I hope to have shown, trickles down from the élite, and the élite is in a position to syphon off everything that crosses its frontiers—or nearly—including charity. Any charity ought to have as its primary goal to make itself redundant. Where social justice prevails, charity is superfluous. It is far better to contribute to a project that will help poor people produce more for themselves than to send direct food aid. Even in this area, however, it is extremely difficult to find types of aid that will not benefit the privileged minority in one way or another. It is, I suppose, morally impossible *not* to send food, for example, to the Sahel; but one should have no illusions that much of it may be used for commercial and speculative purposes.

If your group wants to support a project, it should try to apply other standards I have tried to suggest: how many people will it employ? Will every person in the community have equal access to its benefits? (Not true, for example, of wells in India.) Who is it designed to help? How much land do these people already have? Does it contribute to better organization of the peasants themselves? Which means, will *they* have a decisive say in how it is to be set up and operated? On the whole, better a "micro" than a contribution to a "macro" project—but even if it's a tubewell everyone will be able to use, find out if there will be energy to run the pump.

My personal feeling is that very little can be done to help the rural poor without overwhelming social changes in their own countries. Most projects can therefore be little more than palliative measures serving the élites, in the final analysis, as alibis for maintaining the status quo. Thus I would urge other people to give support to national liberation and minority political groups whose goal is to change the whole society, but there are probably few charitable organizations willing to go that far.

Back on the home front, there are some specific lobbying actions that could have an effect. We should try to stop the scandalous use of fertilizers on golf-courses and cemetery lawns— and make sure that what may be economized gets to the Third World, via, for instance, the new World Food Council Fertilizer Fund. More pressure should be put on legislators (through commodity campaigns and the like) for granting more favorable trade terms to produce of the Third World. Food aid should go to hungry people—not political clients. In spite of outraged cries of offended nationalism, the aid should be in so far as possible administered by impartial managers—foreigners if necessary—to prevent its reaching the hands of speculators. Although this is probably too much to hope for, food aid should be made conditional on real agrarian reform. This could be a reasonable long-term goal for bilateral aid; it would apply to the World Bank as well, but the World Bank doesn't answer to anyone except the governments of its most powerful members.

Food aid is, alas, going to remain necessary for some time to come. If the International Fund for Agricultural Development (see preceding chapter) gets off the ground,* lobbying should be directed towards getting Western governments to contribute to it. This is because recipient nations will be *equally represented* in the Fund's administration, alongside the donors. This is not the case for any other existing multilateral aid channel. Second-best aid is probably bilateral, or government-to-government aid; because people in the donor country, through their elected representatives, can exert at least some pressure on their government and attempt to promote aid without political strings. The same criteria as above (repressive regime? food used for speculation?) should be applied. Third and last place in my book goes to multilateral agencies like the World Bank which no pressure group has a prayer of influencing. This is amply illustrated by the way the US tried to channel aid to Saigon through the Bank consortium when its own Congress had balked. This tactic will be used more frequently as public awareness of the true nature of much aid grows. Watch for it.

Disarmament has become possibly the dullest subject on the international scene. The food crisis, by comparison, is positively sexy. However trite it may sound, we are nevertheless living in an age that is going to have to make a choice between life and death. In 1975, governments spent $300 billion on arms; during the Vietnam war, the US spent $114 billion all by itself—and all for destruction. As many nations at the World Food Conference (not the rich ones) pointed out, a mere 10 per cent reduction in annual arms spending would provide enough funds if not to solve the food crisis in six months, at least to reduce dramatically its present catastrophic proportions. The "guns and butter" slogan should be changed to "bombs or bread." It would be amazing if Western governments started the ball rolling, but that is no excuse for not attempting to keep as much pressure as possible on defense budgets.

It is customary to end books like this with some lyrical, yet appropriately subdued phrase like the one the World Food

*IFAD should normally start operating in 1977.

Conference chose for its swansong. It pledged "that within a decade, no child will go to bed hungry, that no family will fear for its next day's bread and that no human being will be stunted by malnutrition." I have nothing against lofty sentiments or even noble prose when I can manage it. But I am far more concerned by what we can all do, preferably together, to make such declarations unnecessary. Now you know just about as much as I do about the world hunger crisis. So my own final word will be: Let me hear what *you* are doing.

Appendix: Agricultural Inputs

Nothing comes from nothing. To make food grow, something must be given. Traditionally, agricultural "inputs," as they are now called, were the land and water given, or not given, by nature, to which man added the sweat of his brow. Modern inputs come under the headings of fertilizers, pesticides, and farm machinery as well as the financial input of farm credit and the intangible one of research. The following overview is a *technical* one, and tries to give an idea of what could be done to improve food supplies and at what cost. It does not assume that the *political* changes that would make such improvements possible will take place.

LAND

Of the 34 billion and some acres that make up the planet's land surface, 70 per cent are too mountainous, too arid or too cold to be of much use to anyone. At present, the world's farmers are using just 10 per cent of the world's land mass to produce crops. Theoretically, this leaves a margin of 20 per cent more that could be devoted to farming. This is, of course, only partly true. It has been estimated that an extra 1.75 billion acres could be brought into production with relative ease; another 5 billion with greater difficulty and with special precautions, but this would mean, for one thing, chopping down all the forests that now exist on flat land—a rather drastic remedy for the world food problem! Still, with an altogether reasonable investment, a reasonable world could increase its present farming area by about 50 percent—up from about 3.5 to about 5.25 billion acres—without going to ecological extremes. This alone could solve the food crisis for the present global population or for a larger one. Most of this surface is in Africa and Latin America but there is also still some unused land in parts of Southeast Asia. The UN indicates that "all of these regions suffer from specific limitations, often connected with high rainfall and high temperatures, but modern technology is increasingly able to cope with the problem." A campaign to eliminate the tsetse fly in Africa could reclaim an area comparable to that of nearly the whole United States for crops and pasture. It would cost in the neighborhood of $2.5 billion spread over a twenty-year period. Outside of this, the UN states that a reasonable goal between now and 1985 would be to bring 15 to 17 million acres of new land into production per year. After that, with the expertise developed, it ought to be possible to add 25 million acres a year. The first phase of such a program would cost a little over $2 billion a year. For a total of $90 billion over the next ten years, it would be quite feasible to put 175 million more acres under cultivation, to complete large new irrigation projects and to renovate most of the inadequate irrigation systems that now exist. By way of comparison, the world spent $300 billion on armaments in 1975.

WATER

Most of the DCs are blessed with temperate climates and adequate rainfall. Where they are not, complex irrigation systems do the job. The US even has the technical capacity to modify the weather, and cloud seeding is now considered more effective than prayers for rain. Of all the acres the poor nations cultivate, only about one eighth are irrigated, most of them in Asia. Only half of *these*, or a sixteenth, are irrigated efficiently. The other systems are characterized by waste, bottlenecks and general ineffectiveness. Many irrigation projects in the UDCs have been grandiose, but they have not necessarily been valuable to small farmers (see the chapter on the World Bank). Furthermore, in the Third World water is generally bound up with complex social relationships. Especially in Asia, the existence of a well does not mean that there is free access to it. Water, like land, is often controlled by the wealthier members of society. Assuming that obstacles to fairer distribution were eliminated, underground water is probably the best hope for the future in UDCs. It exists in sufficient abundance in most places to make tubewell drilling and pumping a far more valid objective than the construction of spectacular dams which can turn out to be spectacular failures.

The UN thinks that it would be far more useful to invest in improving existing irrigation systems in UDCs than in elaborating new ones. In the next ten years, a realistic target would be renovation of half the existing facilities; that is, efficient irrigation for 115 million acres. This would make it entirely feasible to *double* present crop yields on this area even in the absence of other inputs like fertilizer. If 175 million grain-producing acres that now have inefficient water supplies were to be renovated, the gains in output would be equivalent to one fifth of *all* the cereals produced by *all* the UDCs for the period 1969–71—or tantamount to solving their food problem for many years.

The choice of what to grow is also vital to the effective management of water. René Dumont recounts how

. . . American advisors are telling Bangladesh to use irrigated Green Revolution rice during the dry season. This rice is irreplaceable during the rainy season because it can absorb excess water and can even stand up to limited floods. But during the dry season, with the water needed by an acre of rice, one could water three acres of wheat that would give twice as much grain and three times as much protein as rice. The gap would be even wider for pulses: with the 8,000 cubic meters per acre that rice demands, one could water five or six acres of peas or beans and provide the people with more food, more work and more cash receipts.

FERTILIZER

In simpler, not-so-dear departed days, any farmer could be self-sufficient in fertilizer. To nourish the soil, he merely ploughed under wastes from his previous crop, left the land fallow for a time, rotated his plantings (using, for instance, pulses that help to fix nitrogen in the soil after maize which removes it) or he used organic wastes from his animals and his own family. Any good amateur gardener keeps an eye on his compost piles in various stages of disintegration because he knows the contribution "worthless" matter can make to next year's flowers and vegetables. Still, we can no longer think in terms of simple gardening, and such ideally cyclical "soft technology" using wastes, although it has its place, is wholly inadequate to the needs of modern farming which demands chemical industrially produced fertilizers.

If you were allowed only one indicator to guess the productivity of any given country's agriculture, the best one to choose would be the amount of fertilizer used. You might measure it in two ways: pounds per acre or pounds per capita, but you would come up with the same results. They would be more spectacularly unequal if you chose pounds per acre: you could show, for instance, that Holland uses 470 times as much fertilizer as Ghana, or that Western Europe in general consumes 21 times as much as the whole of Africa. Comparisons per capita would also be revealing: 27 times as much fertilizer used for every American as for every Indian and nearly nine times as much for every citizen of the developed world compared to all those of all the UDCs.

A ton of fertilizer applied in a previously unfertilized area (i.e. most of the underdeveloped world) can produce up to ten extra tons of grain, whereas an extra ton spread in the developed world will not produce more than a maximum of three extra tons because of the law of diminishing returns. While one ton more of fertilizer matters only marginally to those countries that already have the best yields, it matters vitally to those who are still far from self-sufficient in food production.

The Third World, according to the latest (1974-5) FAO estimates, could produce about 17 per cent of the world's fertilizer if existing plants were used to full capacity, but for a variety of reasons this is not the case. In reality, these countries produce about 8 per cent of all fertilizer and consume about 15 per cent. This means—conversely—that those 25-30 per cent of the world's inhabitants who comprise the developed nations' population use 85 per cent of all fertilizer for their own crops.

Even though the poor-world nations thus had to import about half of their fertilizer to satisfy commercial demand (this does not mean, obviously, that they satisfied their real *needs*), until the early 1970s they at least knew the quantities they could count on and the approximate price they would be expected to pay. Then the lid blew off.

There are three kinds of fertilizer: Nitrogen (N), which accounts for about 55 per cent of world production; Phosphate (P) providing 21 per cent, and Potash (K) making up the remaining 24 per cent. All three have undergone dramatic price increases. Urea, which is basic to N, cost $16 a ton in 1971, $95 in 1973, and $300 in 1974; P in its natural form went from $14 to $42 a ton during the same period, while its derivative, triple superphosphate, also tripled in price; figures for K are not quite so drastic, but have more than doubled. UDCs were already paying $550 million in hard currency for fertilizers in 1971. Now, merely to keep up the same level of imports, they would have to pay $2½ *billion*. Several nations willing to make financial sacrifices still were not able to obtain fertilizer in 1974 at any price. The FAO issued a series of alarming bulletins for 1975. The year's spring crops in the poor world suffered from serious shortages of fertilizer and the head of FAO's International Fertilizer Supply Scheme announced that if money was not available through emergency aid very soon, many of the nations the UN calls "MSA" ("most seriously affected") may as well resign themselves to even lower yields for the autumn plantings. A technical document issued by the FAO Commission on Fertilizers in June 1975, which projected supply and demand of fertilizers up to 1981 by regions, showed depressing rows of minus signs for the "Developing Market Economy" (i.e. underdeveloped, non-centrally planned) countries: they will remain in a permanent state of underproduction and undersupply for the foreseeable future. The centrally planned (socialist) economies of Europe and Asia are expected to be mostly self-sufficient in N, P and K; while the developed world will have surpluses—but small ones—and these surpluses are expected to decline as we move into the next decade. It is no wonder that Raymond Ewell, a world authority on fertilizers, insists that there will be a permanent fertilizer shortage "for the rest of history." The FAO projections show that world capacity will just barely be able to cover effective (commercial) demand and that it will come nowhere near satisfying needs if more food crops are to be grown in the poor countries*

Fertilizer is therefore a Disaster Area. Is this pre-ordained? Must the Third World be undersupplied and thus condemned to underproduction

---

*US fertilizer prices dropped in 1975, but were recovering by the end of 1976—and '77 looks good for the industry: "The US farm belt will be planted from fence to fence . . . farmers have lots of cash . . . they'll plow significant amounts of it back into the land as fertilizer." (*Financial World*, October 15, 1976).

of food "for the rest of history?" Why have we reached such a pass? I am prepared to argue that just as war is far too important to be left to the generals, fertilizer is far to vital a commodity to be left in the hands of the fertilizer industry. This industry provides us with a perfect example of how the free-market system works.

First of all, there is going to be very little fertilizer for export to the places where it would do the most good and produce three times the present yields in food. The United States has removed all restrictions on the amount of cropland that can be put into production because it knows it can now sell all the grain it can grow. This has already increased the demand for fertilizer by American farmers, who complain that now they cannot buy enough even though they can afford it. There are also reports that many DC farmers are hoarding fertilizer, fearing further price hikes. The industry prefers to sell to steady customers for whom hard cash is no problem. Thus the US farmer and his counterparts in Western Europe will take priority.

Orville Freeman—as President of Business International he hardly qualifies as an enemy of business—tapped the industry mildly on the wrist in a recent speech:

> With fertilizer, as with food or any other resource, not only production but *distribution* questions of an economic and moral nature arise when supplies are short. As nitrogenous fertilizers became critically scarce in late 1973, the immediate reaction of Japan, the United states and European exporters was to reduce exports and maximize the domestic supply, even though farmers in these agriculturally advanced nations already use high levels and thus get rapidly diminishing returns from each additional amount of fertilizer applied . . . It will also be necessary for nitrogen exporting nations to at least restore exports to 1973 levels, both in aid programs and commercial channels, rather than reducing them as they did in early 1973.

Above and beyond diminishing returns, it takes more and more fertilizer in DCs just to maintain *present* yields: for example in the US it has been estimated that merely to maintain an average yield of 150 bushels of maize, use of nitrogen fertilizer has had to increase from 120 to 480 pounds per acre. In the UK, use of nitrogen has risen from 100 units per acre to 420 units, while wheat yields have only risen from about 120 to 170 units. The increase in meat consumption by people in the DCs also contributes specifically to the demand for fertilizer, as ever-increasing amounts of grain for cattle feed (and fertilizer for grasslands in countries where cattle are still pasture fed) are required. Finally, at least 2 million tons of fertilizer in the US (and at least 100,000 tons in the UK) are used for beautifying lawns, golf-course and other non-food-producing greenery. Some researchers have put the estimate of non-food fertilizer use in the US as high as 10 to 15 per cent of the total consumption, although industry insists it is not more than 3 to 4 per cent.

UDCs cannot always use even the fertilizer-producing capacity that they have. The industry is highly energy intensive, and because of fuel costs, many poor countries have had to cut back. Many must also import the basic feedstocks for production and they often suffer from other classic effects of underdevelopment—poor transportation systems for getting the fertilizer to farmers, shortages of spare parts and plant maintenance facilities, lack of storage and of enough trained personnel, etc. An FAO team has recently reported their concern that "80 per cent of the small farmers in the developing countries had to be without fertilizers . . ." and that they were being "squeezed out of fertilizer use by high prices, lack of credit to meet the higher prices and lack of access to supplies." The team also deplores cases "where fertilizer was going primarily to cash crop plantations while food producers had to do without." This means that from the meager amount of fertilizer actually used in the UDCs, we must still subtract untold numbers of tons that go to cash crops that will, in any event, benefit the developed, not the underdeveloped world. But on the whole, the worst-off countries have very little capacity—properly utilized or not—and production and distribution rest with the industries of the rich countries. It is therefore worth examining in more detail what the latter are doing.

Companies involved in fertilizer production all reported record profits in 1974 and are looking forward to bigger and better things as more acreage comes under production: one top industry executive in the US predicted (in 1975) that "between the surge in wheat acreage and a USDA forecast of between 79 and 80 million acres of corn to be planted . . . demand should set another all time high" . . . "As to our foreign fertilizer markets, we do not see any rapid export expansion since US producers are primarily committed to supply the domestic market." This gentleman, Mr. Joseph P. Sullivan, President of Estech Inc., also feels that the government of his country will not interfere with this situation, in spite of pressure on the part of some concerned about world hunger to increase fertilizer exports: "My own feeling is that we [i.e., the US government] will emphasize grain shipments rather than fertilizer shipments as part of over-all policy." This means that the poor can continue to pay inflated prices for grain, rather than have any hope of achieving food self-sufficiency, even if it meant having to pay inflated prices for fertilizer. This is because it is all-important to the US, economically and politically, to control grain supplies to the Third World, and indirectly its food production.

What has happened in the fertilizer industry in recent years is fairly typical of the free market system as a whole. When production is high, prices tend to decline and industry has no incentive to invest in greater capacity. As demand goes up, so does the price. Industry decisions to invest in new plants follow the price—but just enough to ensure continued high prices and profits, for the industry does not want to see prices decline. Therefore, production capacity must be tightly monitored and controlled. At a meeting of the International Fertilizer Supply Scheme, an emergency operation set up in 1974 by FAO at the request of the UN, the following exchange took place:

Speaking on behalf of the developing countries . . . Suleiman A. Jabati . . . said the "fertilizer problem is going from bad to worse" and asked participants from industry if there was any chance of relief in prices.

A candidly negative reply came from Neal Schenet, Division Vice President of the US-based International Minerals and Chemical Corporation.

"I don't see any hope for a drop in prices in the immediate future," Mr. Schenet said. He added that the fertilizer industry worldwide is "plowing hundreds of millions of dollars back into additional plant capacity."

"There is a fine line," he said, "between expansion to meet expected demand and overexpanding to the point where oversupply results."*

And since Mr. Schenet and his colleagues are in fact interested only in customers who can afford prices set by his industry—prices that are set by scarcity value rather than production costs—he does not find it obscene to speak of a "fine line" and of possible "oversupply" in a world where people will necessarily continue to starve, partly because of the way his industry is run.

We have reached the apex of absurdity in some UDCs: Mr. Steiner of the FAO Fertilizer Scheme explains that paradoxically there are actually surpluses of fertilizer in certain countries:

The major reason for this began [in 1973]. At that time, governments of the Third World were importing fertilizer at very high prices. The results were that most farmers could not afford to use fertilizer. The governments themselves could not subsidize the cost to farmers. Net result: countries were forced to cut back on fertilizer imports, which has left a surplus on the market. Thus the need for fertilizer is still there, but the old problem of lack of effective demand (purchasing power) has forced a reduction in fertilizer use.

Before we shed too many tears for the industry and its troubles in drawing fine lines, let us ask how business was in 1974. One of the giants reports:

In 1974, Estech Inc. (part of the Esmark conglomerate) faced the challenges of wage and price controls, inflation, the energy crisis and numerous other domestic and international problems. However, for Estech, it proved to be a year of record performance in sales and profits. The pace was set by the outstanding performance of the Fertilizer and Agricultural Chemicals group in Swift Chemical Co. All operating units surpassed previous results and the profit goals set for the fiscal

---

*Schenet is not alone. Other executives explained to *Business Week* why, "despite the threat of overcapacity, fertilizer makers' prospects look very good for . . . [1976] and perhaps for many years to come. Back in the 1960s, they say, the glut and the price wars that developed in fertilizer were largely the result of oil companies moving heavily into new markets they did not understand. This time, most of the big expansion projects have been undertaken by established producers who know the penalities if they press too hard." (*Business Week*, January 12, 1976)

year . . . The Swift fertilizer operation had a record year, both in profits and tons of product sold. The emphasis, as always, was placed on service to the American farmer.

Other US fertilizer firms did every bit as well in 1974. In Great Britain, the picture is the same. Albright and Wilson nearly doubled profits during 1972-3, and ICI (agricultural activities profits only) tripled theirs during 1970-73. Fisons may be doing something wrong: their profit increase for the same period was little more than a third.

What about the companies' vaunted "service to the American farmer"? Some do not feel so well served as all that. In fact, the *Wall Street Journal* reports that the

. . . Attorneys General of Washington, Idaho, and Montana filed civil anti-trust suits in federal court accusing eight companies, including subsidiaries of several major oil companies, of fixing prices and eliminating competition in the sale of commercial fertilizers . . . The suits say the alleged price fixing and monopolistic activities of the defendants have put Pacific Northwest farmers at a competitive disadvantage because fertilizer price levels in the area have been higher than elsewhere . . . the suits also charge that the defendants *created an artificial fertilizer shortage during the energy crisis to drive up prices* [my emphasis].

These are not radical economists crying "Fraud," but the top law-enforcement officers of three US states.

Meanwhile the industry is sitting pretty. It intends never again to return to the "surplus" situation of the 1960s when technological innovations reduced production costs by 20 per cent and increased plant production from an average 600 to 1,000 tons a day. Conversions to this new type of plant in the industrialized countries led to rapid increase in volume and several newcomers—including the oil giants—moved into the industry. The result was "overproduction" (always in relation to commercial demand) which sent prices for the main type of N plummeting from $90 to $20 a ton. Many companies pulled out, but those who hung on took over the market and are now reaping super-profits from the prices they are in a position to set at home and abroad.

Investment in new plant capacity triggered by the booming market is estimated (by Estech's Sullivan) at $5 billion between now and 1980, but production will not come "on stream," as industry jargon has it, for at least another two or three years. And as the FAO's projection figures show, it will not result in sizeable surpluses—much less in a glut on the market. Meanwhile, the developed countries will continue to get almost all the fertilizer there is. In 1973, when the situation began to be critical, India's supplies were down 30 per cent, Pakistan's 20 per cent and Bangladesh's 50 per cent. There seems little reason to hope this situation may change.

How could such glaring inequalities be corrected? The chronic fertilizer "shortage" seems destined to condemn the UDCs to permanent low yields if something is not done. Orville Freeman, a former US Secretary of Agriculture, reminded the fertilizer industry that "chemical fertilizers account for approximately one third of all the food produced in the world today. A world without fertilizer would be a world without the capacity to sustain a *billion* [his emphasis] of our fellow human beings." He did not add that the "world without fertilizer" already exists and presently contains *three* billions of our "fellow human beings."

Certain institutions like the World Bank today lament the scarcity of fertilizer in the UDCs. Unfortunately, although fertilizer has been considered one of the keys to solving the world hunger problem for easily twenty years, the Bank itself has done little to help poor nations produce it, and has, upon occasion, even impeded their efforts. Thus, when Algeria proposed construction of its first fertilizer plant, the Bank refused to help finance it, basing its refusal on the contention that the plant would be too large for Algeria's own needs and that the government would have to show purchase-contracts from other countries beforehand. The Algerians went ahead and built the plant solely with national financing. Today it does not even supply half the country's needs.

The most valid proposal for helping to reverse the catastrophic fertilizer situation comes from the Sri Lanka report on fertilizers to the World Food Conference. It is couched in cautious language, but states unequivocally that "unless urgent attention is given to the fertilizer industry and it is retrieved from the vagaries of market forces, all attempts at agricultural development, and the economic development of the Third World, will experience a severe setback." At the moment, this hoped-for "retrieval" can be seen as an exercise in wishful thinking. One does not see the industry divesting itself of its present advantages, although it may adjust its prices to somewhat more realistic levels.

Today's utopia should be tomorrow's realistic goal. Meanwhile, a slight improvement could be made if societies which formerly depended mostly upon organic matter for fertilizer, but which were encouraged to switch to chemicals, could return to "soft," recycling technology. The UN suggests the use of

... various types of plant, animal and human wastes which provide nitrogen, phosphate and potash nutrients as well as other benefits to agriculture. The total potential availability of this fertilizer resource in the developing countries is very large—it is estimated very roughly that the total of waste products in developing countries in 1970-71, which could be used for organic manuring, contained 7-8 times more nutrient [in terms of N, P and K] than the total amount of inorganic fertilizer consumed by them in that year.

Unfortunately, this is not just a technical problem. Pierre Spitz learned from his inquiries in the field in Sri Lanka that peasants had been encouraged to switch to imported chemical fertilizers and that the extension services had implied they were "backward" if they refused. The changeover to purchased fertilizers was eventually made. But then the export price for copra, natural rubber and especially tea—Sri Lanka's biggest source of foreign exchange—declined drastically while prices for fertilizer continued to climb. Now the rural extension workers would like to see the peasants switch back to the old system of compost—but they have discovered that any technological change also means a change in the *social* fabric, and that seesawing from one method to another is not so simple.

China, of course, has brought the use of organic wastes to the status of a fine art, properly treating them before use to remove harmful bacteria. The Chinese have also developed a whole network of "backyard" fertilizer factories. There are now about 800 of these plants, turning coal and water into nitrogen fertilizer. "Together they supplied half of China's consumption of inorganic fertilizer in 1973 . . . In addition, China has planned or is constructing eight fertilizer factories capable of producing a thousand tons a day."* "The American scientists [ten leading agronomists who visited China for four weeks late in 1974] said the backyard fertilizer plants which produce ammonium bicarbonate, a chemical not generally used as a fertilizer outside China, appeared to be using a simple technology that might well be adapted to other areas of the world."

Another step could be to bring production of fertilizer closer to the basic sources of raw materials, known as "feedstocks." Natural gas is about the best feedstock there is for nitrogen fertilizer, because it is cheaper per unit of energy than other sources and also because plants using it require simpler technology and thus less capital investment. At present, the oil-producing nations flare—that is, waste—something like 130 billion cubic meters of gas every year. On-site fertilizer-plant construction for using this natural gas could have an enormous impact on food production in the UDCs, for there is every reason to believe that these countries would receive priority fertilizer shipments from Arab States producers. Trade journals report a number of joint ventures planned or under way between US firms and Middle-East governments.

There are all sorts of proposals aired in various UN/FAO forums concerning the establishment of "fertilizer pools," bilateral or multi-lateral financing aid schemes in favor of UDCs, buffer stockpiling by governments, "Special Drawing Rights" through which poor countries could call, in time of need, on a small percentage of world production, and the like. One doubts that any of these proposals can amount to much in a world where DC industry, hiding behind the "free market," determines the price—and it is the *price* of fertilizer that is the chief problem. Industry will not give up its privileges without pressure. The Third World itself is not likely to supply such pressure, by the simple fact

---

*These plants have been ordered from a US firm.

of its dependency on the industry. Given all this, one solution—although partial—might be long-term, set-price contracts between producers and importers. The FAO Commission on Fertilizers rather dryly remarks that "unfortunately, in the past the international fertilizer market has featured opportunism on the part of both exporters and importers." (Some, as George Orwell might say, are in a position to be more opportunistic than others.) "However, with a built-in pricing formula including minimum and maximum prices, and a reasonable amount of good will between the contracting parties, such contracts could prove to be beneficial to both sides."

International aid should meanwhile concentrate on allowing the UDCs to get the most out of their existing plant capacity, on increasing the efficiency of use and distribution of what fertilizer they have and on directing research towards new types of feedstocks and simpler technology (as in China). Nations receiving food aid should be allowed a choice between food and fertilizer aid. The UDCs themselves will have to resist the temptation to allocate fertilizer to cash crops in the hopes of earning more foreign exchange. It won't help them much anyway in a period of ever-rising prices for food and manufactured goods imports. They must direct it rather to the farmers who can produce food for the country far more economically. But in the final analysis, utopian though it may seem today, the fertilizer industry is going to have to be considered as a public utility—like water or electricity—and not as a source of profits for private business reaping benefits from the hunger of others.

PESTICIDES

What is a pest? The FAO, which is very thorough in such matters, says it's an insect, mite, tick, nematode, fungus, bacteria, weed, rodent, bird, mollusc, crustacea or virus that hurts or damages the animals and plants man uses for his foods and fibers. So what's a pesticide? Any natural method or synthetic chemical substance that can get rid of any of the above. The term thus incorporates insecticides, herbicides and all the other -cides that correspond to the list.

If the UDC situation is bad for fertilizers, it is disastrous for pesticides. In 1970, the US bought 45 per cent of all the compounds available, followed by Western Europe (23 per cent), Eastern Europe and Japan. Total sales in all the UDCs combined amounted to only 7 per cent of the total. This proportion has not improved: in 1974-5 it doubtless worsened, even though the poor nations are planting more and more crop varieties which absolutely demand pesticides in order to prosper. World sales at manufacturers' prices amounted to about $4 billion in 1970; they are expected to reach $10 billion in 1980. This does not make the industry a particularly large one: by way of comparison, consider that a single US farm-machinery manufacturer (John Deere) reported sales in 1974 of nearly $2½ billion! Nor is it an industry which is expanding especially fast, in spite of the need for its products. Finally, it is not an industry in which the small can survive. A limited number of companies will therefore continue to produce what they plan on, according to their own timetables, and will continue to sell to the sure and stable markets of the DCs that have always taken priority.

Pesticides, like fertilizers, depend largely on petroleum products for their basic feedstocks, and the current market situation is very tight. Demand reduced 1973-4 stocks to zero. At that time, the UN Assessment predicted a 20-30 per cent shortage for 1975, noting that "a shortfall of this order could almost eliminate the pesticide supply to the developing countries if the developed countries which produce almost all of the basic feedstocks from pesticides [gave] first priority to meeting their own requirements." One could legitimately claim that a world revolution had taken place if the developed countries did anything else! Since this revolution has not occurred, the prediction has come true: India and Pakistan say they have been particularly hard hit. The longer-term outlook is not much brighter.

Before the stricter stripe of ecologists reading these facts rejoice for the chemical purity of the Third World, they should realize that food lost *on the stalk* through pests and disease in the poor countries is estimated at about *one third* their actual harvest, and that food lost *in storage* can run as high as 40 per cent. The value of world crop losses in a single year can be calculated in terms of 1973 grain prices at $75 *billion*. To strengthen this demonstration, we may take the case of two Asian countries, Japan and India. In 1952, both of them produced about the same amount of rice per hectare. Then Japan introduced massive use of pesticides. (This was not the only change, but it was a major one.) The figures now show Japan producing 58 quintals per hectare and India only 16. India has about 30 per cent of the world's rice growing land, but on this area provides only about 20 per cent of the total crop. Some African countries have rice yields as low as 5 quintals per hectare. Many people feel that Japan has gone chemically overboard, but it ought to be possible to find a middle ground between poisoning the land and needlessly losing precious food.

These figures give some idea of what happens to food from the fields because of inadequate chemical disease prevention and protection. What happens to food on the hoof is just as bad. One specialist counts the world's total cattle population at 100 million head, and says at least *two thirds* are infested by some kind of parasite or disease. In the US—which certainly has reasonably good standards of animal health—cash losses of animals and poultry during 1951-60 reached well over $5 billion. (These are the last years for which figures are available and they are given in the uninflated dollars of the period.) As we have by now come to expect, the situation in poor countries is worse. Mexico and Peru (1960) had animal losses amounting to at least 37 per cent of their total animal production, and it took Guinea five years to replace its herds after a single outbreak of rinderpest. Nobody really knows what this means in terms of losses of milk, eggs and meat.

This book is no advocate of cash crops for the UDCs, but for the moment cash crops are what they produce, and it is *impossible* to grow most of them without pesticides. A test plot at the Experimental Cotton Center in Nicaragua was left totally untreated throughout the growing season. It produced 130 kilos of cotton per hectare. In Nicaragua, a farmer has to get *1,550* kilos per hectare just to break even. After three years of treating cocoa trees against the capsid bug, Ghana discovered it was getting yields nearly 250 per cent higher than before. When no chemical control existed, during the late nineteenth and early twentieth centuries, whole agricultural industries were wiped out: coffee in Sri Lanka, cocoa in large parts of South America, and bananas on thousands of acres in Central America simply disappeared. All this could happen again without pesticides.

What makes the market so tight, and why are pesticide prices climbing? Increased petroleum prices are only a fraction of the story. Agri-chemicals are produced by perhaps the most research-intensive industry on earth. Industry spokesmen point out that they now have to screen up to 10,000 compounds for every one that eventually reaches the market—and it will not reach the market before an average of eight years has elapsed. In 1974–75, the cost of developing a single new active ingredient was $10 million, up from $4 million in 1967. In addition to the long screening process that determines active ingredients, one must find the best method of application (dust, emulsion etc.), and conduct field trials over several years in different areas of the world that include tests for toxicity and residues. Market studies and the registration process also take time.

Even if one is not especially enthusiastic about the activities of multinational corporations, it is only realistic to state that barring total overhaul of the world economic system, they alone are able to invest the necessary capital (with very high costs in trained research personnel) necessary for the development of chemical crop and animal protection. In the entire world, there are only 30 to 35 research centers for the development of new pesticides, and this figure may well decrease in the future since costs are increasing drastically. Five of these firms are in West Germany, ten or twelve more in the rest of Western Europe, less than ten in the US, three to five in Japan. There are a few in Eastern Europe, but their production is not marketed outside the area.

Most UDCs do not have on hand sufficient supplies of the basic chemical products to make even the simplest compounds, and the more sophisticated products necessitating up to five different syntheses lie totally beyond their manufacturing reach. What might they do about this—aside from accepting blights and harmful insects as a permanent part of the landscape? Instead of attempting to start a pesticides industry from scratch, they should probably concentrate on formulation plants that can receive bulk ingredients from foreign suppliers and then prepare the emulsions, solubles, etc. themselves. This would mean they would import smaller tonnages with consequent savings in hard currency. It could also mean that their plants might face a degree of obsolescence and might not be able to handle some of the more highly synthesized products—but better a few broad-range protection agents than none at all.

UDC governments could also consider getting together to project demand and to make common longer-term purchasing arrangements. Industry complains that it cannot foresee the UDC's needs (in commercial terms) far enough in advance to provide for them. UDC governments should also cooperate with the efforts of the FAO and the Codex Alimentarius to establish acceptable international standards concerning toxicity, residues, etc. If a country, especially a small one with a limited market, imposes complicated registration formalities for products which have long been in normal use elsewhere, industry will just say, in essence, to hell with it. The patent-life of a product is not long enough to make further time losses worth its while. Finally, UDCs should devote some of their rural extension-work efforts to showing farmers how to get the most out of the pesticides they do have. Simple "ultra-low-volume" spraying techniques are one example. Tanzania has introduced this system for its cotton acreage—mixing purchased chemicals with its own cotton seed oil—and figures that it economizes 90 million liters of scarce water while using only one third the number of mechanical sprayers it used to employ with conventional techniques.

Such measures are becoming more than ever necessary as the US, the world's number-one hogger of pesticides, puts more farm acreage under production; and as "speculative buying and stocking of feedstocks and finished products" on the part of certain nameless agents cited by FAO aggravate scarcity conditions. Because the pesticides industry is a small one, it may be the first in which supply and demand can be planned in a slightly more rational way than simply by allowing "market forces" to do the job. A hopeful sign is that representatives of 90 per cent of the industry are now cooperating with FAO, giving future supply data on a confidential basis, which FAO then digests and passes on to the UDCs to help them make their own plans.

Scientists working for chemical companies that produce pesticides have made major contributions to controlling and eliminating plant, animal and human disease. For example, a major company has recently isolated a compound that can effectively eradicate bilharzia-carrying snails in Africa. If these companies did not do it, the chances are that no one else would. There is, however, an area in which they are weak, for obvious economic reasons. This is the domain of biological control (inhibition of mating, release of sterile insects and the like). Such measures for the moment can only be applied to insects (perhaps a quarter of all pests) but research is not exactly leaping ahead, since success would eliminate the need for the companies' future services. It is comprehensible, from their point of view, that attention continues to be concentrated in the field of chemical compounds. Yet in the Soviet Union, a Leningrad factory is now producing 50 million helpful insects a day and biological insect control is now used on 22 million acres (as opposed to 300 million still treated chemically). This proves that it can be done, and on a considerable scale. Any public or private non-industry funds that can be found for research should go to the areas of biological, microbial (bacteria secreting toxins specifically harmful to other organisms), physical ("black-light" traps, irradiation) and cultural (crop rotation) pest control.

It may be altogether logical for environmentalists to worry about pesticides in the California valleys or in Japan, but this, to put it mildly, is hardly the problem in the UDCs. These nations could feed themselves even today if they benefited from the kind of crop protection—on and off the stalk—that is a matter of course in the rich countries.

They should, however, be careful what they order, especially from "development" agencies like USAID! "Nothing is forbidden from AID-financed procurements. . . . That is, materials regulated or banned from domestic use (e.g. DDT) are not so regulated for international commerce."* It is also possible in UDCs where manpower is abundant and capital scarce, to use human labor for tasks like weeding, crop surveillance, pest-egg collection and the like. But in tropical countries there is no cold weather period to reduce insect activity, and the fact that we in the West have polluted our own environment should not cause us to militate for zero-level pesticide use in UDCs. For a detailed and authoritative discussion of such matters, I refer those who read French to the book by Joseph Klatzmann, Professor at the Institut National d'Agronomie; especially to Chapter Five, entitled "No Agriculture without Fertilizers and Pesticides." (See bibliography).

FARM MECHANIZATION

Large-scale use of fertilizers and pesticides are largely phenomena of the second half of the twentieth century, but agricultural machinery is a child of the Industrial Revolution and occupies almost a symbolic niche in the modernization process of farming. Poor countries have tended to see the tractor as a panacea, and the rich ones have generally been only too happy to encourage this belief. By the early 1970s, traditional DC markets for tractor producers were almost saturated. Now they, too, are

*"Purchasing Management," *Chemical Marketing Reporter,* 5 May 1975.

benefiting from the new US land policy: the companies cannot even keep up with home demand. Giant manufacturers like Deere, Caterpillar, and Massey-Ferguson all reported production running at full capacity in 1973-4, with employees working overtime—and still they were obliged to put deliveries on an allocation system. Fiat replies to requests for information with glossy promotional brochures rather than figures, but it still claims to sell one out of every ten tractors the world produces. All these companies credit expanding farm production and higher farm incomes with sending their sales zooming. In spite of plans for expansion, they were not able to keep up with demand in 1975 either.

According to Fiat, European farmers ride nearly half of the world's tractors, and North Americans over a quarter. The other quarter of sales goes to the three poor continents, and, of course, to the largest farmers on them. Countries where latifundia are a principal feature of the landscape are the best customers: for example, Massey-Ferguson reports sales up by 80 per cent in Argentina in 1973, and "Brazil remains the second largest of Massey-Ferguson's markets for tractors and the third largest for combines."

So in the department of farm mechanization, the inequality figures are a little less unequal—if we consider only the richest farmers. Obviously, smallholders cannot make economic use of tractors, and most of the UDCs do not encourage collective ownership, regrouping of plots or cooperatives that could make investment in machinery profitable. A major manufacturer, in a study on labor displacement by farm machinery undertaken in 1974, claims that "no more than 6-7 per cent of total world tractor production is required at present by the developing countries. It is therefore understandable that major manufacturers have had little incentive to design machines specific to developing country needs." This contrasts with what Fiat says, but if we accept these figures, then we should assume that 93 per cent of *current* production is now being sold in the developed countries although UDCs may possess about 25 per cent of *existing* machinery in various stages of disrepair. "Requirements" doubtless refers to what UDCs can purchase in a tight market situation, not to their needs. In any event, very little effort is being expended on developing machines—like two-wheeled cultivators—which would be far more useful to small farmers than traditional tractors.

It is not *always* true that tractors reduce the need for labor, especially when they help to prepare additional land for cultivation. But it is increasingly true that farm mechanization can be downright dangerous for the poor.* Combine harvesters replace at least 90 workers wherever they go. Mechanization can be expected to increase productivity *per*

*See also the chapter on technology *supra*.

worker—but not necessarily *per hectare*—and thus it can lower crop production costs. The large, mechanized landholder can then afford to sell cheaper to the merchants, helping to drive smallholders out of business. The cycle is completed when the big man buys up the small one's land, paving the way for more mechanization on larger holdings. On the whole, when it is not community-controlled as in China, farm mechanization increases the dependency of the Third World on Western agribusiness and the domination of the rich landholders over the poor.

RESEARCH

Agricultural research is a vital, if intangible modern input. The latest figures (1970) available in UN documents indicate that developed countries spent more than 5½ times as much money on research as the poorer ones ($1.3 billion as against $236 million). But these figures are deceptive for two reasons. First, they concern only the public, or government research sector. In the United States at least half of all research is done by agribusiness corporations. The second disparity is that at least half the research being done "in" the UDCs is not necessarily being done "for" them. Much of this research effort is made by outside private or international agencies and is entirely concerned with cash crops, which will end up in the rich countries anyway. So the amount of research devoted to food production in the UDCs is tragically low.

Tragically, because research pays. One of the more enthusiastic advocates of the multinational corporations points out that although a machine can be patented, "a better method of applying fertilizer to corn cannot, [yet the companies] still find research profitable." Annual returns, calculated in increased yields, on research investment average about 300 per cent and can go as high as 700 per cent in a single year.

One might object that the UDCs can nevertheless use the research that has been done in the rich world. Knowledge is supposed to be free. Theoretically, yes. Practically speaking, Western efforts are oriented towards food crops, but specifically to food crops that grow in the climatic and other ecological conditions of their own regions. This is entirely normal. It does turn out occasionally that such efforts are applicable to other conditions. For instance, India and Pakistan introduced new Mexican varieties of wheat developed by Rockefeller Foundation scientists after very limited local field trials—but this is not the rule.

Access to scientific information is also supposedly "free," but that does not mean that it is without cost. Pierre Spitz points out that the organization he works for, the Institut National de la Recherche Agronomique, subscribes to 2,000 different agriculture-related publications; that there are something like 400,000 varieties of wheat alone; that in 1972 a single international research center produced 5,500 new strains of wheat. Research centers in the poor countries have nothing like the personnel or the physical means necessary to collect, read, classify and distribute available knowledge. The UN's judgment reinforces such conclusions. Reviews made over a five-year period (1969-74) by FAO show that "the Ministries of Agriculture in several countries of Asia had fewer than 5 Ph.D. and fewer than 10 M.Sc. degree-level scientists in their entire organizations." Throughout the underdeveloped world, "70 per cent of research institutions have less than ten trained research workers and in most regions 50-60 per cent of the institutes have less than five." What is more, these people are poorly paid, compared to their advanced training and to the contributions they could make. You almost have to be a national hero in a UDC to work for a public research institution when you could do much better financially in a private corporation or abroad. The brain drain is particularly severe for qualified agronomists. There also seems to be a tendency in UDC research centers to want to cover too much ground, with the result that none of it is covered very well. Expenditure on agricultural research in UDCs (1970) came to a puny 0.25 per cent of the total value of agricultural production to their economies. By contrast, the wealthier countries spend up to 2 per cent of agricultural receipts annually on research.

Clearly the UDCs need help, and they should be getting it from international, no-strings-attached research centers situated in the poor world itself. A few already exist; some of them are funded by US private foundations. It is far from sure that the latter attach no strings—or at least less visible gossamer threads—to the kind of research that is undertaken and financed. (See Chapter 5, "The Green Revolution.")

Such centers should concentrate on food and food alone, including livestock and poultry. They should, furthermore, concentrate on increasing protein content in cereals, on better methods of cultivation of high-protein crops like pulses which have lately been dangerously downgraded; on local oilseeds that are an important part of poor peoples' diets; and especially on the whole field of tropical agriculture. At the moment, there is very little knowledge about what can actually be grown in the tropical hunger belt—except for bananas, cocoa, sugar, and the other cash exports.

The UN proposes a very modest target for 1985: $1.25 billion to be spent on agricultural research in and on behalf of the UDCs annually. If the multinationals wanted to improve their standing in the international community, together they could easily commit part of such a sum, as well as grant leaves of absence to their own scientists for work—paid by the companies—in regional institutes. But it would be up to the governments of the poor countries to set the research goals themselves. Otherwise they would run the risk of seeing research oriented toward the possible future sales of the corporations' products.

CREDIT

In the sphere of credit the small Third World farmer again gets the short end of the stick. In Latin America just the top 15 per cent of the farming community has access to state or private credit, while in Africa there are only 5 per cent. In most UDCs, very little credit is available to the agricultural sector *as a whole*—rich or poor. There is *no* credit available to some 100 million small farmers who are worst off because they are considered poor risks and because the lending institutions don't want to be bothered with the administrative expenses of setting up very small—to them—loans. "In countries as disparate as Bangladesh and Iran, less than 10 per cent of institutional credit is available in rural areas; in Thailand, the Philippines and Mexico less than 15 per cent; in India less than 25 per cent. And only a fraction of this is available to the small farmer," says Robert McNamara.

The result is that the average small farmer invests only about $6 per hectare—if he can afford that—when to get a halfway decent yield he should be spending anywhere from $20 to $80 on vital inputs. The smallholder is trapped coming and going, because he is financially strapped: he must sell his crop immediately after harvest when prices are at their lowest. He is indebted to the local usurer who "tides him over"— for an exorbitant fee—between harvests. Even supposedly "free" farmers who are neither sharecroppers, squatters or landless can thus be reduced to peonage by the lack of a credit system worthy of the name. Agricultural extension services, sometimes managed or influenced by the international agribusinesses that sell inputs, also tend to benefit the larger landholders on a priority basis.

The small farmer in a UDC who cannot make ends meet usually has only one alternative to starvation—and that is the unsavory "private credit" network. The World Bank has compiled figures for several countries comparing "Institutional Rates" (those of legitimate private or state banks) to "Commercial Rates" (i.e., usury). They disclose that smallholders are paying anywhere from three to twenty times as much for credit from the money-lender as they would have to pay a bank—if it would condescend to look at them. In a tiny minority of UDCs, a substantial number of small farmers can get normal bank credit: in Taiwan 95 per cent, in South Korea 40 per cent, in Colombia 30 per cent. But in Ethiopia, Nigeria or Malaysia only 1 or 2 per cent. Not surprisingly, the small farmers in these countries must then pay whopping rates for private credit: yearly interest rates in Ethiopia are (were?) 66 per cent, in Malaysia 58 per cent; while first prize for all countries goes to Nigeria where usurers can get no less than 192 per cent interest per annum.

A Few Useful Addresses

Two intermediate technology groups:

VITA, 3706 Rhode Island Avenue, Mount Rainier, Maryland 20822 (c/o Tom Fox) and

TRANET, 7410 Vernon Square Drive, Alexandria, Virginia 22306 (c/o William Ellis). TRANET publishes a quarterly on appropriate tools and lists other working groups world-wide.

Interfaith Center on Corporate Responsibility, National Council of Churches, 475 Riverside Drive, New York, N.Y. 10027 (c/o Ms. Leah Margulies). ICCR is doing especially good work on the babyfoods issue.

American Freedom from Hunger Foundation (AFFHF), 1625 Eye Street NW, Suite 719, Washington, D.C. 20006. Fairly "establishment", but publishes free monthly bulletin listing resource materials and describing recent moves by US government.

World Hunger Year, Inc. (WHY), 211 East 43rd Street, New York, N.Y. 10017.

Students in the social sciences may check to see if their university has a group affiliated with the **Union for Radical Political Economics.** National address: URPE, 41 Union Square West, Room 901, New York, N.Y. 10003.

Returned Volunteer Action London tells me that the comparable US group no longer exists. Documents for past or future volunteers available from RVA, 1C Cambridge Terrace, London NW1, England.

The Institute for Food and Development Policy, P.O. Box 40430, San Francisco, California 94140. Publishes a monthly *Food Forum* and can help individuals link up with the action group closest to them.

References

I want this book to be something people will feel they can read on the bus, not something that has to be sat grimly in front of in a library; and I find tiny numbers in the text eye-stopping and distracting. My editor has furthermore told me, "Footnotes do rightly or wrongly give printers, production people and readers the impression of complexity." In the interests of both reading ease and publishing speed, we have therefore decided to adopt a references system that works chapter by chapter through the book listing references and sources. If it turns out not to be a good one, and if any fellow-researcher needs something I have inadvertently left out, I will be glad to supply missing links if he/she will be kind enough to write to me through Allanheld, Osmun.

The General Bibliography is a selection of (a) official or semi-official documents, (b) a winnowing of what I consider to be the "wheat." An enormous amount of chaff is published, and anyone seriously interested in pursuing the subject will not be able to avoid coming across much of it—my help will not be needed. The official documents listed contain plenty of reliable technical information. (The UNRISD studies are in a class by themselves—outstanding—and go beyond technical questions.) Since hunger in my opinion is not, however, a technical problem but a political and social one, I do not list documents emanating from such well known entities as the Club of Rome, US foundation-supported bodies and the like. I do try to give a few titles of sources for general reading I find valuable and which one might be less likely to encounter, but have no pretension to being exhaustive even here.

GENERAL BIBLIOGRAPHY

I urge people who agree with the general thrust of this book (and even more those who don't!) to subscribe to the *New Internationalist*, far-and-away the best regular periodical on development problems, including food: *New Internationalist*, Victoria Hall, Fingal Street, London SE 10 8BP, $12 annual subscription for the US.

Ditto, for more specialized information, the *News Bulletin* of the International Union of Food & Allied Workers' Associations: 100 Swiss francs (or equivalent) from IUF, Rampe du Pont Rouge 8, 1213 Petit-Lancy (Geneva), Switzerland.

Official or Semi-Official Documents

United Nations documents, available from the UN, Sales Section, United Nations Plaza, New York, N.Y. 10017. Sp. United Nations World Food Conference, *Assessment of the World Food Situation*, Item 8 of the Provisional Agenda (of the World Food Conference), E/Conf. 65/3; *The World Food Problem: Proposals for National and International Action*, Item 9 of the Provisional Agenda, E/Conf. 65/4; *Multinational Corporations in World Development*, ST/ECA/190

United Nations Research Institute for Social Development (UNRISD): various titles pertaining to the global study on "The social and economic implications of large-scale introduction of new varieties of foodgrain" (i.e., the Green Revolution), available from UNRISD, Palais des Nations, 1211 Geneva 10. (Each title $2.50.)

Organization for Economic Cooperation and Development (OECD): Seminar on *Science, Technology and Development in a Changing World*, 21-5 April 1975, publication expected 1977, available (as are other publications of the Development Center) from OECD Publications Office, 2 rue André Pascal, 75775 Paris CEDEX 16, France.

World Bank documents, including *Annual Reports*, *Speeches* by President McNamara to the Board of Governors, and various rural-development studies (request the catalogue) from the World Bank, 1818 H Street NW, Washington, D.C. 20433.

FAO has a huge catalogue of publications, which can be consulted in most libraries. The *Action for Development* office at FAO periodically publishes a useful summary of development literature: write to Development Education Exchange (DEEP), Action for Development, FAO, 00100 Rome, Italy. This office, in conjunction with the Freedom from Hunger Campaign, also publishes *Ideas and Action* on activities in favor of rural development in both DCs and UDCs.

For information on *multinational corporations*, you can start with their own annual reports and PR handouts. I simply wrote to the whole membership list of the Industry Cooperative Program of FAO—otherwise you can get necessary addresses from the *Standard and Poor* stock reports or *Moody's Industrial Manual* (containing detailed and up-to-date data on companies quoted on the US stock exchange). If not available in libraries, try the local Chamber of Commerce or the office of a broker dealing in securities.

US government publications (like Committee Hearings) from the Government Printing Office, Washington 20402; and the United States Department of Agriculture, Publications Division, Washington, D.C. 20250, particularly for the annual report on PL 480 (Food for Peace).

Both the *Reader's Guide to Periodical Literature* and the *Business Periodical Index* provide invaluable guides to magazine articles (mostly from the US), indexed by subject. Beyond that, I recommend regular perusal of the *Harvard Business Review*, the *Columbia Journal of World Business*, *Fortune*, and especially *Business Week*.

Books or special issues of periodicals:

Algeria, Democratic and Popular Republic of. *Petroleum, Raw Materials and Development* (Memorandum submitted by Algeria on the occasion of the Special Session of the United Nations General Assembly) and *Annex* to the above on *"Basic products of agricultural origin": Statistical data concerning production, consumption, exports, imports*, Algiers, April 1974.

Idem. Mémoire présenté par l'Algérie á la Conférence des Souverains et Chefs d'Etat des Pays Membres de l'OPEP, Alger, mars 1975.

American Association for the Advancement of Science. *Science*, Vol. 188, No. 4188, 9 May 1975 (special issue on food).

Amin, Samir (ed.). *L'Agriculture Africaine et le Capitalisme*, Anthropos-Idep, Paris, 1975 (case studies, concrete).

Amin, Samir and Vergopoulos, Kostas. *La Question Paysanne et le Capitalisme*, Anthropos, Paris, 1974 (*highly* theoretical).

Barnet, R. J., and Müller, R. E. *Global Reach: The Power of the Multinational Corporations*, Simon & Schuster, New York, 1974 (good on MNCs in general, little on agribusiness).

Barraclough, Geoffrey. Articles on the world food/energy crisis in the *New York Review of Books*, issues of January 23, 1975 and August 7, 1975.

Collins, Joseph, and Moore-Lappé, Frances. *Food First*, forthcoming, Houghton-Mifflin, 1977. (I haven't read it, but I trust the authors!)

Comité Information Sahel. *Qui Se Nourrit de la Famine en Afrique?* Maspéro, Paris, 1974.

Croissance des Jeunes Nations. *Les Riches Mangent Trop*, novembre 1974 (special issue on food and development).

Dumont, René. *Croissance . . . de la Famine*, Le Seuil, Paris, 1975.

INRA (Institut National de la Recherche Agronomique, Groupe d'Etude de Relations Economiques Internationales. Various publications, particularly on foodgrains and soybeans, as well as *Les Exportations des Etats-Unis au Titre de l'Aide Alimentaire: Bilan Chiffré 1955-1973*. Available from the GEREI, INRA, 6 Passage Tenaille, 75014 Paris. Request list of publications.

Jeune Afrique. *Les Dossiers "Bis" de Jeune Afrique*, special issue on the World Food Crisis ("La Crise Alimentaire Mondiale," janvier–juin 1975). Available from Jeune Afrique, 51 Avenue des Ternes, 75017 Paris.

Klatzmann, Joseph. *Nourrir Dix Milliards d'Hommes?* Presses Universitaires de France, Paris 1975.

Lerza, Catherine, and Jacobson, Michael (eds.). *Food for People Not for Profit*, Ballantine, New York, 1975 (collection of articles, some excellent).

Mason, E. S., and Asher, R. E. *The World Bank Since Bretton Woods*, The Brookings Institution, Washington D.C., 1973 (A 5 pound volume on IBRD up to the end of 1971).

Pirie, N. W. *Food Resources Conventional and Novel*, Penguin, 1969.

Rhodes, Robert I. (ed.). *Imperialism and Underdevelopment: A Reader*, Monthly Review Press, New York, 1970.

Spitz, Pierre. *De la Recherche en Sciences Sociales du Développement aux Etats-Unis*, Paris, 1971 (mimeo, and, I am sorry to report, virtually unavailable although very important to the preparation of the present work. One copy in INRA library at above adress; reprinting possible in 1977).

Transnational Institute. *World Hunger: Causes and Remedies*, Amsterdam and Washington, 1974. Available from Institute for Policy Studies, 1901 Q Street NW, Washington, D.C. 20036. $2.00 (See Foreword. Can be read especially as a companion piece and an antidote to the *UN Assessment*, op. cit.)

Unesco. *Le Courrier de l'UNESCO*, special issue on hunger, in English or French, May 1975.

Weissman, Steve, *et al. The Trojan Horse*, Ramparts Press, San Francisco, 1974 (an examination of US "aid": includes contributions on food aid, the Green Revolution, the World Bank *inter alia*).

REFERENCES

Any references to sources in languages other than English have been translated by me unless otherwise noted. "Op. cit." preceded by the name of an author refers to a source cited in the general bibliography above or already cited in the references. "Idem" means the same source as the one noted immediately above.

PART ONE

Chapter 1: Rich Man, Poor Man: Who's the Thief?

On eating too much meat and how still to get protein while eating less, see Frances Moore-Lappé, *Diet for a Small Planet*, Ballantine, New York, 1971; long introduction plus recipes. **Figures on how world grain production is consumed,** *UN Assessment*, op. cit. **Figures on US farmers** from USDA and AP dispatch, "Farming in US tends to fewer, larger holdings," *IHT*, 7 Jan. 1976. **Concentration of growers** in the US: *Fact Sheets on Food*, Union for Radical Political Economics (URPE Food Research Collective, c/o URPE, 41 Union Square West, New York, N.Y. 10003), undated, but apparently around December 1973, mimeo. **Tenneco** information from its annual reports. **North Carolina super-farm:** AP dispatch by Robert B. Cullen, Knight newspapers, incl. the *Akron Beacon Journal*, Section E, 10 November 1974. **Feedlots:** from corporate publications, sp. the Merck Sharp and Dohme *International Review*, several issues. **Soviet animal raising system:** various press reports, confirmed by J.-P. Berlan of INRA, visited USSR in 1975. **Generalization of US energy/grain-intensive agricultural model to rest of world:** Susan Sechler and Susan de Marco, a digest of the *Agribusiness Accountability Project Report* ("The Marketplace of Hunger") in *Ramparts*, July 1975. See also same authors, *The Fields Have Turned Brown*, Agribusiness Accountability Project, 1000 Wisconsin Avenue, NW, Washington, D.C. 20007, 1975. *Fortune* article on **corporate growers and processors:** Dan Cordtz, "Corporate Farming: A Tough Row to Hoe," August 1972. **Ray Goldberg encourages individual US farmer to integrate himself into the agribusiness chain:** "US Agribusiness Breaks Out of Isolation," *Harvard Business Review*, June 1975. **"Social inefficiency" of the US** (breakfast) **food industry:** hearings of the Senate Select Commission on Human Nutrition, statement by Robert Lewis quoted in *The Elements*, December 1975 (published by Institute for Policy Studies, see above). **Few Americans employed in farming, but many in food:** Alain Giraudo, "Trois américains sur dix travaillent pour le complexe agro-alimentaire," *Le Monde*, 25 November 1975. **US crop increases 1972-3:** First National Citibank *Monthly Economic Letter*, October 1973.

Harvests in 1972 not really "catastrophic:" Figures given at World Conference on Soya Proteins, Munich, 11-14 November 1973, Report by J.-P. Berlan and J.-P. Bertrand of the GEREI-INRA *(rapport de Mission Janvier 1974)*, p. 5. **How much more grain the DCs could have produced** if land used to capacity: *Washington Post*, 21 October 1974. **US Bureau of Census report on "sick or starving" Americans** in *Characteristics of the Low-Income Population 1972*, cited by URPE, Fact Sheets on Food, op. cit. **Malnutrition:** see *UN Assessment*, op. cit., Section I, Ch. 3; Dr. Elie Shneour, *Le Cerveau et la Faim*, Stock, Paris, 1975 (original title in English: *The Malnourished Mind*). Some information summarized from lectures by Prof. Henri Dupin, Rennes School of Public Health, and

Prof. J. Lederer, University of Louvain, given during the *Cycle d'Etudes sur la Nutrition dans le Tiers Monde et ses Incidences Socio-Economiques*, Paris, 5 January-15 March 1976, organized by the Centre de Formation des Coopérants and the Association Médico-Pharmaceutique contre la Faim dans le Monde. See also the work of Dr Fernando Mönckeberg, *American Journal of Clinical Nutrition*, Vol. 25, 1972, p. 776; "Factors Conditioning Malnutrition in Latin America with Special Reference to Chile" in P. Gyorgy and O. L. Kline (eds.), *Malnutrition is a Problem of Ecology*, Karger, 1970; J. Cravioto and E. de Licardie, "La Malnutrition chez l'enfant," *Revue Tiers Monde*, IEDES-PUF, Paris, juillet-septembre 1975, p. 325 (excellent bibliography). Also Alan Berg, "The Crisis in Infant Feeding Practices" in *Ekistics*, January 1975 (special issue, "Food from One Earth"). Berg is the World Bank's nutrition expert. **Africa infested by tripanosomiasis:** *UN Assessment*, op. cit. **IQ figures** from Mönckeberg, *Am. Journal Clinical Nutrition*, op. cit. **Rural poverty figures:** World Bank, *Rural Development, Sector Policy Paper*, February 1975, pp. 4-5; and *Land Reform*, Rural Development Series, pp. 44-7 and tables in annex. **Landless workers,** idem, pp. 47-9 and table 11. **Largest holdings produce least food:** In Latin America, World Bank idem, Table 2.2 p. 32; and in India, Jeune Afrique, op. cit., p. 102. **Lord Salisbury quote** from R. C. Dutt, *Famines and Land Assessment in India*, London, 1900, Appendix O, p. 197 (kindly supplied by P. Spitz). **Cash crops:** Three poor continents used to export grain: Ray Goldberg, "Agribusiness for Developing Countries," *Harvard Business Review*, Sept.-Oct. 66. An account of the **banana "OPEC"** (UPEB) attempt in Penny Lernoux, "The Great Banana War," *The Nation*, 29 June 1974; also *Business Week* of 16 June 1973 ("At War with Chiquita Banana") and of 22 June 1974 ("A Banana Brouhaha over Higher Prices"). A long account of **how Brazil was prevented by General Foods from exporting its own soluble coffee** in Case Studies of the Harvard Graduate School of Business, "Maxwell House Division of General Foods, The International Coffee Agreement," Case 4-371-479 AI 308. **Bangladesh jute:** *New Internationalist*, August 1975. **Brazil soybean processing by US firms:** Centre Français du Commerce Extérieur: *Le Développement de la Production du Soja au Brésil*, coll. Enquêtes à l'étranger, enquête par P. Vautrin et J.-P. Guilhamon, November 1973. **Value of banana crop does not stay in producing countries:** Fredéric Clairmonte, "L'empire de la banane," *Ceres* (FAO magazine), January-February 1975, and UNCTAD, *"The Marketing and Distribution System for Bananas,"* TD/B/C.1/162 December 1974. **Cash crop increases faster than food crop production in Africa:** Ingrid Palmer, "Food and the New Agricultural Technology," UNRISD, 1972, p. 55 and tables. **Mali cash crop export revenues:** *Qui se Nourrit de la Famine en Afrique?* op. cit., pp. 134-9. **Possible grain imports in future by UDCs:** *UN Assessment*, op. cit., para. 28, 31. **Land surfaces occupied by cash crops:** Ernst Utrecht, "Insoluble Agricultural Problems," paper presented at the Conference for the Appraisal of the Relationship between Agricultural Development and Industrialization in Africa and Asia, United Nations Economic Commission for Africa, Tananarive, 4-14 July 1975. *Croissance des Jeunes Nations*, op. cit., sp. Dr. Henri Dupin and Thierry Brun; also idem, Thierry Brun, "Les Vrais Responsables de la Famine," May 1974; Senegalese government promotional document for its groundnut exports. **UDC animal-feed production by MNCs:** Overseas Private Investment Corporation, Annual Reports for 1973, 1974, 1975. **Beef exports:** Bernard Roux, "L'Integration dé l'Amérique Centrale au marché mondiale de la viande bovine," *Revue Tiers Monde*, IEDES-PUF, Paris, avril-juin 1975. **FAO average consumption statistics by country** in *UN Assess-*

ment, op. cit., pp. 51-4. **Calorie intake according to income:** idem, pp. 60-63. **Women:** *UN Assessment* para. 130; FAO Press Release 75/14, 7 March 1975; Palmer, op. cit., p. 33; René Dumont, op. cit., p. 45. **Self-provisioning:** Pierre Spitz, op. cit., pp. 125-41; German study cited by Spitz: K. H. Junghaus, "Pauvre à la Campagne, Misérable à la Ville" in *Ceres* (FAO magazine), July-August 1969, pp. 24-8. **Small farmers' desperate attempts to sell anything but their land:** N. S. Jodha, "Famine and Famine Policies: Some Empirical Evidence," *Economic and Political Weekly,* 11 October 1975. **UN "vicious circle" conclusion:** *Assessment,* para. 185. **Climate/Weather:** *UN Assessment,* pp. 35-7; Bowen Northrup, "Feasibility of Forecasting Weather Trends over Long Term Stirs Debate among Experts," *Wall Street Journal,* 28 May 1975; Conference on "The Coming Climate Change and Famine" as summarized in the *Report* of the Center for the Study of Democratic Institutions, February 1975; *National Geographic,* Thomas Y. Canby, "Can the World Feed its People?," July 1975. **Bangladesh famine 1974:** Steve Raymer, "The Nightmare of Famine," *National Geographic* idem.; René Dumont, *Courier de l'UNESCO,* op. cit., Prof. Anisur Rahman, "The Famine," University of Dacca, 7 November 1974, mimeo (quoted with the author's kind permission). **Famine flashpoints:** FAO press releases 75/127, 75/128, 75/75, 75/54, 75/77, 75/64, 76/7, 76/8, 75/4, 75/56; *International Herald Tribune,* 21 March 1975 (Somalia); idem, 16 May 1975 (India); idem, 12 January 1976 (Ethiopia); World Food Program press releases 76/57, 13 October 1976 (Sri Lanka); 76/68, 16 November 1976 (Lebanon). **Low levels of grain stocks:** Ray Goldberg, op. cit., *Harvard Business Review,* June 1975; Simon Winchester, "Little in Store," *Guardian,* 5 January 1976, tables; FAO press release, "Grain production, trade and prices up, stocks relatively unchanged," 75/71, 10 October 1975; World Food Program press release 76/66, 15 November 1976.

PART TWO
Chapter 2: *The Population Myth*

Best overall supplementary source: *New Internationalist,* special issue for World Population Year, May 1974. Also *Scientific American,* special issue on "The Human Population," September 1974, in which **article by Roger Revelle,** "Food and Population," appears.

Dumont quote in "Population et Cannibalisme," *Forum du Développement Nations Unies,* Septembre-Octobre 1974. (Like other UN publications—*Ceres,* etc.—also exists in English under title *Development Forum.*) **Cartoon** by Fischetti, *International Herald Tribune,* 5-6 April 1975 (reprinted with permission). **McNamara quote** from Speech to Board of Governors, Nairobi, September 1973. **Heinrich von Loesch study:** summary of German book, "Standplatz für Milliarden?" kindly supplied to me in English by the author (publ. Deutsche Verlags-Anstalt, Stuttgart, 1974). **"Doomsday"/Infinite Population** in Pirie, op. cit., p. 22 and note, p. 194. **UN data on population growth** in 1973: *Le Monde,* 7 February 1975. **Food production grows faster than population even in most UDCs** ("54 out of 86 developing countries for which data is available" acc. *UN Assessment,* p. 3); also idem, p. 31, and table, p. 30. **Brazil growth trends:** data from World Bank, *Atlas,* 1974, pp. 6-7. **Land concentrated in few hands:** World Bank, *Land Reform,* July 1974, Annex I and sp. table 6, p. 55. **Land distribution figures,** idem, table 2, p. 51 ("Cropland in relation to population by countries"). **Ratios Bolivia/India/ Holland** in document written to launch *Transnational Institute Report,* op. cit. Figures were supplied to us by David Baytleman. See also TNI, pp. 35-8.

Population/copulation quote in *New Internationalist*, op. cit., p. 11. **"Appropr-ate technology"** quote from The Victor-Bostrum Fund for the International Planned Parenthood Federation: *Food and Population*, Report No. 19, Summer-Fall 1974 (article by J. G. Harrar, President Emeritus of the Rockefeller Founda-tion). **Population Council study** in TNI, op. cit. **D. Bannerji on Indian popula-tion control:** "Family Planning in India: the Outlook for 2000 A.D.," *Economic and Political Weekly*, 30 November 1974, pp. 1984-9. **William Rich study and chart:** *New Internationalist*, op. cit., pp. 8-9 (reprinted with permission). **Han Suyin on China:** AP dispatch from United Nations, *Rome Daily American*, 19 July 1975. **Economic system in China encourages population limitation:** G. F. Sprague, "Agriculture in China" in *Science*, op. cit., p. 551 (emphasis added-.

Chapter 3: Local Elites—And How to Join Them

Pierre Spitz deals with this subject extensively in *"De la Recherche en Sciences Sociales du Développement aux Etats-Unis*, op. cit. I am also indebted to him for passing on his copy of *Winning the Cold War*. **All quotes from "Winning the Cold War: The US Ideological Offensive"** in *Hearings before the Subcommittee on International Organizations and Movements of the Committee on Foreign Affairs*, House of Representatives, Eighty-Eighth Congress, Second Session: Part VIII, US Government Agencies and Programs, Agency for International Develop-ment, Department of State, January 15 and 16, 1964, US Government Printing Office, Washington, D.C., 1964. Emphasis is added. **"Geography of Disgrace"** article in *Saturday Review/World*, 15 June 1974. **Lord Cornwallis/Lord Bentinck** quote in Noam Chomsky, *American Power and the New Mandarins*, Pantheon Books, New York, 1967, pp. 251-2. **America "the creative society"** says Brzezinski, idem, pp. 30-31. **Harry Truman** also quoted by Chomsky, p. 268. **Officials' views of peasants in Sri Lanka:** Susantha Goonitalake, "Imperialism and Development Studies: A Case Study" in *Race and Class*, Vol. XVI, No. 2, p. 130. **Bannerji on India:** *Economic and Political Weekly*, op. cit. **Background on Rockefeller and Ford Foundations** from Pierre Spitz, "Les Fondations Carnegie, Rockefeller et Ford" (mimeo), Paris, January 1974. **Whole section on Ford Foundation/US university actions in Indonesia** summarized from David Ransom, "Ford Country: Building an Elite for Indonesia" in *The Trojan Horse*, op. cit., pp. 93-115. **Effects of military takeover on Indonesian food situation:** Ernst Utrecht, op. cit. (in Part One, cash-crops references). **Origins of the Civic Action Program of USAID:** Steve Weissman, "An Alliance for Stability," *The Trojan Horse*, op. cit., p. 77. **Hollis Chenery quote:** Pierre Spitz, *De la Recherche . . .*, op. cit., p. 168 (not verbatim quote because translated back into English by me). The original is to be found in "Report for the Behavioral and Social Sciences Survey Committee of the Social Science Research Council," Washington, D.C., June 1967 (mimeo, and of which I do not have a copy).
Indian Emergency Food Act 1952 provided training for local elites: Pierre Spitz, "Les Aides Alimentaire, Technique et Culturelle dans la Politique Agricole des Etats-Unis depuis la Défaite du Kuomintang," *Mondes en Développement*, No. 4, 1973, pp. 55-6. **Harvard Development Advisory Service** in Pierre Spitz, *De la Recherche . . .*, op. cit. 88 ff. **Chomsky on "modernizing elite"** in *American Power . . .*, op. cit., p. 358. **Dumont on Third World education systems** in a mimeographed paper prepared for the meeting of the "Group of Eminent Persons" prior to the World Food Conference. **Frantz Fanon and national bourgeoisies** in *The Wretched of the Earth* (trans. Constance Farrington), Grove Press, New York, 1964; Penguin, 1967.

Chapter 4: Technology: Now Who Pays to Do What and to Whom?

This chapter would not have been nearly so complete if I had not been fortunate enough to attend, as an observer, the *Seminar on Science, Technology and Development in a Changing World* organized by the Development Center of the Organization for Economic Cooperation and Development (OECD) in Paris on 21-5 April 1975. Experts on both agricultural and industrial technology from developed and underdeveloped countries presented a number of extremely useful papers and engaged in very stimulating discussion during the course of the Seminar, and I would like to thank Mr Jean-Jacques Salomon of the Development Center for allowing me to listen.

Crop transfers and resulting social effects: Pierre Spitz, "Notes sur l'Histoire des Transferts de Techniques dans le Domaine de la Production Végétale;" paper for OECD seminar. **Soybeans in Brazil:** Centre Français du Commerce Extérieure, op. cit. (See references to cash crops in Part One.) **On traditional Western "development" theory:** Richard DuBoff, Keynote Presentation, "What is Authentic Development?" for the Conference on International Development Issues organized by the American Friends Service Committee, 26-7 April 1974 (mimeo). **Andre Gunder Frank essay:** "The Development of Underdevelopment" in Rhodes, *Imperialism and Underdevelopment*, op. cit. **Senegalese example:** P. Kane; "Problématique du Changement des Techniques Agricoles en Afrique," paper presented at OECD seminar. **Norwegian project in Kerala:** Johan Galtung, "Technology and Dependence" in *Ceres-FAO Magazine*, September-October 1974 (quoted with the kind permission of the author). **Study Commissioned by Massey-Ferguson:** *The Pace and Form of Farm Mechanization in Developing Countries*, available from M-F, 200 University Avenue, Toronto 1, Ontario, Canada (sp. pp. 13 and 19). **2 1/2 million jobs lost in Latin America due to mechanization:** K. C. Abercrombie, "Agricultural Mechanization and Employment in Latin America," *International Labor Organization Review*, July 1972. **Pakistani World Bank economist:** Mahbub ul Haq, "Facing up to What Went Wrong" in *Ceres-FAO Magazine*, November-December 1972. **Two different approaches to "working with the people" in Maharashtra:** Pierre Spitz, "Rapport de Mission en Inde, Sri Lanka et Thaïlande, du 1er août 1974 au 10 novembre 1974," INRA, mimeo, mai 1975. **Student/peasant cooperation in North Vietnam:** Mme Vo Thi Tuc, Professor of Organic Chemistry, University of Hanoi, personal communication. **Sri Lanka metallurgy:** oral communication by Dr. D. L. O. Mendis at OECD seminar. **UNICEF worker report on non-working tubewells in India:** the *New Internationalist*, February 1975, pp. 13-15. **Examples of Ernst Shumacher's intermediate technology** from the *Center Magazine* (Center for the Study of Democratic Institutions), Santa Barbara, California, January-February 1975, pp. 43-9. See also *Small is Beautiful*, Blond & Briggs, London, 1973 and *International Labour Review*, July 1972. **Women and technology:** FAO brochure, *The Missing Half: Woman 1975*.

Other very useful contributions to the OECD Seminar which have influenced this chapter without being specifically quoted are those of A. Rahman ("Inconsistencies in Developing Countries"); Jon Sigurdson ("China's Autonomous Development of Technology and Sciences"); Samir Amin ("Technological Dependence"); Genevieve Dean ("China: A Case of Autonomous Development?"); Ignacy Sachs ("Crisis in Development Strategies: Towards an Identification of

New Objectives") as well as the closing remarks of Mr. Salomon. For **disadvantages of "package" technology:** see also H. A. B. Parpia, "Problems of Technology Transfer in Food and Agricultural Industries in Developing Countries," FAO, AGS:MISC/73/32, May 1973, sp. pp. 10-11.

Chapter 5: The Green Revolution

Origins of the GR: see Lester Brown, *Seeds of Change*, published for the Overseas Development Council by Praeger, New York, Washington, London, 1970. **Idem for subsequent quotes of L. Brown:** see also his article "The Agricultural Revolution in Asia," *Foreign Affairs*, Vol. 46, No. 4, 1968, pp. 688-98. **For effects of GR in Mexico where it was first implanted:** Cynthia de Alcantara, "Modernization without Development: Patterns of Agricultural Policy and Rural Change in the Birthplace of the Green Revolution," UNRISD, op. cit., November 1974. **Director of IRRI cautions against "miracles:"** H. Lowenstein, "Un miracle avec des si . . ." in *Ceres-FAO Magazine*, January-February 1969. **Increase of surface planted to HYVs:** "The social and economic implications of large-scale introduction of new varieties of foodgrain: Summary of conclusions of a global research project," UNRISD, op. cit., 1974. **Supplying farmers can be big business,** Brown, op. cit., p. 59. **Other sources than Brown concerning "pressure on India:"** *New York Times*, 24 and 29 April 1966; idem, 14 May 1966; *Christian Science Monitor*, 5 December 1966 (cited in Spitz, *De la Recherche* . . . op. cit., p. 144). **Philippine agro-service centers closed:** *Business Week*, 21 November 1970. **Francine Frankel study:** *India's Green Revolution: Economic Gains and Political Costs*, Princeton, Princeton University Press, 1971; **commented on by Richard Franke:** "Solution to the Asian Food Crisis: Green Revolution or Social Revolution?," *Bulletin of Concerned Asian Scholars*, Vol. VI, No. 4, November-December 1974. **How the GR has been spread through local elites:** Harry Cleaver, "Will the Green Revolution Turn Red?" in *The Trojan Horse*, op. cit., pp. 175-6; also Krishna Moorthy, "India's Food Struggle," *Far Eastern Economic Review*, 24 January 1963. **GR's effects on nature:** Ingrid Palmer, UNRISD, op. cit., p. 51. **Private corporations and seed production,** idem, pp. 52, 65-6. **Australian geneticist agrees:** Sir O. H. Frankel, Fellow of the Australian Academy of Science, "Les Dangers d'ordre génétique de la Révolution Verte," *Union Agriculture*, October 1970. **Danger of blights:** Cleaver, op. cit., p. 190. **Javanese malnutrition:** Palmer, op. cit., p. 62. **Great number of edible plant species:** René Dumont, op. cit., p. 171. **Indian Food Minister's remarks:** Mohan Ram, "Les Contradictions de la Révolution Verte en Inde" in *Le Monde Diplomatiqr-é*, October 1974. **Landlord/Tenant dialogue** based on "Summary of Conclusions . . ." UNRISD, op. cit., sp. pp. 21-9. **Cornucopia or Pandora's Box:** Clifton Wharton, *Foreign Affairs*, Vol. 47, No. 3, 1969. **Social mayhem caused by GR:** Spitz, op. cit., pp. 103-4; also Cleaver, op. cit., p. 185. **Indian Congress Party leaders hold more land than legal limit:** Pierre Spitz, "L'Inde: Par la Loi, mais aussi par la Force," *Le Monde Diplomatique*, Avril 1973. **Increase Indian Police Forces:** Bernard Weinraub, "Legislators Protest India Outlays on Police," *International Herald Tribune (NYT)*, 25 October 1974. **Criticism of GR:** sp. in *Ceres:* Flores, May-June 1969; Pearse, July-August 1969; Barraclough, November-December 1969. **Statements of Rockefeller Foundation and Inter-American Development Bank officials to Congressional Committee:** *Proceedings of the Subcommittee on National Security Policy and Scientific Developments:* House of Representatives, 91st Congress, 5 December 1969, p. 20 and p. 57-58. **North Vietnam "GR:"** Yves Lacoste, *Le Monde*, 4 January 1975. **Improvement possible even with limited reform:** UNRISD, op. cit., "Conclusions," pp. 32 ff.

Here, once more, I want to acknowledge my debt to the research Pierre Spitz has done on the GR, especially the chapter devoted to it in *De la Recherche...*, op. cit.

Conclusion to Part Two

World Bank quote from McNamara, Speech at Nairobi, 1973, op. cit. See also studies mentioned under **self-provisioning. Dumont quote** from paper for Group of Eminent Persons, Rome, November, 1974, op. cit.

The verses from Isaiah are from the King James Version.

PART THREE

Chapter 6: Planned Scarcity

André Udry quote from "The Profits of Famine," *Inprecor*, 16 January 1975. **Famines in the Middle Ages:** M. Ganzin, "Pour entrer dans une ère de justice alimentaire," UNESCO, *Le Courrier de l'UNESCO*, May 1975, op. cit. **"Little that might elevate prices has not been tried"** quote from Thomas T. Poleman, "World Food: A Perspective" in *Science*, op. cit., p. 513. **FAO official quoted by Udry**, op. cit., p. 57. **Extra grain could have been produced 1969-72:** *Washington Post*, 21 October 1974. **Rice stocks and prices,** *UN Assessment*, op. cit., p. 20. **Soybean magnate contribution to Nixon:** Irwin Ross, "Dwayne Andreas' Bean has a Heart of Gold," *Fortune*, October 1973. **Oil price increases contribute little to Western inflation:** see Geoffrey Barraclough, "Wealth and Power: The Politics of Food and Oil;" *New York Review of Books*, 7 August 1975 (excellent, long article). *Chemical and Engineering News* on **fertilizers:** 5 July 1974. **Barry Commoner calculations** in Dumont, *Croissance...*, op. cit., p. 154. **For the whole question of energy vs. food/fertilizer cost increases and consequences for Third World,** see Algeria, documents cited in bibliography. **Cargill:** "Cargill at a Glance," undated PR document from Cargill, Inc., Cargill Bldg, Minneapolis, Minnesota 55402. See also **NACLA report,** cf. note in text. **Barron's on satellite data for USSR:** Richard Donnelly, "Commodities Corner," 9 June 1975. **Satellite crop identification:** A. B. Park, "Inventorier la Planète, *Ceres*, January-February 1975. **On the "grain robbery" and the grain trade** see A. V. Krebs, "Of the Grain Trade, by the Grain Trade and for the Grain Trade" in Lerza and Jacobson, op. cit., p. 353; James Trager, *The Great Grain Robbery*, Ballantine, New York, 1975; INRA/GEREI team, "Blé et Soja: Pénuries sur Commande?" in *La Recherche*, No. 56, May 1975, p. 408. *Cargill press release on sales:* F. M. Seed, 2 November 1972; *URPE Fact Sheets on Food*, op. cit.; and sp. *Hearings* before the Subcommittee on Livestock and Grains, House of Representatives, 14, 18, 19 September 1972; INRA/GEREI team, "Pénurie Naturelle ou Pénurie Sociale?," INRA, mimeo, November 1973. **Earl Butz's remarks about grain companies and farmers** are in Krebs, op. cit. An earlier article on **Cargill:** Hubert Kay, "The Two-Billion Dollar Company that Lives by the Cent," *Fortune*, December 1965. **Soybeans:** see INRA/GEREI in *La Recherche*, op. cit.; Alain Leplaideur, *Le Marché du Soja: Vers l'Organisation Oligopolistique des marchés des produits du soja,"* doctoral thesis for University of Paris I (Pantheon-Sorbonne), mimeo, IEDES, June 1975; Marcel Marloie, *Le Marché Mondial des Tourteaux Oléagineux: Une Nouvelle Division Internationale du Travail*, INRA, mimeo, February 1974. **Soybean trade:** *The Times:* four-page special report on the occasion of the opening of the London futures market, 3 April 1975. **For an explanation of why prices cannot be kept up to 1974 levels, and how one country might react to the US food offensive** see the paper delivered to an audience of French military people by Marcel Mazoyer, reprinted in *Defense Nationale* ("Pénurie Alimentaire et Développement de la

Production"), October 1975. **Report on Munich Soybean (TVP) Conference:** J.-P. Bertrand and J.-P. Berlan: "Compte-Rendu de la Conférence Mondiale sur les Protéines de Soja, Munich, 11-14 November 1973," INRA, mimeo, January 1974. **On stocks and stockholding policies:** "A Campaign for Famine Insurance," *Business Week*, 2 November 1974. **McGovern quote:** Transnational Institute, op. cit., p. 56. **Commodities futures markets:** see *Understanding the Commodities Futures Markets*, published by Bache & Co., 36 Wall St, NY. 10005. **The "ideal hedge"** from testimony by C. M. Roberts before Senate Agriculture and Forestry Committee, 20 May 1974, reprinted in *Cargill Crop Bulletin*, June 1974. **How the commodities markets have overtaken the stock markets:** "Commodity Trading... more, more, more," *Business Week*, 15 March 1976; Ray Goldberg, *Harvard Business Review*, June 1975, op. cit. **Speculation and commodity prices:** Lawrence Mayer, "We Can't Take Food for Granted Anymore," *Fortune*, February 1974. **"The only cure for high prices is higher prices:"** "Dwayne Andreas' Bean has a Heart of Gold," *Fortune*, October 1973, op. cit. **Future requirements for various foodstuffs:** *UN Assessment*, op. cit., para. 217. **Sugar profits:** Amstar in *Business Week*, 16 November 1974; see also *Tate & Lyle Annual Report* 1974 and J. Baudet, "Sucre: Pénurie ou . . . ? in *Actuel-Développement*, November–December 1974; "Brewer's Boom" in *Duns Magazine*, July 1974. **US sugar worker wages:** IUF *Bulletin*, op. cit., No. 1-2-3, 1975, p. 7. **Decline of sugar prices, hardship for UDCs, competition from corn-syrup:** *Wall Street Journal* 21 October 1976 and 2 November 1976; **Bonanza for bakery products, soft-drinks:** *Business Week*, 4 October 1976. **IUF Dairy Conference: IUF Bulletin**, No. 9-10. 1974. **Livestock industry not doing well:** FAO press release CO/6, 14 May 1975 and Industry Cooperative Program, *Seventh Session of the Working Group on Integrated Meat Development*, Rome, 8-9 May 1975, FAO DDI:G/75/61.

Chapter 7: There's No Business Like Agribusiness

Ray Goldberg definition of agribusiness: "Agribusiness for Developing Countries," *Harvard Business Review*, September-October 1966. **US government paves way for private agribusiness in UDCs:** *Proceedings of the Subcommittee on National Security Policy* (op. cit., notes in references on Green Revolution), statement of Charles S. Dennison, Vice-President of International Minerals and Chemicals, p. 121. **Louis Lundborg speech "The Agribusiness Approach"** in *Vital Speeches*, 1 October 1967, p. 756. **Goldberg concurs:** "Agribusiness for Developing Countries," op. cit. **Orville Freeman, "a well-run agribusiness project can bring in 30 per cent a year:"** untitled paper (mimeo) 12 June 1974, obligingly communicated by Business International. See also Orville Freeman, "I Have a Plan," *Saturday Review/World*, 14 December 1974. **Freeman on tropical explosion of production** (footnote): *Fortune*, "We Can't Take Food for Granted Anymore," op. cit. **On IBEC:** see Rodman C. Rockefeller, "Turn Public Problems to Private Account," *Harvard Business Review*, January 1971; "Do-Gooders," *Newsweek*, 21 June 1971; Wayne G. Broehl, Jr, "The Company with a Cause," *Columbia Journal of World Business*, July-August 1968; an extraordinarily complex example of corporate infighting involving IBEC's entry into the Iranian poultry market in R. A. Goldberg, *Seminar in Agribusiness Systems in the International Environment*, Harvard University Graduate School of Business Administration, mimeo, 1971 (case ICH 12G 24 A1 242); also Sechler and de Marco, op. cit. and IBEC's *Annual Reports*. **IBEC sells Venezuelan supermarkets:** "Latin America opens the door to foreign investment again," *Business Week*, 9 August 1976, p. 37.

On concentration in US food production and failure of small farms: see Larry

Casalino, "This land is their land," *Ramparts*, July 1972. **Standard and Poor** *"Industry Surveys"* **on food industry** 21 November 1968. **Breakfast food industry outlays:** J.-P. Berlan, "US Agro-Industry," INRA, typescript, 1971. **Low research and development investments in food industry:** Thomas Horst, *At Home Abroad*, Ballinger Publishing Co., Cambridge, Massachusetts, 1974, p. 56. **Chemical additives to processed food:** Colman McCarthy, "Bon Chemical Appétit," *The New Republic*, 30 November 1974. **Concentration and conglomeration:** Leon Garoian (ed.), *Economics of Conglomeration*, Oregon State University Press, Corvallis, 1969, sp. the paper by John Narver, "Conglomeration in the Food Industries." **Acquisitions by food companies;** Berlan typescript, op. cit. **Recent mergers** (footnote): "Finance Briefs," *Business Week*, 19 July 1976. **Increase of junk-food consumption in US:** USDA, *Consumption, Food Prices, Expenditures 1966 and 1971 Supplement* cited by URPE, op. cit. **Profits of food firms:** *Business Week*, 10 March 1973. For the **expansion of US food-processing industry abroad,** Senate Emergency Committee on American Trade, *The Role of Multinational Corporations in US and World Economies;* compendium papers submitted to the Subcommittee on International Trade of the Senate Finance Committee, 1973; and several chapters in Horst, op. cit. **Hawaiian cannery operations moved to Philippines, Thailand:** IUF *Bulletin*, op. cit., No. 7-8, 1974. **Unilever fires 11,000:** *Business Week*, 13 April 1974. **Unilever profits soar 227%:** *IHT* 19 August 1976.

Dietary changes induced by MNCs in UDCs: Alan Berg, "Industry's Struggle with World Malnutrition," *Harvard Business Review*, January 1972; see also Barnet and Muller, *Global Reach*, op. cit., pp. 183-4; H. Walter, Chairman of the Board, International Flavors and Fragrances, "Marketing in Developing Countries," *Columbia Journal of World Business*, Winter 1974; document of International Organization of Consumers' Unions (for World Food Conference), 9 Emmastraat, The Hague, Netherlands. **Plantations/Land ownership:** Del Monte President quoted in *Business Week*, "At War with Chiquita Banana," 16 June 1973; Ernst Utrecht, "Insoluble Agricultural Problems," op. cit.; Bernard Wideman, "Dominating the Pineapple Trade," *Far Eastern Economic Review*, 8 July 1974. **Amazonia ranching:** José S. da Veiga, "Quand les multinationales font du ranching," *Le Monde Diplomatique*, September 1975. José da Veiga has been kind enough to supply me with his much longer working document on this question, "Les Ranches Modernes de L'Amazonie Brésilienne," typescript, INRA, May 1975. See also, Industry Cooperative Program, FAO, *Report of the ICP Mission to Brazil: Agro-Industrial Potential of Legal Amazonia*, FAO doc. DDI: G/73/53 24 July 1973. **Sri Lanka tea:** IUF *Bulletin*, op. cit., No. 5, 1974; *Liberation of Tea*, Logos, Vol. 14, No. 1, February 1975, publ. by Center for Society and Religion, Talahena, Malabe, Sri Lanka. **Little food produce remains in producing country:** Ernst Utrecht, op. cit.; Ernst Feder, *Strawberry Imperialism: An Enquiry into the Mechanisms of Dependency in Mexican Agriculture*, Institute of Social Studies, The Hague, Netherlands, 1976. **Flowers more profitable than food:** Barnet and Müller, op. cit., p. 182. **Pet foods/people foods:** "One of the Family," Merck, Sharpe and Dohme, *International Review*, Summer 1974; "Pet food sales $2.1 billion, SAMI says," *Advertising Age*, 30 September 1974. **Costa Rican beef exports increase:** Sechler and De Marco, op. cit. **Gulf & Western in the Dominican Republic:** José del Castillo *et al.*, *La Gulf & Western en Republica Dominicana*, Publicaciones de la Universidad Autonoma de Santo Domingo, 1974; Robert Ledogar, *Hungry for Profits*, IDOC, N.Y., 1976; IUF *Bulletin*, op. cit., No. 3, 1974. **Balaguer quote** from *El Caribe*, 10 May 1973, quoted in del Castillo, op. cit., p. 221. **G. & W.'s President's "interest in food:"** *Business Week*, 20 January 1975, p. 56. **Labor-brokering in Amazonia:** da Veiga, article and working document, op. cit. **Worker discontent in the Philippines:** Wideman, op. cit. **Brazil and US fertilizer:** da Veiga, op. cit. **Tax advantages for agribusiness abroad:** see G. L. Baker, "Good Climate for Agribusiness," *The Nation*, 5 November 1973, pp. 456-62. **Iran as host country for agribusiness:** Frances Fitzgerald, "Giving the Shah Everything He Wants," *Harpers*, November 1974, p. 55; "How Iran Spends its New Found Riches," *Business Week*, 22 June 1974; G. L. Baker, op. cit. **"Zeroing in" on foreign land:** "Brewer's Boom," *Duns Magazine*, July 1974. **But Brewer's President resigns** (footnote): *Business Week* 23 June 1975. **LAAD/PICA/ADELA/Agribusiness Council:** R. A. Goldberg, *Seminar in Agribusiness Systems in the International Environment*, op. cit.; LAAD Annual Reports 1974, 1975. The Agribusiness Council ignored my two requests for information. **Nestles:** First *New Internationalist* article ("The Baby-Food Tragedy"), August 1973; follow-up ("Kicking the Bottle"), March 1975. **Change in advertising:** "Code Adopted on Baby Food by 8 Makers," Reuters dispatch, *International Herald Tribune*, 2 December 1975. **Nescafe to toddlers:** Dr Henri Dupin in *Croissance des Jeunes Nations*, op. cit. **Nestles Greek contract** in IUF *Nestlé Bulletin*, No. 18, May 1975. **United Brands negotiations with USSR:** IUF *Bulletin*, No. 7, 1973.

    Booker McConnell sugar project Mumias, Kenya: Documents supplied by Bookers, Bucklersbury House, London EC4N 8EJ, sp. J. E. Haynes, Director: "The Mumias Sugar Company: A case study of development in Kenya," mimeo, undated; brochure "Sugar from Mumias," in color, illustrated, undated; the *Financial Times*, "Small Farmers' Role in Boosting Output," 16 May 1974; see also color brochure "Bookers in Agriculture" and *Annual Reports*. **Buhler and Alfa-Laval** documents also supplied by the companies. Comment on **Les Grands Moulins in Senegal** from lecture, Dr Henri Dupin, lecture cycle, op. cit. **IUF statement to the World Food Conference,** "Contribution de l'UITA à la Conférence Mondiale de l'Alimentation," November 1974. **Examples of agribusiness workers** from several IUF *Bulletins*, op. cit., 1974 and 1975. **Orville Freeman's praise of MNCs:** "Demands of a Changing World," *Columbia Journal of World Business*, Summer 1974.

Chapter 8: Food Aid? . . . Or Weapon?

Early history US food aid: see Pierre Spitz, "L'Arme de l'aide alimentaire: les années d'apprentissage, 1914-1947," *Critiques de l'Economie Politique*, No. 15, January-March 1974. **Herbert Hoover:** see Walter Cohen, "Herbert Hoover Feeds the World" in *The Trojan Horse*, op. cit.; Herbert Hoover, *An American Epic*, Henry Regnery Co., Chicago, 1964 (four vols., Vol. IV concerns the Second World War and post-war period); *Hoover Institution on War, Revolution and Peace* (descriptive brochure), Stanford University, Stanford, California, January 1963. For the **pre-PL 480 period,** one may also see Chester Bowles, *The Conscience of a Liberal*, Harper & Row, New York, 1962. **Senator McGovern quotes** from his *War on Want*, Walker and Co., New York, 1964, sp. pp. 24-5. **"Can Agriculture Save the Dollar?":** *Forbes*, 15 March 1973. **Role of agriculture in US balance of trade** see also INRA/GEREI in *La Recherche*, May 1975, op. cit. As noted in text, all quotes and figures are from **PL 480 Annual Reports**, 1966 to 1974, emphasis is added—sp. **Expansion food/feedgrain market Iran**, 1972, pp. 17-18; **in Korea**, 1969, pp. 16-17; **sales made by private traders**, 1972, p. 15; **Yugoslav women guinea pigs**, 1970, p. 61; **overall statistics on Title II** from 1973 and 1974 tables. **Effects of food aid on India:** B. R. Shenoy, *PL 480 Aid and India's Food Problem*, East-West Press Ltd, New Delhi, 1974, sp. Chapters 2, 3 and p. 93. **20 year food sweepstakes winners:** Tables 2 and 18, 1974 **Political Preferences** Table 3, 1974. **"Ford Warns UN Food**

May Blunt Oil as a 'Weapon,'" *IHT*, 19 September 1974; **Le Monde comments,** 20 September 1974. **Food Weapon against China advocated:** Chomsky, op. cit. p. 337. **Triage:** see Lord Ritchie-Calder, "Triage equals Genocide," *Center Report* (Center for. the Study of Democratic Institutions), June 1975; Sol Yurick, "The Profit Profile and Mass Genocide" *IHT*, 16 January 1975; Charles Foley, "The New Let 'em Starve Theory," *Observer*, 20 April 1975; article about William Paddock, "A Modest Proposal," *Forbes*, 1 December 1975; **Food aid just because people are starving weak reason:** Dan Morgan, *IHT*, 10 December 1974. **Triage recommended in 1946** (footnote): "The Food Scandal," *Fortune*, May 1946. **CIA Report:** Henry Weinstein, "CIA Study Says Food Crisis Could Increase US Power," *IHT*, 18 March 1975. **Humphrey quote:** *Hearings*, Senate Agriculture and Forestry Committee, 1957, p. 129; **Butz quote:** *Business Week*, 15 December 1975. **Food stocks go down, so does aid:** Lyle P. Schertz, *Foreign Affairs*, April 1974. On **food power,** see also *NACLA Report*, op. cit.; "Earl Butz: Plowing New Furrows for US Agriculture," *Nation's Business*, June 1973; Victor Zorza, "Use of US Grain as a Strategic Weapon," *IHT*, 26 December 1975; Hugh Sidey, "More Powerful than Atom Bombs," *Time*, 12 January 1976; Jonathan Power, "The Concept of Power Viewed in Oil vs. Food," *IHT*, 18 November 1975, etc.

Chapter 9: Et Tu, UN?

Much of this chapter was prepared from notes on conversations with people inside and outside the Industry Cooperative Program and the Investment Center at FAO in June 1975. Major documents used were:

Information on the Industry Cooperative Program (also contains addresses of members); DDI: G/74/84 rev., 1 October 1974.

Annual Report of the Industry Cooperative Program March 1974-February 1975; DDI: G/75/28, 6 February 1975.

Industry: An Effective Partner in Implementing the World Food Conference Recommendations (Report on meeting of General Committee ICP); DDI: G/75/41, 28 February 1975.

Consultation with Agro-Industrial Leaders (Toronto) 10-11 September 1974: DDI: G/74/89, 26 September 1974.

ICP; Press and Media Coverage World Food Conference Rome 5-16 November 1974.

Several reports on *ICP Missions* to various countries. The missions to Brazil (Amazonia) and to Ethiopia (Meat Development Group) are cited in particular: respectively DDI: G/73/53, 24 July 1973 and DDI: G/74/77, 10 July 1974.

See also G. S. Bishop, CB, OBE (Chairman of Booker McConnell and now chairman of ICP), "The Contribution of International Business," Speech at Grosvenor House, meeting on *World Food Supplies*, 1-2 May 1974.

FAO Bankers Program, brochure, undated.

FAO Bankers Program, Note on operations 1972-74, mimeo, undated.

FAO Bankers Program Meeting, Amsterdam 23-24 October 1974: Summary Record, mimeo.

Letter-Report to Bankers Program participants, 30 January 1975.

Other specific quotes in the chapter not related to one or another of these documents are: **On staff and projects of FAO:** Ray Vicker, *Wall Street Journal*, 11 November 1974. **New FAO Director** (footnote): William Tuohy, "Controversial new head of FAO cuts staff and paperwork," *IHT*, 30-31 October 1976 and *FAO press release* 76/43 CL2, 20 July 1976. **ECOSOC resolution on MNCs:** ECOSOC press release 3667, 5 December 1974; **Ray Goldberg MNC/USDA meeting:** *Harvard Business Review*, op. cit., September-October 1966. **Iranian agribusiness** investments abroad: *Business Week*, 22 June 1974. **Egyptian imports of foodgrains from US:** UPI dispatch, *IHT*, 23 January 1976. **Campbell Soup Company 1963 tomato contract:** Camden, New Jersey, Form AI 219. **Chile loans curtailed by US private banks:** Barnet and Müller, op. cit., p. 142.

Chapter 10: IBRD, or Is the Bank Really a Developer?

Material in this chapter is based on:

Speeches by President Robert McNamara to the World Bank Board of Governors in Nairobi (1973), Washington (1974 and 1975), Manila (1976).

Annual Reports, 1973, 1974, 1975, 1976.

Questions and Answers: World Bank and IDA, January 1974.

World Bank Atlas, 1974.

Agricultural Credit, World Bank Paper, Rural Development Series, August 1974.

Land Reform, idem, July 1974.

Agriculture, Sector Working Paper, World Bank, June 1972.

Rural Development, Sector Policy Paper, World Bank, February 1975.

FAO/IBRD Cooperative Program, FAO Brochure, PI/Cl933/11.71/E/1/-10000.

International Finance Corporation: *IFC in Africa, IFC in Asia, IFC in Latin America, IFC-General Policies, Annual Reports*.

Speeches by William S. Gaud: "Private Investment and Local Partnership," London, 7 November 1973; "How IFC Works with Banks," Tokyo, 13 March 1972.

United Nations Yearbooks, Sections on IBRD, IDA, IFC, 1966-72.

See also: *The International Monetary Fund and the World Bank: A Long Cold Look at International Benevolence*, a four-part study in *Peace Press*, available from ICDP, 6 Endsleigh Street, London WC1, £1 plus postage. Also E. S. Mason and R. E. Asher, *The World Bank since Bretton Woods*, op. cit.

Tarbela Dam, Pakistan: World Bank *Report*, July-August 1975. Also IBRD annual report p. 58. **Dumont on Sri Lanka:** Dumont, *Les Dossiers "Bis" de Jeune Afrique*, op. cit., p. 113. **Destruction of fruit and vegetables in EEC:** *Le Monde*, 3 January 1975. **Ethiopian sugar investment in Awash Valley:** from *HVA annual reports, UN Yearbooks, IFC annual reports* and especially Lars Bondestam, "Population et capitalisme dans la Vallée de l'Aouache" in Samir Amin, *L'Agriculture et le Capitalisme*, op. cit. (Normally this study should be available in English from the IDEP, BP 3370, Dakar, Senegal, as it was prepared for a conference held there.) **Lome Agreement:** "Accord Historique à Lomé, *Le Monde*, 1 March 1975. **Question of OECD/OPEC aid:** McNamara's *Address to the Board of Governors*, Manila, 4 October 1976 and Table, p. 40. **Comparisons OECD/-OPEC GNP**, McNamara, *Address . . .*, Washington, 30 September 1974 p. 21. Algeria, documents cited in bibliography; OECD reports OPEC gives 1.8% GNP in 1974, *Le Monde*, 22 April 1975. *Peace Press*, "Petroleum, Raw Materials and Development," March-May 1975 (address above); Jonathan Power, "OPEC as Aid-Giver," *IHT*, 5 March 1975; Philippe Simonnot, "Les Tiers Mondes,'" *Le Monde*, 27-8 October 1974. **Cartoon** by Mauldin, *IHT*, 15 September 1975 (reprinted with permission). **OPEC Special Fund loans:** *IHT*, 12 November 1976.

Swedish paper by "Henri Labouret:" "Landsbygdsutveckling—en ny syn pa lönsamhet" ("Rural Development—A New View of Profit") in *Rapport Fran SIDA*, July-August 1974. **Guardian quote on Bangladesh:** Paul Boucher, 12 June 1975, cited in *Peace Press* (No. 2 of series) op. cit. **Aid to African socialism:** David B. Ottaway, *IHT*, 6 May 1975. **Le Monde report on Bank's secret consortium for**

aid to Saigon: Jacques Decornoy, 7 March 1975. **McNamara's rationale for aid:** *The Essence of Security, Reflections in Office*, Hodder & Stoughton, London. 1968.

Conclusion to Part Three

I am indebted to Claude Bourdet for the central concept of this conclusion, which has always seemed to me a useful tool of thought. He has stated it in various articles and books, most recently in *L'Aventure Incertaine—De la Résistance à la Restauration*, Stock, Paris, 1975, pp. 48-9 and Chapter 18.

PART FOUR

Chapter 11: What Can "They" Do?

Alternative food sources: Prof. A. J. Vlitos, *Total Crop Utilization*, Tate & Lyle Ltd Group Research and Development, doc. MPP 74/9, 9 August 1974; **including alternate feeds for livestock:** research to multiply food production: "Was Malthus Right?," *Business Week*, 16 June 1975. **Single-cell proteins:** Dr H. S. Bondi (Chemap AG) "Single-Cell Protein: A Survey of Present Technology and Future Prospects," paper for Swiss Industry and Technology Exhibition, Peking, 1974, kindly supplied by the author; C. A. Shacklady and T. Walker, BP Proteins, Ltd, "New Sources of Proteins as Components of Animal Feeds," Fourth International Congress of Food Science and Technology, Madrid, 23-7 September 1974; W. A. Peet, "Proteins from Oil," *Chemical Processing*, December 1973; C. A. Shacklady, "The current State of Research on the Safety and Use of Yeasts Grown on Alkanes," Lemigas Symposium, Central Java, Indonesia, June-July 1973; same author, "Response of livestock and poultry to SCP," Symposium on Single-Cell Protein, Rome, 7-9 November 1973. **Village-level production of high-protein foods:** in Vlitos, op. cit., p. 12. **Harold Geneen wants government crash program in alternate foods:** "Feed the people," *New York Times*, 16 June 1975. **Bill on food production research submitted to House of Representatives:** HR 6153; also Congressional Record, House of Representatives, 17 April 1975, kindly communicated by Repr. John F. Seiberling. **Plant regulants:** *Business Week*, op. cit., 16 June 1975; "Plant regulant chemicals give nature a hand," *Chemical Week*, 5 March 1975.

The new UN Bureaucracy: The World Food Council: Hannah's background: Irving Horowitz, "Michigan State and the CIA: A Dilemma for Social Science," *Bulletin of the Atomic Scientists*, September 1966 and *OPIC Annual Report 1973*, p. 5. **Chart** drawn from data in UN PRE S/1, "Background Note on the World Food Council," February 1975; various World Food Council documents relating to the agenda of the 23-7 June meeting in Rome, WFC/1 through/12, April, May 1975; WFC press release 75/1 "First Meeting of World Food Council to Launch New Assault on Hunger." **Jurisdictional disputes:** Paul Hoffman, "World Food Unit has Doubts about its Role," *IHT*, 28 April 1975. **Press accounts of first WFC meeting:** Alain Giraudo, "Trente-six pays pour lutter contre la faim" and "Coup nul au Conseil Mondial de l'Alimentation," *Le Monde*, 24 and 29-30 June 1975; Juan de Onis, "Third World at Food Talks Asks Aide, an American, to Resign," *IHT*, 28-9 June 1975. **WFC Second Session** (footnote): Helge Ole Bergesen: *Norsk Utenriks-politisk institutt (NUPI)*, Report no. 30, Oslo, November 1976, p. 54-60. **Food aid requirements 1975-6:** World Food Council document WFC/5, 5 May 1975. For a declaration on **some practical steps that could be taken to ease present crisis,** see also International Institute for Environment and Development (27 Mortimer Street, London W1A 4QW): "Declaration of the Rome Forum on World Food Problems" (statement of the Group of Eminent Persons that preceded the

World Food Conference). **Part of US Establishment prefers cooperation with OPEC to Kissinger confrontation strategy:** Geoffrey Barraclough, op. cit., *New York Review of Books*, 7 August 1975.

What can "they" do in UDCs? UDC productive capacity under-utilized: Yves Lacoste, "L'Aide: Idéologies et Réalités, *Esprit,* July-August 1970. **Land reform: Dacca wedding feast:** Dumont, op. cit., p. 60. **Ancient Greek land reform:** Marcel Mazoyer, oral communication at OECD Seminar, op. cit. **Components of land reform,** see Transnational Institute, op. cit.; Ernst Utrecht, "Land Reform," *Bulletin of Indonesian Economic Studies,* November 1969; Al McCoy, "Land Reform as Counter Revolution: US Foreign Policy and the Tenant Farmers of Asia," *Bulletin of Concerned Asian Scholars,* Winter-Spring 1971.

Chapter 12: What Can I Do?

After (I swear!) I had finished this chapter, the *New Internationalist* came out with a special issue titled, "Yes, But What Can I Do?" (November 1975), full of examples of development-oriented actions, present or possible. Required reading! There is also a chapter on action in Lerza and Jacobson, op. cit. The anti-General Mills action example and some ideas for women are taken from this section, p. 412. **Commodity campaigns** are described and evaluated by Ivan Rebeiro: *Commodity Campaigns and the Third World: An Evaluation of Education and Action Programs in Europe,* Action for Development, FAO, May 1974. **Volunteer action in Third World countries:** Ex-Volunteers International, "Thinking About Power," undated.

Those interested in understanding how Establishment social science has encouraged everyone to "study the poor, not the rich," and why it is high time for a change, are again referred to Pierre Spitz, *De la Recherche en Sciences Sociales du Développement aux Etats-Unis, op. cit.*

Appendix: Land

Total land mass and arable land: FAO Production Yearbook 1972; World Bank *Land Reform,* op. cit., Table 1. **Future possibilities:** see *UN Assessment* para. 32; *UN Proposals,* op. cit., para. 209. See also all of Chapter 5 in the *UN Assessment.*

Appendix: Water

Present irrigation and future possibilities in UDCs: *UN Assessment,* op. cit., para. 281 and Chapter 5. **Dumont on Bangladesh over-irrigated rice:** *Croissance. . .* op. cit., pp. 142-3. The September-October 1975 issue of *Ceres* is devoted to water problems and prospects.

Appendix: Fertilizer

Figures in this section are extrapolated and adapted from

1. *FAO Document AGS:F/75/7 May 1975:* "Commission on Fertilizers, Second Session; longer term fertilizer supply/demand positions and elements of a world fertilizer policy."

2. The *Transnational Institute Report,* op. cit., which itself relies heavily upon the *Sri Lanka Government Report on Fertilizers* for the World Food Conference. The latter is available from the UN (ECOSOC): ref. E/Conf 65/PREP/L2.

3. Ken Laidlaw (to whom I am particularly grateful), World Development Movement, Bedford Chambers, Covent Garden, London WC2: *Summary of Findings on Fertilizers* (typescript).

See also *Business Week,* 8 June 1974: "The Boom in Agrichemicals."

Poorest nations unable to obtain fertilizer in 1975: FAO press release 75/13 PL1, 25 February 1975. **Orville Freeman speech to fertilizer industry:** "World Food Scarcity: The Challenge to the Fertilizer Industry," address before the Fertilizer Institute, White Sulphur Springs, West Virginia, 11 June 1974. **Increasing use of fertilizer in DCs, ornamental uses:** Ken Laidlaw, op. cit. **FAO concerned that 80% small farmers without fertilizers, most going to cash crops:** FAO press release 75/25 PL2, 25 March 1975. **Industry spokesman predicts increased demand but no increase in exports to UDCs:** Joseph P. Sullivan (President, Estech Inc.) speech on "Outlook for Fertilizer," *High Plains Journal*, Dodge City, Kansas, 17 February 1975. **The "fine line" between expanded production for commercial demand and possible oversupply:** FAO press release 75/13, op. cit. **Mr Steiner of FAO explains fertilizer surpluses:** Interview with Ken Laidlaw, op. cit. **Figures on industry profits** from annual reports and Laidlaw (for the UK). **Eight companies accused of fertilizer price fixing:** *Wall Street Journal*, 12 June 1975. **World Bank non-assistance to Algerian fertilizer production:** Government of Algeria, *Petroleum, Raw Materials and Development*, p. 40. **"Soft" technology for supplementary fertilizer sources:** *UN Proposals*, op. cit., para. 148. **Chinese techniques:** Boyce Rensberger, "They Recycle Everything in China," reprinted from the *New York Times* in Lerza and Jacobson, op. cit. **Bring production closer to raw materials:** FAO document AGS:F, op. cit.; "Ammonia Output in Mid-East: Money, Resources and Logistics are Said to Make it a Sure Bet," *Chemical Marketing Reporter*, 17 February 1975.

Appendix: Pesticides

Definition of pesticides (and much other useful information) from *FAO Document CL 66/21 May 1975:* FAO Council, Sixty-Sixth Session, "Ad Hoc Government Consultation on Pesticides in Agriculture and Public Health," 7-11 April 1975 (definition, p. 19). **Pesticide purchases by UDCs:** C. J. Lewis (ICI), "The Manufacture of Pesticides in Developing Countries," paper for UNIDO workshop on pesticides, Vienna, 28 May-1 June 1973. **Size of industry, world sales:** D. F. Strobusch (BASF), "Economic Factors in the Discovery and Development of Pesticides," paper for FAO/Industry seminar on Pesticides in Agriculture and Public Health, Nairobi, 3 October 1974. **Crop losses due to pests and disease:** "Crop Protection and World Crops," Groupement International des Associations Nationales de Fabricants de Pesticides, Brussels, 1974. **Examples of crop and animal losses:** several articles in *Span*, periodical published by Shell International Chemical Co. Ltd, Vol. 16, No. 2, 1973; also "Pesticides in the Modern World," symposium prepared by the Industry Cooperative Program with FAO, London 1972. **Costs of product development:** Strobusch, op. cit. **Small number of research centers:** H. Metzger and D. F. Strobusch: "Development of a new pesticide" in *Pesticides*, Vol. VIII, No. 7, July 1974. **Getting the most out of available pesticides:** E. Sandner (Hoechst), "Application of pesticides without using water as demonstrated by the use of Thiodan ULV for the control of cotton pests in Tanzania," 1974. **DCs and speculators hog supplies:** FAO/ICP Document DDI: G/74/76, 12 July 1975, "Mesures d'urgence concernant l'offre d'engrais et de pesticides." **Biological control of insects in the USSR:** *Le Monde*, 16 September 1975.

I would like to thank Drs Hendrie of Shell Chemical Life Sciences Division; Maier of Imperial Chemical Industries Plant Protection Division; Metzger of GASF AG; Sandner of Hoechst for their kindness in sending scientific/technical material relevant to this section.

Appendix: Farm Mechanization

Annual reports and corporate literature from Fiat, Massey-Ferguson, John Deere, and Caterpillar. See also TNI, op. cit., pp. 27-8. **Very useful figures on response of yields to irrigation, fertilizers, pesticides and figures on mechanical equipment and consumption of fossil-fuels in agriculture** are to be found in Dr H. A. B. Parpia (Food and Agricultural Industries Service), FAO; "Global Interaction between Agriculture and Industry;" paper presented at the Eighth International TNO Conference, Rotterdam, 27-8 February 1975.

Appendix: Research

Public funds spent on agricultural research: *UN Proposals*, op. cit., para. 320. **Pay-off of research in DCs:** Lester Brown, *Seeds of Change*, pp. 47-50. **Scientific knowledge "free" but not accessible:** Pierre Spitz, "Notes sur l'histoire des transferts de techniques dans le domaine de la production végétale," op. cit. **General problems of research in UDCs:** *UN Proposals*, op. cit., pp. 84-98.

Appendix: Credit

World Bank, *Agricultural Credit*, 1974, op. cit.

Index